First Qur'anic Command:
Seek Knowledge

Dr. Ghulam Jilani Burq

First Qur'anic Command: Seek Knowledge

Dr. Ghulam Jilani Burq

ISBN 978-1514885383

English Rendering by
Iqbal Muhammad

Published by
Dr. Manzoor Memon
at
Tayyeb Iqbal Printers,
Royal Park, Lahore

Composed/Designed by
M. Naveed at Color Choice Lahore
colorchoice2008@yahoo.com

CONTENTS

Publisher's Note (Dr. Manzoor Memon)

By chance (or destiny), I found DOU (TWO) QURAN earlier this year in my collection. I had brought it along with my medical books when I left Pakistan back in 1965 for England for post graduation. I had read the book ten years earlier while still a medical student.

Reading fifty years on for the second time, I was deeply affected as the world had moved on what with 9/11 (USA) and 7/7 (UK) and general doom and gloom in Islamic world as well as rapid mind blowing medical and scientific progress in this part of the world.

I could not believe that there existed this rare Islamic scholar Dr. Burq in pre-partition days who worked so hard and gathered facts got to see the WISDOM in Quran. I realized for the first time how the FINAL BOOK was meant to be for the entire mankind not only for Muslims.

I requested my friend Maqbool Farhat (he has passed away since) who introduced me to Hussain Kaisrani who also saw the beauty like me in the book and kindly agreed to help to translate it in English.

I recently visited the exhibition at The Royal College Of Physicians in London where the Golden Age Of ISLAM it was shown discovering medicines along with manuscripts from 9th century to 17th century and their contributions to mankind.

Unfortunately the road has been downhill after that despite the oil boom and as the time has progressed Muslims have fallen off the ladder altogether.

The reason is obvious. The Muslims turned away from the very first Commandment that is IQRA "READ" and KALAM "Pen". There are 1.6 billion Muslims and almost

75 percent never go to School. Muslims have produced only two noble laureates while Jews outnumbered 100 to one by Muslims have won 79.

ALLAH (SWT) is very fair. Those people who take notice of HIS creations and work hard get the reward while the Muslims stayed with rituals. Dr Burq noted only 150 Ayas for rituals of prayers, loan, divorce etc while 756 Ayas for "RESEARCH". The 150 Ayas as it turned out to be the STARTERS while the rest are MAIN COURSE and DESSERTS.

An estimated 3 million people in England volunteer in hospitals, health charities and social organisations, providing support for bereaved families and help older people in need (British Medical Journal 16.3.13). As visiting Islamic scholars these shores have said that we see Islam here but no Muslims while back home we see Muslims and no Islam.

I dedicate this translation work To the victims of terrorism, violence and injustice irrespective of their beliefs, colour and nationalities for these are not permitted by the CREATOR.

Dr. Manzoor Memon

Prelude

More than half a century back, a man took onto him the enormous responsibility to write a book on Qur'an and to establish linkages between what is now scientifically proven and what was ordained in the Qur'an some fourteen centuries back. Hardly, one comes across a book on the Holy Qur'an that deals so scientifically, so elaborately and so conclusively with the mysteries of universe. The masterful manner in which Dr. Burq has dealt with the inscrutabilities of nature, the massive scientific discoveries and the artful creation of linkages of these discoveries with the Qur'anic verses, could only have been done by the person of his standing and caliber.

I have however a wish and a complaint (sort of): easier Urdu, lesser 'poetic prose', not that much 'tinge' and the things would have been lot easier to read, understand, and appreciate. Since my wishes might not be reaching Dr. Burq, I would make the same requests to other (intending and serious) Urdu writers to write in simple plain Urdu. By adopting such an approach and by putting to task their intellectual acumen, they would certainly add to the Qur'anic know-how and ensure that what was revealed centuries ago, was not the figment of human imagination but the doings of the Supreme Creator. This way, their readership would greatly increase and with that, the intended impact. Since what has already been done, cannot be undone, I would expect the would-be authors, especially those that have better understanding of Qur'anic thought and of course, of science, to be kind to their readers by writing everyday Urdu.

Dr Manzoor Memon of London, UK sent me a copy of

"Dou Qur'an" to read and attempt its rendering into English. After reading the book, I was convinced that it was a highly commendable project. I accepted the challenge because I understand that a copy of the Book should reach every household and should adorn the bedside table of every person to serve as a useful reference and guide to properly understand the Message of Allah, but with scientific evidence.

This English rendering of the book "Two Qur'ans" provides practical help to understand what the author has expressed in Urdu. The rendering describes the Book in not-very-technically-difficult English. This will (hopefully) make it helpful especially for those who communicate in English as a second language.

Feeling a moral responsibility to convey, as far as possible in the rendering, original meanings and purposes, I have tried to use words that would convey to the best of my judgment what the author intended to. Thus it is distinguished from a typical translation.

Dr. Burq's original thoughts, undoubtedly regarded by me at first a stumbling blocks in making sagacious English rendering, have proved helpful instead of being ineffectual. This way, carefully and deliberately arrived conclusions by the author, have helped me to gear my efforts towards message rather than verbosity. This helped me greatly to convey what was intended.

Care has been taken that this rendering should prove to be:

- A careful rendering and explanation of the meanings of words and phrases used in the book.

- Helpful in elaboration of historical backgrounds, features, and implied information.

- Rendering aided by examples and footnotes and explanations: footnotes fill a much-needed niche, even for those whose primary language is English.

For those who are only acquainted with metric system of measurements, I have tried to convert, for example feet to meters, pounds to kg, ounce to gram and miles to kilometers. Then certain scientific discoveries and explanations of mid-1900s needed substantiation through today's findings. That has been done, as far as possible by adding footnotes to the (relevant) text. To bring uniformity to the name of the Supreme Creator, I have used mostly "Allah" instead of "God". I have also changed "Lord" frequently used in the English translation of the Qur'anic verses to Allah, where appropriate.

I wish that all the books that can substantiate divine talk with scientific findings, would be a great service to Muslim community especially to those that believe that the Qur'an is just the figment of imagination of a person.

I further believe that in order for the reader to benefit the most, all such books be written in English and later, translated in French, German, and Spanish. If we could do this, we would certainly be taking our message right across Europe, Africa, and South America, besides English speaking-and practicing countries.

Finally, let me make it clear that this rendering would have never been as elaborate as it is now, without the tremendous guidance and help that I got from "Wikipedia" (historical evidences), "Google" (general information), and "HamariWeb" (Urdu-English translations). All of my thanks to these three giants of information treasures! Add to this the determination of Hussain Kaisrani to see to it that the book gets published, internationally and that it reaches every nook and corner of the world.

Any improvement over the quality of English, ease of explanation, and any additional scientific material substantiating Qur'anic philosophy shall be most helpful for me to improve the quality of next edition of this wonder-book by Ghulam Jilani Burq, PhD.

Iqbal Muhammad
Lahore - Pakistan (2013)

Prologue
(Back in 1938)

I was sitting in the library of *Ummat-e-Muslima*[1] in Amritsar and going through old newspapers and journals that I got hold of a special edition of Daily *Inqilab*[2]. After turning a few pages, I came across *Qur'an-e-Hakim aur Ilm-ul-Aaafaq*[3]. After reading the article, I liked it. Its author was Ghulam Jilani Burq, then MA; now PhD. I said to myself how good if he could also write for *Al-Bayaan*[4]. After sometime, I started sending him copies of the Magazine and expressing my wish (to write for "*al-Bayan*"). Just after a few days, his first article reached the office of *Al-Bayaan*.

Today, when I reflect, I feel the strange instruments of Nature. Then, I couldn't even think that he would write a book on Qur'an that would conclusively prove to be the first of its kind enriching Urdu literature, so much so that he would ask *me* to write its Preface; and that in fact, I will have the privilege to do so. It was not even in my wildest dreams that I will do what I am doing right now.

For about two-and-a-half years, we kept on publishing his articles till we received the first installment of his book "Two Qur'ans". At first, we thought that this too would be like a long article of a few installments. On the contrary, the sequence kept on for good fourteen months.

We could not reckon that it would be such a long spell of writings, likewise, it was equally impossible to adjudge the gratitude that he earned from his readership. It was only because of the insistence of readers that inspite of paper

---

[1] Muslim Nation
[2] Revolution
[3] The Qur'an and Knowledge of Universe
[4] The Statement

being very expensive; his thoughts were compiled in the form of a book. Office of *Ummat-e-Muslima* deserves our deepest gratitude that it took onto itself to print the book under extremely adverse circumstances.

As its name implies, there is Qur'an available in all the houses of Muslims (and saved in the hearts of all the Huffaz)[5], and there is Qur'an unfurling the mystries of universe. Its latter facet includes (but is not limited to) the mother earth, the sun, the moon, stars, galaxies, clouds, flowers, chirping birds, oceans, mountains, coal, aluminum and iron, and the deserts, all referred to in the Qur'anic verses. One Qur'an has verses while the other has moving and performing verses. One Qur'an has rules and regulations and the other has its explanations.

It is the Qur'an and its wonderful connect with Nature that has been repeatedly commanded (by Allah). Hard luck of the Muslims that instead of prying in to the secrets of glittering truth, they started looking for some other truth. In fact, life and probity are not two different phenomena. There is no light in the dark hermitages while death prevails equally in monasteries and graveyards. There are no signs of life in recitations and scholarships and in human miracles making human arms paraplegic and freezing the brains. And there is no heat of action and movement. Where is the doubt in the haplessness of Muslims that instead of embracing the oozing and sparkling life, it has opted to make death as its sleeping partner?

Let's not lose sight of the fact that Qur'an is not the religion of the (so-called) Muslims. It is rather the religion for the welfare of the entire mankind. Of all the ages and of all the places and in real and true sense, it is the religion of

---

[5] Those who have leant the Qur'an by heart

life. A book that leads man away and induces him towards a
difficult-to-understand probity could not have been
authored by the Creator of Universe.

How Qur'an induces man towards most horrendous and
most trivial things, will be available to you in the pages that
follow however I feel it necessary to point towards
something of relevance. Just a few days back, I was reciting
Surah *Nahal* wherein man's attention has been drawn
towards the gorgeous exploits of honey bee. The Surah says
that in honey bees, there is lesson for those who think deep.
Just by coincidence, I had the opportunity to read a small
article on honey bees. The article said that a man, in his
entire life, can at the most, vouch for three things: health,
wealth, and wisdom. All the three valuables are available to
honey bees. It is because she flies in sunlight, fresh air and
beautiful flowers and fruits and while toiling hard, stocks
honey. After reading that article, I asked myself: Is there
any lessons for us in the osmosis of honey bee?

Life in itself is religion. This is *the* fundamental principle
that must be kept in mind while reading (and
understanding) the Qur'an.

Dr. Burq has in fact rendered such a great service to
Qur'an that no Muslim before him could perform in the
entire Indian sub-Continent. There is not a single Ayat that
he did not explain in the perspective of science (and logic).
For this purpose, how much literature he might have
studied, how much time he might have spent and how hard
he must have worked, is difficult to imagine. All that I can
say is to thank him, on behalf of all those Muslims who
want to quench their thirst from the oozing spring of
Qur'an, in the cup of science.

This feat was accomplished by Tantavi Jauhari of Egypt
but being unacquainted with Arabic, Muslims of India

could not make use of it. Today, the Muslims of India can say with pride that they too have a Tantavi of their own.

I in fact had picked up the pen to write the preface, but could not. And then I thought let it not be preface, but at least an introduction to the book. Unfortunately, I couldn't do that even; because a good intro is devoid of praise. I can, at the most, express my pleasure and that too, as much, as I feel from within; about being able (if at all) to introduce this book to the (would-be) readers.

Muhammad Iqbal Salmani
Preet Nagar,
December 20, 1943

Chapter-I

Preamble

The study of Qur'an reveals that there are two Qur'ans: Divine Book, and Nature's Treatise (Universe!). Allah has called each period (of history) as Ayat [verse]. Quite obviously, it is known about the Qur'an *"tilka aayaat-ul-kitab-ul-mobin"*: contents of the Qur'an are the evidence of kitab-e-mobin[6].

First Argument

Different scenes of the Book on Universe have been shown to have similarities, with evidence.

There are clear indications for the wise ones in the creation of earth and skies and in the difference between night and day. There are also (clear) evidences for rational human beings in the creation of universe, alternation of day and night, in the purposeful sailing of boat in seas and in the clouds that are floating between the earth and the skies. Al-Baqarah, 164.

It is further said:

The creation of earth and skies and the differences in your languages are clear indications of Allah's doings. And then, there are evidences of Allah's doings in your birth and the rearing of animals. Jasai, 4.

Second Argument

Both the Qur'an and the Treatise on Universe are apparently asymmetrical. Contiguity and consistency in

---

[6] An unambiguous, visible book

the Qur'an has always been a riddle for the *paraphrasers*[7] while the apparent disorganization of the universe is no secret. Dispersal of planets, high and mighty mountain peaks, differences in human world, apparent disconnect in plant life and provocation of insect and animal lives have always created unease (and challenge) for the seekers of knowledge. Any of the two are apparently disjointed but in fact are governed by a strong system. The way the secrets of Qur'an are apparently hidden from human eye, similarly, all the treatises of universe are unknown; though perceptible (to those who seek). Western scholars have consumed lifetime efforts in pursuit of unfolding the secrets of universe. All of their efforts however give them the message of their helplessness and are forced to declare:

Ma'aloomum shud kay haich ma'aloom na shud[8]. In simpler words, this means "the more I know, the more I realize that I know not".

Third Argument

The way no one, no matter how great a scholar of Islam he might be, can develop even a single (Qur'anic) verse. Likewise, the greatest scientist of the world is unable to create a plant leaf, even a minutest particle.

Importance of the Study of Nature

The way the study of Qur'an (and its understanding and acting upon) is obligatory (for mankind), it is equally (if not more) obligatory to study the universe.

---

[7] Mufassirin [scholars!] explaining Qur'anic verses with reference to the context

[8] I have known that I know nothing

Allah says:

O' Rasul! Command the mankind to move around and keenly observe how Allah started the process of evolution. A'nkaboot, 20.

The way it is fatal to defy Qur'an [*These people turned away from Divine Message. Aal-e-Imran 87.*], it is equally like inviting the wrath of Allah if one denies the (existence of) universe.

Allah further says:

There are innumerable visible things in the universe that man goes by and (alas) turns his face the other way. Yousaf, 105.

At one instance, death has been prescribed for those that indulge in the denial of the study of universe:

Do they not ponder over the creation of skies and earth? It appears that their days are numbered. A'araaf, 185.

The significance of study of nature can be gauged from the fact that Qur'an has ordained ablution, prayers, fasting, charity, pilgrimage, divorce, loan, etc. All of these have been described in 150 verses, in total. On the study of nature however there are 756 verses[9]. Qur'an is the last Divine Message for all the ages and all the nations on earth. If today, this Book does not guide us in geology, mountains' wealth and treasures in seas and cannot make us equal to the developed societies then (God forbid), it is worthless. Today, why the westerners are profiting from the knowledge of extremely far-off objects and forecasting information of the forthcoming rains and thunders? It is just because that after due enquiry and study of nature, they are using the science and its application, the technology, for the welfare of mankind.

Visualize! There are layers of white, red, and black rocks

---

[9] Rest of the nations disobeyed Allah and only studied the doings of Allah. And that is why they could not make proper use of it. We on the other hand, have given on both words and deed. That is why we are neither this way nor that way. Al-Bayan.

hidden in the mountains. Also study the different colors of human beings and animals and remember: of all of His subjects, only scholars are troubled. Fatir, 27, 28.

This verse clearly indicates that true knowledge can be sought by studying the nature. And the concern can only be the prerogative of scholars of universe. The way it is important to study the writings of Shakespeare, Roussos, Luqman, Saadi, Bu Ali Sena, and Iqbal and to understand their greatness, it is equally important to understand the greatness and exaltation, the apex of creation, the evolution and the intricacies of universe. For this, one would need to deeply study the universe. If an author cannot be appreciated without reading his writings, likewise, it is not possible to do so without deep thinking over what He has done and created in the universe (for the good of mankind).

As a hungry man thanks when given food, a thirsty man thanks when given water, an ignorant person thanks after getting knowledge. Hazrat Ibrahim used to thank Allah so:

I thank Allah who gave me two sons in my old age – Ismael and Ishaq. Ibrahim, 39.

After getting freedom from captivity, Hazrat Yousaf says:

How great beneficence of Allah, who released me from jail. Yousaf, 100.

How apt an Arab poet had been when he said:

I thank Allah who adored me with the linen of Islam. But instead of self-seeking, the Muslim has been commanded to thank Allah (for his immense bounties). All the approbation is (only) for Allah.

How vast sympathy has been bestowed onto those who pry into the secrets of nature. Allah likes only true praise. And that is why those nations have been honored that are thankful to Allah in the truest sense. On the contrary, we, the Muslims, have gone deep in to disrepute just because of our lip service to the greatness of Allah; though our mosques are full of (apparent) worshippers and praying people but Allah says:

Those who are in fact thankful to Me, are very few. Saba, 13.

There is a fantastic treasure of mines under the soil. Latent forces of listening and seeing (radio, television) are active in their own right. Today, man is tremendously benefiting from electricity, steam energy, gasoline, etc. And the fact is that Allah says:

All the treasures of earth have been created for your benefit. Baqrah, 29.

Nature has gifted us with the senses of seeing, feeling, listening and understanding, but unfortunately, we have not used these faculties properly. And that is why we are bearing the punishment for our lapses. And that is why Allah says:

Man would be asked about the proper (and improper) use of eye, nose, and heart. Bani Israel, 36.

Islam has called *inquisition* as the best act. A Hadeeth says: In this world, deep thinking for a while is far better than worshipping for a whole year.

One morning the Prophet said:

Last night, a verse was revealed onto me. Death be for him who would read it but not think it over. Let there be second and third time wrath of Allah (on them).

And then the Prophet read this verse:

The creation of earth and skies, the difference between day and night, the beneficial ships sailing in the seas and inducing life in the dead earth through rains, the moving winds, and in clouds that stay between earth and sky, there are lessons but for seekers of knowledge. Baqarah, 164.

The Qur'an was descended to annunciate the Momineen about exaltation and acclivity.

Should you remain committed, you will be acclaimed the

world over. Aal-e-Imran, 139.

Today, only that nation can have freedom and honor which, in its truest sense, is benefiting the mankind, and those who lighten the world, and know the proper and rational use of gasoline and coal, or those who will cause death and destruction to mankind?

And verily, He revealed iron, wherein is mighty power and (many) uses for humankind. Hadid, 25.

Qur'an has bestowed on us the title of those "ordering for acknowledged virtues". It is also acknowledgement that of the natural resources of earth, we can create powerful and dreaded things that can do away with the Satan.

Create that strength to meet your enemies together with strong cavalry with which you can strike terror in the hearts of your enemies and Allah's enemies. Anfaal, 60.

A man is well-wisher of his peoples only if he can cause goodness, justice, equality, and peace and stability. Since delivering order is the sole prerogative of the ruler, therefore he must be the well-wisher of his nation. These days, no government can stay without the use of worldly powers. The word 'renegade' has all the ingredients of vice. Slavery is the greatest evil on earth and because of this, not an iota of dignity is left in a slave nation that has reached the last stages of evil, ignorance, and torture. Such a nation is just like a herd of goats. The way goat's milk, meat, skin, even bones are sold, similarly, a ruling nation deprives a conquered nation of all of its produce, wealth, grains, land, even their lives and uses it for its benefit. Can such a nation be called the best of nations?

O' Muslims! You are the best of the nations and have risen for the betterment of the world. Your job is to order for goodness and stopping from evil. Aal-e-Imran, 11.

The phrase *ukhrijat lin-nasé*[10] signifies that to become the

---

[10] Stand up for the welfare of mankind

well-wisher of nations, attention must be paid to the welfare of the world. And this can only be possible when we have all the basic ingredients that ensure welfare of the people. Along with that, we must also own universal knowledge, tremendous strength, and heart-rendering character. If on the one hand, world acknowledges our moral values, on the other, all the forces of evil must be trembling even by just a cursory mention of ours. This is exactly what leads to welfare of the people.

A Fact

The way sun rises from east and sets in the west, the same way, the sun of knowledge and civilization keeps on moving. Researchers agree that the sun of civilization shone first in the east. True to this agreement, civilizations of China, India, Babylon, and Egypt are far too old. Gradually, Greece, a part of west, became the center of knowledge and inquiry. In 336 B.C., Alexander annihilated the grandeur of Persia and later on, conquered Egypt in 331 B.C. After the demise of Alexander, Greece was divided into small states and wars started that lead to their destruction and oblivion.

In 248 B.C., Parthia[11] rose up and in no time, became a powerful state. After about two centuries, Rome started coming into life and quickly became a tremendous Empire. Rome first defeated Parthia in 38 B.C. and inflicted a second defeat on it in 163 A.D. In 216 A.D., the last signs of Parthia disappeared from the world map and the sun of civilization

---

[11] An 800 km landmass stretching between Khurasan and Astar Abad. After the assignation of Julius Ceasar, when a war broke out between Mark Antony and Brutus, Parthia sided with Brutus.

once again started shining on the west.

After some time, Persia started getting new life and the flag of Sassanid Dynasty started fluttering over Madayin. On the other side, the Roman Empire started showing signs of weakness till the middle of seventh century A.D. That was when in the desert of Arabian Peninsula, knowledge started spreading out in all directions that benefited both east and west.

After a few centuries, the sun of knowledge and civilization once again drifted to the west. Moving through Germany, France, Spain, and England, it ended up in America. We are observing once again that the sun of knowledge and civilization has started rising in the east, creating awareness in India, Iran, and Turkey. Allah has turned the attention of the wise through this Verse:

O' Allah! Whosoever You want, make him the owner of earth and whosoever You want, make him slave. Both respect and disgrace are in Your power. All the heights are in Your control. You control anything and everything and You own everything and have the power to convert freedom in to slavery and night into day. It is Your prerogative to create life in dead nations and to cause death to those living nations that have gone lazy. Imran, 26, 27.

These facts can be observed only by alert eyes and a heart full of farsightedness. But alas! Muslim nation is deprived of this wealth.

These people shirk from the significance of universe.

Quantities

Both cotton and wheat have originated from eight elements. Because of differences in combination of quantities, somewhere it came up like wheat and elsewhere, in the shape of cotton. Water has two parts of hydrogen and one part oxygen. If this combination is altered even a little bit, it will become poison. If these two parts are mixed in equal quantities, even then, poison would be the ultimate result - deadly compound. Both oxygen and hydrogen are deadly gases and when mixed in different combinations, millions of compounds can be prepared, each one of which would turn to be a deadly poison. But if mixed in proportions of two parts of hydrogen to one part of oxygen, a compound (of these two poisons) would make water that provides life to all the living beings.

And We have created life from water. Anbia, 30.

Think! How much knowledge Allah has of the destinies and how He creates innumerable things by the combination of different quantities of different elements.

And We have created everything through pre-determined quantities of various elements. Qamar, 49.

Both lemon and black pepper are made up of 10 molecule[12]s of hydrogen and twenty molecules of Carbon. But because of difference in atomic structure, both have different shapes, colors and tastes. Same way, coal and diamond are made up of carbon. But the difference in their atomic structures, one is black (coal) and the other is white (diamond). One is breakable and the other is solid and strong. Now let's link this explanation with the Qur'anic Verses:

(1) We have treasures of all the things. And We descend everything in pre-determined quantities. Hijr, 21.

(2) And We are never unmindful of creation. Mominoon, 17.

All the things of universe are created by mixing precise amounts of elements. If some alteration occurs in these

---

[12] Molecules are made up of atoms held together by chemical bonds. These bonds form as a result of the sharing or exchange of electrons among atoms.

combinations, the system of life would immediately be turned around. If today, Allah reduces the quantity of hydrogen, even a little, all the rivers and oceans would be converted to floods of poison and no living thing would be able to survive. All the plants have similar combination; it is just the difference of qualities. Think! How deep is the knowledge of Allah of elements and their quantities.

Har Gulay ra rang o boo-ye deegar ast

Every flower has different color and fragrance

Arrangement of animals and plants is the result of a string of combinations of oxygen, hydrogen, carbon, nitrogen, and some other elements. The same elements cause the creation of bones, nerves, blood, even hair. And the same elements have resulted in trees, leaves, flowers and fruits. And of course, bitterness, sourness, and sweetness and colors and styles are all because of these elements.

We created everything in proper proportions. Hijr, 19.

Qur'an has ordained Muslims seven hundred and fifty six times to contemplate on nature's bounties and rules. Ibne Rushd[13], Farabi[14], Sena[15], and Razi[16] all have guided us

---

[13] Ibn Rushd or by his Latinized name Averroës (1126 – 1198 A.D.), was a Spanish Andalusian Muslim polymath, a master of Aristotelian philosophy, Islamic philosophy, Islamic theology, Maliki law and jurisprudence, logic, psychology, politics and Arabic music theory, and the sciences of medicine, astronomy, geography, mathematics, physics and celestial mechanics. Averroes was born in Córdoba (Spain), and died in Morocco.

[14] Al-Farabi, known in the West as Alpharabius was a renowned scientist and philosopher of the Islamic Golden Age. He was also a cosmologist, logician, and musician. Through his commentaries and treatises, Al-Farabi became well known among medieval Muslim intellectuals as "The Second Teacher", that is, the successor to Aristotle, "The First Teacher".

See next page

towards contemplation. Unfortunately, we did not care to ponder, with the result that today, other nations are moving as if sitting on electricity and winds and we are facing the bitter slaps in desert lives. Allama She'arani understands well the physical facets of Islam. And he was sure that if a Muslim remained Muslim in real sense, he will one day reach the pinnacle of progress and prosperity like he (once) excelled in the Islamic system of governance. That is why, it is said:

Islam in the beginning was just jurisprudence but would become reality in the last ages.

And now is (the period of) 'last ages' where we need to concentrate over earth and skies and strive to prove Islam as a solid reality.

And Look! In the heavens and the earth are indications for believers. Jasiah, 3.

And in your creation, and all the beasts that He scattered in the earth, are portents for those whose faith is sure. Jasiah 4.

Redemption for today's Muslims is in the study of nature and universe. Today, only those nations are knowledgeable, prosperous, and powerful that derive strength from the study of nature and spend lives in their pursuits. On the other hand, heedlessness and ignorance have humiliated the Muslims and thus have lost the balance of nationalism. Their empires destroyed, their frontiers are

---

[15] Ali ibn Sena or by his Latinized name **Avicenna**, was a Persian polymath, who wrote almost 450 treatises on a wide range of subjects, of which around 240 have survived. In particular, 150 of his surviving treatises concentrate on philosophy and 40 of them concentrate on medicine.

[16] Al-Razi, known as Rhazes or **Rasis** after medieval Latinists (865 – 925 A.D.) was a Persian Muslim polymath, a prominent figure in Islamic Golden Age, physician, chemist, philosopher, and scholar.

unsafe and all of their defensive strategies have reduced to naught. If today, we constitute a commission to pinpoint our deficiencies and find solutions, all of our efforts would go waste because we lack experts in economics, politics, science, and other skills.

In Europe, they constitute a commission for any deficiency where great experts come and give testimony. Such a commission, after going through all the material evidence collected, prepares a report and sends it to the Government. Today, if before an international committee, a need arises about arms control, economics, balance of power, and distribution of wealth, do we have even a single expert of the 1.6 billion Muslims who could effective plead our case, whose testimony would be worth anything? Alas, that we were sent to this world as evidential.

We have sent towards you a witness. Baqarah, 143.

In other words, we were commanded that we would excel in all the walks of life such that our testimony would be the final verdict. But alas, because of our ignorance, our testimony is not considered worth the paper it is written on.

Use of Body Parts

Allah has given us eyes (to see) and ears (to hear) and brain (to think). A nation that does not use these body parts and their faculties, is in fact blind, dumb, and devoid of brain. People of wisdom only can see the universe from the perspective of reality and listen to each and every sound emanating for each and every particle of the universe.

Why don't they study nature so that they understand and so that their ears get the resonance of knowledge? Al-Hajj, 46.

The digression of a nation is in fact, the deterioration of senses.

For indeed it is not the eyes that grow blind, but it is the hearts, which are within the bosoms, that grow blind. Hajj, 46.

Certain nations on earth are travelling in cars and planes while we sit either under cool shades and rest or move *snailishly* on camels. As a result, our backwardness is a foregone conclusion.

Fortunate are those people who select the best means of transportation:
Good tidings (O Muhammad) to my bondmen Who hear advice and follow the best thereof. Zumar, 17, 18.

Significance of Ka'bah

Muslims are scattered the world over who, inspite of color and creed, different languages, cultures, etc. have been kept together through a few things: one Allah; one Prophet; one Book; only one language (in prayers and worships); and one Qiblah. Our (religious) scholars and the learned ones were commanded to congregate each year at Ka'bah and find means to strengthen bond among the Muslims. *"Tafakkar fil Aafaaq"* is the best means for the stability of Muslim Ummah. To grasp the knowledge of the Rule of Survival prevalent in the universe is the greatest means of redemption and of life.

Allah has made the Ka'bah, the Sacred House, an asylum of security and Hajj and Umrah for mankind, and also the Sacred Month and the animals of offerings and the garlanded[17], that you may know that Allah has knowledge of all that is in the heavens and all that is in the earth, and that Allah is the All-Knower of each and everything. Ma'idah, 97.

---

[17] People or animals, etc. marked with the garlands on their necks made from the outer part of the stem of the Makkah trees for their security.

But unfortunately, today there is no such center of learning that could lead us to the unlimited knowledge of Allah. Just think that a fish egg in the deepest of oceans, would only produce a fish. In a dark cave of Koh Qaf, a mosquito will only give birth to a mosquito. In the wombs of animals, sperms take proper and suitable shapes. In the heart of sea shell, a drop of water transforms into pearl, not coal. Of all the life forms, nothing is invisible from the watchful eyes of Allah. Everything is happening systematically and in proper proportions. There is no chance for error, aberrance, or disorganization.

Look again and again: Can you see any disarray? Mulk, 3.

Is there any school in Ka'bah to estimate the gorgeous knowledge of Allah? No! That is why intent of the Giver is not being fulfilled. Today, Hajj has become just a tradition, when a massive crowd gathers to perform certain rituals, willingly or unwillingly, and returns back to their countries. They do not return by getting new ideas or any lessons of life. Such responsibilities that should have been performed at Ka'bah, are being taken care of in Oxford and Cambridge, and in Harvard and Princeton where seekers of knowledge come from around the world[18].

Pro-Moderation

Qur'an has called Muslims as those who tread the path of moderation. We are moderate from a number of angles. We served as a medium for the spread of Greek knowledge to the east. Unfortunately, we preached dry spirituality to

---

[18] Just to the extent of *"Yashahd wa munafa lahum"* and being oblivious of the fact "Wa yazkoro ismillah". And both of these objectives have been described in Surah Al-Hajj. By forgetting the second objective that holds, even the first objective becomes incorrect.

other believers (Hindus, Christians, Buddhists, etc.). We created amicability between body and spirit and religion and worldly life. Scholars of physical knowledge, who were being crushed by the Roman monks, were provided the blanket security of our religion and of our physical strength. And then geographically as well, we are the residents of middle-eastern countries. In other words, we are like a lamp that glows in the middle of a party. It was our religious and geographical liability to glitter the world with knowledge and mysticism, but alas, our ignorance instead, darkened our own houses.

Parable

A king used to decorate his palace with gems. World's best craftsmen decorated his palace with their artful work. Carpets from Iran and golden curtains, vases with best flowers, etc. would give an aura of awe and grandeur. And then how great cruelty if his dear wife, children and courtiers, devoid of the sense of appreciation, would not like it all and thus behave like animals, not impressed by all of his efforts.

Same is the case with Muslims. How beautifully, the Owner of earth and skies has decorated our universe but we do not have the vision to appreciate it, and we do not have the capability to enjoy it.

We beautified the sky with stars and We divided the skies in a number of sections for the beholders. Hijr, 16.

Is there anyone to enjoy, to like, to see?

For You

If this is correct that we are the first and the last addressees of the Qur'an, then listen to what it says:

Allah is He Who has created the heavens and the earth and sends down water (rain) from the sky, and thereby brought forth fruits as provision for you; and He has made the ships to be of service to you, that they may sail through the sea by His Command; and He has made rivers (also) to be of service to you. And He has made the sun and the moon, both constantly pursuing their courses, to be of service to you; and He has made the night and the day, to be of service to you. And He gave you all that you asked for. Ibrahim, 32-34.

In this Ayat, *"Lakum"* (for you) has been used five times. Meaning thereby that all these bounties were for Muslims and through them, for rest of the world. But today, sun, electricity, light, and all else have been conquered by the westerners. They are ruling the oceans, they have conquered the seas and skies and giving the power of light to the world. And we get wonderstruck by looking at an electric bulb. Why all this? Because of our atrocities:

And Allah guides not the people who are atrocious to themselves. Baqrah, 258.

Earth Floor

Allah has made the earth a resting place for you. Baqrah, 22.

And how very strange, that we even don't know the composition of our bed. We have absolutely no idea of the various elements of earth, how and when was it created and on whose will does it stay, what is in it and where did the water come onto it. Our "all knowledge" mullah says that all this has happened because of Allah's prowess. But is it not our obligation to get knowledge of how it happened? And if not, then what is the purpose of this Verse:

It is because that you may know that Allah has knowledge of all that is in heavens and in earth. Ma'idah, 97.

Things made up of steel, for example, planes, ships, tanks, and guns keep on horrifying the world. How powerful are those nations that have excelled in the use of steel and how miserable are those that have no knowledge of it. About 1,400 years earlier, the Prophet of Islam gave this Divine message to the Muslims the world over:

And He revealed iron, wherein is mighty power and (many) uses for humankind. Hadid, 25.

Unfortunately, Muslims did not think it over and as a result, have been subjected to humiliation and detraction. Even today, if our "so-called" Islamic governments get modern knowledge, their present weakness would at once be transformed into ascendancy.

In the presence of such Ayaat, who could dare say that Qur'an is not a guide for all the ages? In fact, the message given by the Prophet is that gorgeous constitution (the Qur'an), acting upon which would invariably result in power, grandeur, conquest of land and water and the rule on earth. And there have been a great stress on the study of nature that when not obeyed, would invariably result in national destruction.

It is pertinent to ponder that jurisprudence-related Ayaat usually start in response to "ask you" [*yas alunaka*], for example:

They ask you (O' Mohammad) about alcoholic drink and gambling. Baqrah, 219.

A Historical Incident

Once Hazrat Aziz[AS] was passing near *Bait-ul-Maqdas* that had then been devastated by Bakht Nasr. He kept on thinking if it would ever be possible that this town is again brought to life. Allah caused him to die for one hundred years and then revived him and said:

Look at your food (figs) and your drink (milk). None of these have become stale or got rotten even in hundred years.

Baqrah, 259.

There is a lesson for us in this Ayat: not to rot during such a long time is not a miracle, because today, experts keep them fresh in cans for years.

Another piece of the same Ayat:

And look at your donkey; and We will make you a sign for the people. And look at the bones [of this donkey] - how We raise them and then We cover them with flesh.

While looking at the present knowledge of explanation of life, Hazrat Aziz[AS] thought over the donkey, and its bones. He was visibly impressed by Allah's workmanship and cried:

Then Aziz cried that now I have understood the knowledge of Allah. Baqarah, 259.

This is the knowledge that results in modesty but simultaneously, creates vigor in hearts.

And when His Verses are recited to them, they enhance their Faith; and they put their trust in Allah. Anfaal, 2.

Today, in western labs, animals are dissected to observe the workmanship of Divine hand and studies are conducted to figure out the systems so skillfully put together such that human mind becomes dumb-founded. As against their fantastic achievements, Muslims are not only ignorant but consider such knowledge (courtesy, our very Mullah) as against the spirit of Islam. For centuries, we are being punished for our delinquencies and Allah knows how long this system of tyranny would prevail.

They forgot Allah and Allah made them so embarrassed, that they don't know their own status. Hashar, 16.

The Beginning of Khalil[AS]

The entire universe was lying bare in front of Hazrat Abraham[AS] with all its beauty and grandeur. Of all these beautiful scenes, he had to select a deity. His deep sight went tearing across all the glittering toys and straight far above them all and then made this heart-rending announcement:

I cannot worship those heavenly bodies that set down. An'aam, 77.

This was the first infestation of Khalil that is followed by research. And Hazrat Abraham[AS] hated following in the footsteps of his ancestors. In this regard, Allama Iqbal said:

Had conformity been a good habit

The prophets too would have been treading the path of their ancestors

And that is why, Hazrat Abraham[AS] said:

O' Rabb! Show me the scene wherein life could be infused in a dead body. Baqarah, 260.

As such, four slaughtered birds were infused with life right in front of him. And that was his second infestation.

When Hazrat Ibrahim[AS] fully qualified in both the infestations, and proved his being a man of inquisition and research, Allah ordained on him the leadership of the kingdom in these words:

O' Abraham! I am going to make you the leader of Islamic world. Baqarah, 124.

Ibrahim asked Allah about his children, Allah said:

Those of your children, who would defy the path of righteousness, would lose the leadership. Baqrah, 124.

Ignorance is the greatest vice. Today, the successors of Hazrat Ibrahim[AS] are down-trodden and humiliated because they are ignorant of Qur'an and the universe. They don't know that without using the underground treasures, no nation can survive even for a few hours.

Vision

Qur'an has many a time ordained:

Observe the earth and the skies. Younas, 100.

Literally, vision would mean to see, to observe, to inspect, to think. In the perspective of universe, vision would mean to keenly observe it, think it over and looking at all of its facets. Can we perform such an act by just looking at the things through naked eye? No! Why? Because the (physical) range of our eyesight is very limited. If our eyesight is weak, we can wear glasses. But since Allah has commanded us to 'look', it becomes our foremost duty to fulfill His Command in the best possible manner. Today, a number of high quality instruments –telescopes; microscope - are available that can observe even the most hidden sides of various creations.

A Muslim has been ordered to offer prayers. Now it is the responsibility of a Muslim to keep his body clean, wear clean clothes, go to the mosque, and offer prayers. It is not the responsibility of Allah to wash his clothes, arrange for his ablution, and ask the angels to pick him up and take him to the mosque to offer prayers. Exactly like the prayers, it is also the responsibility of a Muslim that he studies the universe and unfurls its mysteries, for the sake of knowledge and for the benefit of mankind.

Dedication

When a person is useful for nation from any perspective, his name is kept alive (after his death) by naming a building, or a road after his name. For example, Ganga Ram Hospital, Jinnah Terminal, Allama Iqbal International Airport, Kitchener Road, Alphinstone Street, Faisalabad, etc.

Allah has given such an importance to animals, insects, and plants that He has ascribed certain Surahs to their names. For example, Surah Baqarah has 2,612 words and

286 Ayaat. It has reference to paradise, hell, Eiman, dispute, prophets, and lot more. But it has been given the name Baqarah (cow); not paradise, Musa, book, etc. Similarly, other surahs have names like Namal (ant), Nahal (honey bee), Safaat (flying bird), Teen (chain), Asr (period), Najm (star); Naas (man), etc.

Now think how much importance Allah bestows on various scenes of the universe.

Man can be related to the following things:

1) Water: making drinks, medicines

2) Earth: water, gasoline, minerals, food

3) Air: breathing, flying

4) Fire: steam, ammunition

5) Plants: food, medicines

6) Animals: milk, meat, transportation

7) Body: anatomy, physiology

8) Man: poetry, music

It implies that in each and everything, there is a hidden facet to it. Each and every particle gives us the message of the unlimited energy. Unfortunately, we haven't cared:

These people close their eyes to the scenes of nature, while moving. Yousaf, 105.

Rays

While discussing cosmic radiation, Prof. Arthur Aldington writes that those radiations that had started from the universe before the creation of earth, have reached just now. These rays are too small in quantity but too strong.

These are the cause of diversity in plants and animals. In the beginning, there must have been just one flower on a plant. But when it withered and its seeds dispersed, some cosmic rays might have penetrated some seed that must have caused a change in its structure. As a result, its structure and color changed from other seeds. All the flowers and plants that we see today, is the result of those cosmic rays.

Junction of Radiations

Of just an inch of atmosphere, all those radiations are piercing through water, grasses, buildings, and sun and stars. If we look at it through a microscope, we will observe that in just one inch space, millions of radiations emanating from natural objects are crisscrossing. Even the feeblest radiations of North Star are piercing through the most powerful radiations of sun. A huge railway junction is thus like a miniature compared to this one inch space.

Strength of Light

Light is a gorgeous source of energy. If somehow, we could collect it over a space of a tennis court, we could run a 200 Horse Power engine till eternity.

Price of Light

We make use of electricity in our houses and mills whose primary source is sun. A European physicist has estimated that the entire world consumes about 15 g of electricity that costs 340 million rupees. On the other hand, sunlight that penetrates earth in just a day, weighs about 180,000 kg. Compared to the cost of electricity, this light costs 150 trillion US$. Western scientist believe that sun will be giving us light for about 10 billion years. Look at the bounty of Allah that without spending a penny, we have access to such an unlimited treasure.

Then which of the Blessings of your Lord will you both (jinns and men) deny? Ar-Rahman, 13.

Cradle of Earth

In the earliest forms, earth was covered with water. If it is flattened to day, water will cover its entire surface to a depth of about 10,000 ft [3,000 m]. After sometime, because of its internal heat, all the material hidden inside, will ooze out and there will be mountains all around. It was because of earthquakes and the changes in water that have played a crucial part to keep its surface uneven. Its unevenness is in itself a benevolence of Allah, otherwise it would not have been the abode for animals and mankind.

Allah is the one Who made the earth your cradle. Tahaa, 53.

Divine Habit

Some animals use some body parts more. It causes increase in their sizes. And then some parts are used less that keep on diminishing till they disappear. Plants also follow the same principles of nature. A couple of centuries back, banana had seeds like guava that was used for its cultivation. Gradually, instead of seeds, farmers started planting its branches. When the nature observed that seeds are no more used, it gradually finished the seeds in banana and today, we have seedless banana. It is the principle of Omnipotence that keeps those nations alive that are useful and destroys useless nations, like the seeds in banana.

Only that is sustained on earth which is useful for the world. Ra'ad, 7.

Does this verse not wake us up from slumber that we, the (so called) Muslims, will not be sustained if we remain useless as we are?

Allah Listens

Today, because of undulation of sound-waves, we can listen to others from thousands of kilometers away; in Europe and America through wireless communication. Here naturally, a question arises whether this sound is within the authority of Allah, or is it outside it. If inside, then any attention-grabbing sound and movement, no matter how feeble, is not hidden from Allah. The theory of sound waves has ensured us that *Allah listens and sees.*

Mr. William, a professor at Imperial College of London was once observing the structure of human ear. Getting impressed by Nature's craftsmanship, he yelled:

He who planted ear
Shall he not hear?

Imagine! how much belief did the Professor have in the infinite attributes of Allah.

Congruity/Coherence with Environment

The entire structure of universe is composed of electrons. Electrons mingled with protons and the result was neutrons. A few neutrons came together and became atoms the collection of which was called molecule. Each atom and each molecule is a small treasure of electricity.

The composition of Plants is also the result of these particles. It is just the difference in name. In plants, the arrangement of elements is due to cells. Each cell is a compound of electrons and protons and its ingredients are called protoplasm. The cell is not a "dead body" rather it is an extremely sensitive and complex treasure of life, in comparison to which, a watch or some other man-made machine is extremely simple. Each protoplasm has a wonderful property of transformation.

In earlier times, plants appeared on sea shore. When their seeds dropped, birds, winds and rains shifted them to new environments where certain changes occurred in their structure. For example, a rose plant growing in a garden had always the fear of being browsed by animals. To protect it from animals, nature grew thorns on it. On the other hand, roses that were within a safe compound, had lesser danger of damage and so, got lesser thorns. And then, a lot of difference can be observed in terms of color, delicacy, and smell in wild and garden-grown roses. Care of gardener and appreciation of the people added further attraction and delicacy to roses.

Shirley says that in the corner of my garden, I saw a flower that had its outer edges somewhat white. I wished that flower to be white. Next year, it was whitish and after a few years, absolutely white.

Like plants, animals also get new limbs in a new environ. Some bones of birds have gases that reduce their weight and thus could easily fly. A bladder that frog uses in water to swim, functions as lungs while on land. Similarly, all the necessities that a fish needs in water, it gets. Here naturally a question arises: could this have been possible without the craftsmanship of a *Hidden Power*? Is there no brainwork behind this great universal machine? Is it all because of man's wishes? Absolutely not! How wonderful of a western intellectual, when he said:

The idea of mind behind and mind within seems as rational

and working hypothesis as any.

The very thought that a *Brain* is busy within and without the universe, is a rational and believable phenomenon.

Speed of Creation

It took millions of years in the evolution of earth. There was a time when universe was devoid of intellect. This deficiency was taken care of, by the creation of man. In other words, the "invention of man" was the last chapter of the history of "creation". There might still such brains come, for which we might act as the beginning. Where this world is leading to, only Allah knows! What type of men would be there, after say a million years? And how deep their thinking might be, is anybody's guess. A British intellectual, Bernard Shaw said that after a few hundred thousand years, man would have invented cars and planes thousands of times faster than the present ones. And the way today, we have arms and cannons and other artifacts of earlier and medieval ages decorating our museums, same way planes and cars of our age would be considered the products of dark ages and kept in the museums of coming generations.

There is a universal principle that a thing has always been replaced by a better one. Look at cars, their beauty, safety, aerodynamics, fuel-efficiency, and versatility that has been on the rise. How fitting Allah had been, when He said: when we remove a thing or a scene, We create a better one or of similar qualities.

Atonement of mafaat

Think over human body. A surgeon drills a hole in human body and inside a wonderful machine is busy making skin and flesh. Had there been no natural atonement of mafaat, thousands of patients would have died without operation. Similar sequence is working in the realm of morality. We can compensate for our past sins and wrong doings by abjuration and atonement. As for the philosophy of Brahmins that there can be no atonement of sins, is not true.

Forgiveness is only incumbent on Allah toward those who do evil in ignorance (and) then turn quickly (in repentance) to Allah. Nisa, 17.

Capital of Allah

If in a winter night, a Martian descends on Bombay where he will see tall buildings, glittering lights, rushing cars and decorated shops, would he think that all this happened by itself? No! Just look at the sky in a dark night; how magnificently starts twinkle, billions of these presenting an awe-inspiring scene. It clearly shows as if sky is the capital of some magnificent Emperor.

Are they equating them (the kings) with Allah? Allah is far Greater and Pure!

After due thinking over the universe, Einstein said:

The Universe is ruled by Mind; whether it be the mind of a mathematician or of an artist, of a poet, or all of them. It is the ONE reality that gives meaning to existence, enriches our daily life, encourages our hope and energizes us with faith wherever knowledge fails.

At yet another instance, Einstein says:

He, who can no longer pause to wonder and stand rapt in awe, is as good as dead and his eyes are closed.

The above quote of Einstein seems to be an approximate translation of the following Ayat:

Have they not considered the dominion of the heavens and the earth, and what things Allah has created, and that it may be that their own term draws near? A'raaf, 185.

While standing in front of the Himalayas, one shudders with fear and awe: those wide and deep valleys, that nerve-shattering calm, and those limitless grandeurs and horrifying scenes. Do they not create tremors in man's mind? Is the creator of these ranges the same who created the beautiful valleys of Kashmir, the world of flowers, the chirping birds, the babbling streams?

Look at those huge waves of ocean that strike the rocks and go back. How gorgeous is this world of waters! On the other hand, in a moonlit night, how enchanting is the scene of a serene lake, those beautiful flowers of all colors and hue, that fragrance-laden breeze, those half waking storks and ducks over calm grass. O' my God! How beautiful and soothing is all this. How apt a western naturalist, when he said:

> When we stand and gaze upon the scene before us, we grow to feel a part of it. Something in it communicates with something in us. The communication brings us joy and the joy brings us exaltation.

The Chairman

Astronomers have estimated that in the blue atmosphere, there are infinite numbers of stars that are larger by millions of times than our sun; make it look like a miniature. They are flying with tremendous speed. And our sun looks like a minutest particles in comparison to them. And then all these stars and satellites when combined together, are hardly an insignificant part of the whole of universe. And the man is presiding over this infinite company. How great an honor!

And we created man as best of the universe. Bani Israel.

How vast is the clan of man. From the planet of a galaxy

to the desert, all are composed of the same source (electrons) and all are created from the same self (neutron). As such, all these oceans, mountains, sun, etc. are blood brothers of mankind; though man is smaller both in life and stature but (as has been said):

Even if man is smaller in stature, is far better in value

To substantiate the point, Allah says:

Allah is the One who created you from a single source (neutron). Aaraaf, 189.

Allah had sent us, the human beings, as leaders of this grand universe. But unfortunately, we have been consistently breaking the laws of nature; though all the rest of creations are working in accordance with their mandate; and man?

By the declining day, look: man is in a state of loss. A'sr, 1,2.

Is this just a Coincidence?

Our planet earth is the derivative of sun. That is why earthly neutrons also have their source from sun. These particles have today been transformed into various objects on earth. Now the question arises as to who shaped all these things. Does it all happen as a matter of coincidence? We believe that 'coincidence' does exist on earth, but coincidences could be good as well as bad. If yes, then why is it that all '*good coincidences*' have been used in the creation of universe while '*bad coincidences*' have not been even touched upon? Therefore, there is no alternative other than accepting that there must be an *EYE* supervising and some immense brain has been busy making the things happen.

It is because of these creations and cosmologies that Prof. William McBride said:

Can anyone seriously suggest that this directing and regulating power originated in change encounter of atoms?

Can the streams rise higher than its fountain?
And We have created above you seven paths, and We are never
unmindful of creation. Mominun, 17.

Map of Construction

Mango's seed is a small box (or frame) that has the sketch
of a minuscule mango tree complete with roots, stem, leafs,
branches, fruit, etc. is present in the seed. After getting food
from earth, air and sun, the seed first transforms into a tiny
plant and gradually, becomes a whole tree. This seed is like a
map that an architect develops before the construction of a
building. Now a very pertinent question arises: when the
first mango grew on earth, where was the map, the plan? The
answer is: it was in the mind of the Creator.

Not an atom's weight, or less than that, or greater, escapes
Him in the heavens or in the earth, but it is in a clear Record.
Saba 3.

Latent Energy

The entire universe seems to be under an imperceptible
energy. Though it does not exist physically however it is
present. It can be explained through an example that we can
listen to some speech or some drama from thousands of
kilometers away, and sometimes when impressed, we even
cry. Now the speaker is in a far-off place and we get
impressed by an imperceptible power which is anyhow,
something that can be felt but not circumscribed. A still
clearer example is that after falling from tree, an apple
neither flies up, nor runs towards horizon; it is rather
attracted by the force of gravity towards earth. Have you
observed how great an impact an imperceptible power had
on apple? More or less in similar fashion, there is an

imperceptible power busy day in and day out. And that is Allah.

His throne includes the heavens and the earth, and He is never weary of preserving them. Baqarah, 255.

The way all the hills and flatlands, gardens, humans, animals and plants when combined, is called Pakistan and its residents as its brain. Then at some special occasion (for example, a public gathering, a ceremony), a person is selected as its president, who represents the true feelings of the people, likewise Allah is the President of the universe and a pivotal source of man's power, wishes, and emotions.

Impressed by the cosmology, a western intellectual says: The more we know, the more we find there is to know. The farther we go, the greater is our joy. The deeper we penetrate the higher is our exaltation. So on and on we shall go laymen and scientists alike, we shall never stop, because the lure is too great.

Look at what Francis Thompson says about the universe:

All things by immortal power near
And far hiddenly to each other linked are
That thou cannot stir a flower
Without the trembling of a star

Allah is Great! How better could one expect to write on the Oneness of Allah?

This is the real source of inspiration that after hundreds of years of meditation and deep thinking, comes out of the depths of soul. Will Allah throw such people in Hell whose entire lives were spent in studying His acts, who saw Divine light (message) in each and every leaf, looked in every particle the treasure of light (energy), saw Allah's workmanship in every drop and then opened up all this to make us understand the true nature of the vastness of

Allah's Power?

Where does a man stand in comparison to all the breath-taking worlds of Allah? In all fairness to himself, man is not even an insect crawling on earth. And then look at the bounties of Allah who sometime sends a prophet (for his welfare) and shows his glamour at others, He even allows a dialogue with man. Remember Hazrat Musa^{AS}?

How befitting a Hebraic poet has been:

When I consider the heavens, the moon and the stars which thou hast ordained, what is man that thou art mindful of him and the son of man thou visited him.

After observing the details of human anatomy, Professor David Fraser of London University said:

Our minds are overwhelmed by immensity and majesty of nature.

At yet another instance, the Professor says:

We hardly know which to admire the more: the mind that arranged nature or the mind which interpreted?

The Creator of universe likes poignancy; by creating immense things from just an electron, created billions of people, but because of His love for heterodoxy, never let one face look exactly like another. And then look at colors, fragrances, shapes and types of flowers, millions of animals and insects, tens of thousands of tastes. When one thinks over all these things, should one not be struck by awe (of Allah's infinite prowess)?

Tennyson, the naturalist, when impressed by the craftsmanship of nature, said:

What a marvelous imagination God Almighty hath.

Impressed by the horrifying might and immensity of universe, Sir James Janis says:

The universe more looks like a great thought than a great machine.

Look at what Pascal has to say:

The universe is a circle whose centre is everywhere but circumference is nowhere.

Equilibrium

Our planet has two motions: one around itself and the other, around the sun. Earth moves with a speed of one thousand miles [1,600 km] per hour around its axis, and at a speed of 67,000 mile [ca. 108,000 km) per hour around the sun. However, the earth is in such an equilibrium that you don't feel any bumps. While looking at this mind-boggling equilibrium of earth, Sir James said:

The trembling universe must have been balanced with unthinkable precision.

Incident

Once while studying a water drop, Sir David Boaster observed that each of its atom was much more complicated than the machine of a watch. Dumbfound, he said:

Oh God! How marvelous are thy works.

True:

Only scholars of nature are in awe of Allah. Fatir, 28.

Monotony of Universe

1) Adjustability with environment is a universal fact. Long fur of animals in cold regions, black color in warm areas, weak animals like hare and deer having earth-like color (for the purpose of camouflage), fish's recognition senses, and feathers of a bird are all testimony to the universal laws. Animals that cannot go along an existing environment, are annihilated; the way Muslims have given up on

science and instead spending all their energies on rituals, flowing beards, and loose dress.

2) All the things have their origin in electrons

3) Mutual cohabitation is a universal phenomenon. Without salts and bacteria, plants would perish and without plants, animals would not be able to survive.

4) See the wonders of monotony that a heart beats about 70 times and a lung inhales breath about 17 times in every minute. And then the level of water is uniform everywhere. Air is lighter than water wherever you go. A goat would always give birth to a goat. Spring and autumn, winter and summer, life and death, movement of stars and satellites, in short everything is governed by a tremendous proportion and equilibrium.

Do you see any disproportion or deficiency in the creations of Allah? See again and again and see if there is any deficiency. Malik, 3.

The best explanation of this Ayat can be seen in what a naturalist says:

One plan, many variations. One design, many modifications. One truth, many versions.

In furtherance of his thoughts, Samuel Rodgers says:

The very law which moulds a tear and bids it trickle from its source. That law preserves the earth and guides the planets in their course.

Now let's see what Allah has to say in this regard:

It is Allah who lifted the sky in the atmosphere and created equilibrium in the universe. Rahman, 7.

Samuel Rodgers says:

We are at a loss to know which to admire the more: the mathematical accuracy of the universe or the beauty of its design?

Light and Electric Engines

Light and heat are inseparable however in the rear end of a glowworm, Allah has created such a light that has no heat. Today, scientists are making different instruments by analyzing glowworm. Now the problem is that the worm does not speak and thus, scientists are unable to understand the mystery. First they don't understand the logic behind its light, and second, why its light has been devoid of heat[19]. A western scientist says that had there been heat in the tail of glowworm, it would have caused fire burning the entire garden.

Not long ago, man discovered electricity. But electric engines are already in place in the universe since time immemorial. For example, eel hunts with electricity and can create so much electricity, by constricting its muscles, that can kill its prey. Then there is another fish that has strange ways to hunt. When it sees a prey coming closer, it lights up a bulb on its head. It dazzles the prey's eyes; and what happens to the prey, is not a rocket science.

Now think over the glowworms and the fishes that, in addition to several other characteristics, can also produce electricity.

How interesting a western philosopher is when he says:

We must take notice of such qualities of organisms such as varying, growing, multiplying, developing, feeling and endeavoring. As study of such facts, interests, educates,

[19] That was the age of relatively lesser knowledge. The light created by glowworms is known as bioluminescence, a light resulting in chemical reactions that take place inside its body. It is also called "cold light" because luminescence produces hardly any heat. These cold light reactions take place in its abdomen region, where the skin is translucent enough to allow the luminescence to shine through.

enriches and helps to take alive the sense of wonder, which we hold to be one of the saving graces of life.

Each and every particle of universe is like a musical instrument that sings hymnody in the praise of Allah. Think over the human body. According to Sir Arthur Keith, a Scottish Anatomist and Anthropologist, when we take just one step, there are full hundred muscles that work in unison; to make us move. Even if a single muscle malfunctions, we won't be able to take a step. Now just imagine the number of other body parts that might be in action during our movement.

Each man-made machine needs an operator, a cleaner, a maintenance specialist. Obviously, man is not the driver of his body. This poor creature has no idea of the enormity of this machine (that he himself is). Naturally, a question arises: which is that IMMENSE BEING that is operating and maintaining machines of billions upon billions of human, animals, and plants.

Allah says:

And tell them (O' Mohammad) that it is Allah that creates and then repeats the process of creation. How then are you misled? Younas, 34.

Except his buffalo, goat, horse, wife, and farmland to an ignorant person, everything else is 'useless'. He is oblivious of the beneficial values of innumerable plants, trees, stones, minerals, etc. He has no idea that everything in the universe has been created with a purpose. Till this day, about 400,000 plants have been discovered. Of these just a few hundred are used by man. Similarly, there are a lot of unknown domains of animals and insects. We would become 'complete human beings' only when we are in a position to conquer, understand and make use of them. Only then we would be in a position to appreciate and understand that it is Allah that has created anything and everything but with a purpose.

Do you know whose responsibility has this been? Hear what Allah says in this regard:

Such as remember Allah, standing, sitting, and reclining, and consider the creation of the heavens and the earth, (and say): Our Lord! You created not this in vain. Al-Imran, 191.

Today, we don't have those scholars in our midst, who could tell the purpose of creation of even a fly and whose knowledge is based on observation, analysis, and explanation. Mamoon-ur-Rashid, an Abbasid Caliph, had known the purpose of Islam. During his tenure, tens of observatories were established to study the cosmic bodies. During his tenure, more than 26,000 books had been published on animal life, plants, etc. He made watches, tried to run engines, measuring the earth and measuring the distance between sun and earth. But alas,! We have given up on the ways of our forefathers.

West's Passion for Learning

Main entrance of the America's Institute for Creation Research, has the following quote:

"Open thou mine eyes, that I may behold wondrous things out of thy law." Psalm 119:18

Some earlier Scientists of Nature

Here, it will be appropriate to mention certain scientists who spent their entire lives in the study of universe; in search of truth. Though they did not have such lab facilities as we have today, their findings are however considered credible even today.

1) Thales, a Greek philosopher (624-546 B.C.):

considered earth as a floating disc on water

2) Anaximander, Greek philosopher (610-546 B.C.): concurred that earth was suspended in the air

3) Anaximenes, a Greek philosopher (585-528 B.C.): thought that starts are made up of glass and decorated in the sky like diamonds

4) Pythagoras, mathematician philosopher (582-507 B.C.): thought that all the objects of universe are revolving around the earth

5) Anaxagoras (460 B.C.): was the first scholar who called moonlight as 'acquired'

6) Heraclites, a pre-Socratic philosopher (535–475 B.C.): was the first to theorize that earth was moving and that it completes one round in 24 hours.

7) Aristarchus, Greek astronomer and mathematician (310–230 BC): also considered earth to be moving and considered the sun as the center point around which all the universe was revolving. He also measured the volume and length and breadth of moon and sun.

8) Eratosthenes, a Greek astronomer (276-194 B.C.): measured the diameter of earth.

9) Hipparchus, astronomer, geographer, mathematician (190-120 B.C.): found the length of year[20].

10) Hero (of Alexandria), in the year 100 A.D.: invented steam engine and pump

---

[20] There is just a difference of six minutes between what we have today and what he measured thousands of years back

11) Leucippus, the developer of the theory of atomism (460 B.C.) and Vemqratis (470-460 B.C.) declared that everything is basically composed of various imperishable, indivisible elements called atoms.

12) Marcus Varro, a philosopher, chronologist (116-27 B.C.): in his book "Res Rustical", wrote that bacteria flourish in dirty ponds.

13) Julius Caesar (100-44 B.C.): corrected the calendar.

14) The Romans invented arch.

15) Copernicus, mathematician and astronomer (1543-1473 B.C.): considered the sun as the center of universe, but Tycho Brahe (1546-1601 A.D.) theorized that all the heavenly bodies revolve around earth. He also declared that distance between earth and sun was 95 million miles [ca. 154 million km].

Chapter-II

Spring of Plants

Allah says:

He it is Who sends down water from the sky, and therewith We bring forth buds of every kind; We bring forth the green blade from which we bring forth the thick clustered grain; and from the date palm, from the pollen thereof, spring pendant bunches; and (We bring forth) gardens of grapes, and the olive and the pomegranate, alike and unlike. Look upon the fruit thereof, when they bear fruit, and upon its ripening. Lo! herein verily are portents for a people who believe. An'am,99.

In these Ayaat, after the mention of rains and plants, Allah commands *"think over fruits"*. He also said *"there are miracles and lessons for those who believe"*. It is thus our obligation to think deeply over these matters.

Earth and Plants

The way herbivores eat grass, similarly, plants eat earth (soil); its food being nitrogen, calcium, potassium, and hydrogen. Plants get these elements from (dead) leaves, cow dung, bones, blood and hair. Leaf-fall in autumn is a great blessing of Allah, providing food to soil. This is like spreading manure over immense tracts of land; something beyond human reach. Similar was the case of irrigating thousands of square miles/km of land. To make for the former need, Allah spread tree leaves as manure. To solve the difficulty of irrigation, Allah threw sunrays over oceans to pick water vapors, transported by winds and causing rains. Look at the Allah's bounties that billions of tons of water is picked up from the Bay of Bengal and transported as far away as Peshawar, causing massive rains and with that, irrigation of lands.

Allah is the one who send winds towards oceans wherefrom they pick water vapors and this way, He irrigates the dead lands. Fatir, 9.

Our Friends

There is a world of animals (bacteria!) residing in plant roots. Their basic function is chemical. They suck nitrogen from earth and release special juices that contain immense quantities of nitrogen, a very important component of plant life. Had there been no such bacteria, no plant would have ever grown. Now think how Allah has arranged a wonderful system for our sustenance and how needy the human being is to even such a minute animal. Had these bacteria been visible, it would have been consumed by other animals; and would not have been available for plants. Its invisibility is thus another bounty of Allah.

There are a lot of bacteria types that have different functions but the same purpose: production and completion of plant life. Over each acre of land, the labor of bacteria is equivalent to 12 persons. In other words, if a 100 acre farm is ploughed by ten farmers, there is an army of 1,200 invisible laborers working along with the farmers. Now let's be honest: how much is the share of man and how much of Allah in farming.

Have you seen that which you cultivate? Is it you who foster it, or are We the Fosterer? If We willed, We verily could make it chaff, then would you cease not to exclaim. Alwaqiah, 63-65.

If manure is plant food, it is also food for the bacteria so that these 1,200 laborers of hundred acres can perform their duties well. Animal dung and urine is the best food for plants but unfortunately, these are mostly wasted. Some is burnt while almost all the urine is wasted.

On the sea shores of southern America, feathers of water birds fall in great quantities. They keep on piling because of the scarcity of rains. This part of the world is considered one of the best 'mines' of nitrogen. Till 1930s, about 100 million tons of manure was extracted and used.

Scientists estimate that over each square mile of atmosphere, there is a huge treasure of 20 million tons of nitrogen. Due to the deficiency of our knowledge and technology, we have not been able to make use of it.

Electricity

When lightening occurs in clouds, the surrounding oxygen is converted to nitrogen and raindrops bring it down to earth. A Chemist of 1871, Cavendish has proved that if air and oxygen is electrocuted, nitrogen will be created that will have some quantity of manure (alkali). Nitrogen is food for plants and plants are our food. In other words, each lightening in the clouds brings message of life to us.

Now-a-days, a lot of diseases are treated using electricity and there are a lot of hospitals using electricity for medical treatment. Like human body, earth also suffers from a lot of diseases. Atmospheric electricity is the cure for all such diseases. When electric waves pass through the air and touch the land, it creates life in it and becomes ready for production of plants. Now let's be honest and think as to who is more involved in farming? How big a bounty of Allah! In the past, people considered the atmospheric electricity a curse of deities and used to worship it. They never knew that each act of Allah was for the welfare of all of His creations, not a curse.

And of His signs is this: He shows you the lightning for a fear and for a hope, and sends down water from the sky, and thereby quickens the earth after her death. Lo! Herein indeed are portents for the people who understand. Rum, 24.

The very same nitrogen that is a bounty of Allah, can also be used in making of explosives. Each year, billions of tons of nitrogen is used in it. In the beginning of World War One, when Germans captured nitrogen mines in Chile, the Allied Forces had great difficulty.

Earth Crust

The upper layer of earth is made of broken mountains. For this action, there have always been four factors responsible: river, rain, sun, and plants. Plant roots can penetrate even the hardest rocks. Avalanches and volcanic mountains also help in this regard. A good farmland needs four items: clay, sand, calcium and manure. None of these items is useful individually, but when combined, they make a very useful mix.

Lack of calcium causes TB to land, besides reducing its acidity and making it plant worthy. If calcium is spread more than its need, it reduces the quantity of iron thus making the land lifeless. Clay is heavy and cold in nature while sand is deficient in nutrients and dry. But their combination makes an excellent land. Clay retains moisture longer while sand reduces the heaviness of land making it conduct the underground gases reach the plant roots easily. Had land been clayey and hard, these gases would not have been reaching the plant roots and we would not have been able to have wheat, maize, or others crops.

Wonderful System

Besides calcium, land also needs sulphuric acid,

phosphoric acid, nitric acid and potassium. All these elements are generally available in mountains. If we would pick up pick-axes and shovels in search of these items, it would take us hundreds of years, but without any result. Our Beneficent Allah has solved this problem for us by accumulating snow on mountains that seeps in the crevices when it melts. And when it comes out as a spring, it brings a world of potassium and sulphur. These springs when combined, become rivers and rivers when converted to canals, brought a world of these elements right up to our farmlands. This way, one of our most needed requirements is met.

Let's try to link these logical explanations to the Qur'anic verses:

> Do you not see that Allah sends down rain from the sky and makes it flow as springs [and rivers] in the earth; then He produces thereby crops of varying colors; then they dry and you see them turned yellow; then He makes them [scattered] debris. Indeed in that is a reminder for those of understanding. Zumar, 21.

Male and Female

A flower has generally two parts: male and female. Unless female is fertilized by the male flower, fruit or seed cannot come. Male part of flower has a dust called pollen while the female part has tiny hair. When pollen falls on the hair, it captures the pollen and this way, it becomes 'pregnant'. Some plants like hazel have male and female flowers separately but side by side. Male flower is tilted down while female flower, upwards. The reason being that when pollen falls, it should be captured by the female flower.

Some plants have separate males and females. Pollen (of

male plant) is carriers to the female by, for example, honey bees, butterflies, and other insects. Some other trees, for example, Chir, Blue Pine, Deodar, etc. growing in hilly areas, have neither flowers not fragrance and thus cannot attract bees. The job of transportation of pollen is thus done by winds. Since wind keeps on changing its direction, a lot of pollen is wasted. To counter the losses, these trees generate far greater amounts of pollen to ensure fertilization of female trees.

Now consider what would happen had there been no winds: no fertilization of female trees, no seeds, no new trees. This way gradually, the entire mountains that are so beautiful because of trees, would have been devoid of the lush green pine trees besides all the attendant ecological losses.

Let's now revert to the Qur'an that spoke of wind and pollen, hundreds of years back:

And We sent such winds that were laden with pollen. Hijr, 22.

Western botanists established the idea of male and female plants after a lot of research. Our Prophet was communicated this, through Divine Message, some 1400 years back:

And all things We have created by pairs. Zaariyaat, 49.

What other proof do we need about the Qur'an being a Divine Book that told us about something, that the western scientist came to know about just recently?

Sometime back, I told a Hindu friend - a Botanist - that the theory of male and female plants is already mentioned in the Qur'an. He said that this can never be so. Qur'an is an old book while this theory is absolutely new. When I showed him the English translation of Qur'an by Pickthall, he said that if he got satisfied, he will declare the authenticity of Qur'an publicly and no one would be able to stop me from praising the Prophet.

And you (Mohammad) see the earth barren, but when We send down water thereon, it does thrill and swell and put forth every lovely kind (of growth). Hajj, 5.

Trees are a great bounty of Allah. They eat like us, breathe, grow and create children. Their mechanism is as wonderful as ours. Like us, they too are struggling for their existence and fight with one another. For example, a larger tree does not allow smaller ones to grow under its shade and if two trees are close by, they will keep on struggling. These facts are clear indication of the fact that the right to exist is only to the stronger ones, while the weaker ones (lazy, ill-tempered, renegades, liars, cunning, shrewd, etc.) have no place to live and prosper.

And verily, We have written in the Scripture, after the Reminder: My righteous slaves will inherit the earth. Anbia,105.

Plant Diversity

The way some of us are brave, others cowards, some active and others lazy, similarly diversity is also found in plants. Jasmine is beautiful and delicate while butterfly weed (ak) is ugly-looking and stinks. Cypress is cylindrical while Acacia [*Phulai*] is irregular. Wild grass and Mesquite are obstinate; the more you remove them, more they spread. Then there is a plant that is so sensitive that even by breathing, it withers.

Importance of Plants

All the beauty of earth is because of plants. Pastures, forests, tracks, and gardens would have become deserted had the beauty of plants not attracted mankind. It is because of plants that man and animals have been living.

Wheat, rice, maize, fruits, Coco, drinks, squashes, etc. are all the products of plants. Similarly, sugar, butter, honey, and milk are because of plants while our clothes are also the result of plants. Rubber, a very important need of modern life, is obtained from trees. Similarly, gasoline and coal buried under forests, are in our service. Imagine just a small quantity of coal, if burnt in a room (for heating), can kill man. But think of its usefulness in human life and how powerful it has made nations. To the other side, how downgraded are those nations that have no idea of the importance of coal.

In appearance, coal is bad-looking but in use, it can transform a dead nation into a living one. How aptly has this been said in the Qur'an:

> It is so easy for Allah to bring forth the living from the dead and bring forth the dead from the living. Younas, 31.

What I was saying is that plants are not only life-sustaining but have also become part of our society and civilization. At certain instances, plants would transform themselves such that you won't be able to recognize them. Do you know where did you get a soap from that you rub on your body? It has been manufactured from plant oils. In other words, you are not using soap but rubbing a tree on your body. Our silk shirt, muslin [*malmal*] turban, and pajamas made of calico [*latha*] are in fact, a small forest. And these books in the shelves, newspapers, envelopes, etc. are all made up of plants that were harvested and brought to factories for conversion into various paper products.

The US publish daily 112,000,000 newspapers that consume 15 acre forests. Now just think over the enormity of situation and listen to what the trees say, while reading the newspapers. On this, I recall that a poet was passing by a vineyard. There was a barrel of wine under a tree. The poet's thoughts went into the past and reached the times of

Shirin-Farhad[21]. When these lovers died, their bodies slowly decayed into soil and became the manure and food of a branch of grape plant. Elsewhere, water containers and bricks were made of it.

In short, the sea animals of the early days appear today in the form of calcium while trees have become coal, humans soil is transforming into bricks and flowers and where this world is moving to, only Allah knows.

We mete out death among you, and We are not to be outrun, that We may transfigure you and make you what you know not. Al-Waqi'ah, 60-61.

River in a Pitcher

There are a lot of plants in India having seeds that are one-twentieth of the size of poppy seed. Nature has kept hidden the following things in it: (i) a pair of twin leafs; (ii) a bud that transforms in to soil to become the stem root; (iii) a knot that converts into main stem; and (iv) a few days food before the plant firms up its roots.

Now just think how complicated this small machine might be and look at the nature's craftsmanship that a just a minute particle, but has a full tree hidden in it. If such a minute particle has the capacity to become a tree, then think of a man that gets determined, how wonders can he perform.

---

[21] The title of a famous Persian tragic romance by Nizami Ganjavi (1141–1209), who also wrote Layla and Majnun. It tells a highly elaborated fictional version of the story of the love of the Sassanian King Khosrow II for the Armenian Princess Shirin, who becomes his queen. The essential narrative is a love story of Persian origin which was already well-known from the great epico-historical poem. Shahnameh and other Persian writers and popular tales, and other works have the same title.

Scale of Justice

In winter, the sound of axe resounds from the jungle. How heartlessly does the man cut the trees! Go next year to that spot and you will see flowers and plants all around. Why so! Because earlier, seeds brought by birds and winds could not get enough space and light to prosper. Now when the area has been cleared, the same spot is full of plant life. It is the principle of nature that if it takes one thing, it gives another; even more. As an analogy, when a man loses his eyesight, he is compensated by tremendous hearing qualities.

Ducks have small tails but long necks. An uneducated man has untrained brain but is physically robust. Conversely, a scholar has a large mind, but weak physique. Those having wealth are devoid of knowledge and the ones with knowledge, have no (monetary) wealth. If a nation (like today's Muslims) becomes lazy and easy-going and looses mental capabilities, the nature annihilates it and instead raises another nation.

And if you turn away He will exchange you for some other people, and they will not be the likes of you. Mohammad, 38.

System of Plant Growth

According to plant growth, there are two types of plants: one, whose seed sprouts two leaves, for example, trees, and two, that has one leaf at sprouting. The first two leafs are the source of food of plants and act like breasts of a mother. When plant stabilities, the two leaves that sprout in the beginning, dry up.

Plants' arrangement occurs through cells. Of all the cells, the exterior wall is composed of oxygen, hydrogen, and carbon. There is a 'cap' towards the end of root made up of hard cells that can penetrate even rocks. When this 'cap' abases, a new cap replaces it. Each plant has a colored matter called chlorophyll. It is prepared through the action of sunlight and because of this, plants have green color. It has also the quality of getting carbon from the atmosphere and converting into carbohydrates and sugar, the two basic requirements of plant life.

Godly Glory

For plant life, moisture, air, heat and certain other elements like phosphorus, potassium, and nitrogen are needed that get dissolved in water and absorbed by roots. Since the quantity of these elements is very small, therefore, plants need a lot of water. These elements are made part of the plant and excess water is transpired through transpiration. To understand the quantity of water transpired by, for example, flower-bearing trees, is about 5,000 tons per hectare [2,000 tons per acre].

We see that underground water is taken up by hundreds of feet to be stored in overhead water tanks. In comparison, tree roots deep in the soil suck water and take it to its extreme height. Here a question arises as how could this happen especially in the presence of gravity and without a pump? This happens because of 'surface tension'. This can be explained by taking a narrow glass tube and dipped in water. Because of surface tension, water will go up. Similarly, tree roots are small tubes that have the capacity to convey underground water to the top of a tree. Now think! How has the nature made an excellent arrangement to ensure that all the parts of a tree get the required amount of water; to convey the essential nutrients up. Today, if Allah would suspend the principle of surface tension, all the plans would dry up. And with that, the entire life on earth would become extinct.

Such is Allah, your Lord. There is no God save Him, the Creator of all the things, so worship Him. And He takes care of all the things. An'am, 102.

Tree Leaves

Besides adding luster, tree leaves have other special functions as well. A leaf has tiny pores through which it 'breathes'. 'Poison' (carbon[22]) created by animals is inhaled by plants along with oxygen. It converts carbon as its essential body component and exhales oxygen. These tiny pores shut down in the night; as if plants also sleep in the night. If a tree does not get sunlight for an extended period of time, it will die because of suffocation. Some plants get withered in winters. That is because of extended nights especially in cold regions of the world that causes reduction in the availability of food. There are however other plants in northern pole regions that are not affected by long nights.

Plants convert carbon into hydrates and store some of it for use in winter while the rest is used for making seeds. Since carbohydrates cannot fully dissolve in water to be conveyed to various parts of trees, that is why some of it is converted into sugar. And then it mixes sugar in water and sends to its various parts where it is again converted into carbohydrates.

Some tree leaves shrink in cold nights so that the heat obtained from sun is conserved from cold night winds; just like a man in cold night sleeps by recoiling his body to conserve body heat.

---

[22] Carbon is the basis of all organic molecules. It makes up our genetic material (DNA and RNA) and proteins, which are essential for life. Carbon is a major element within our bodies.

Different shapes of leaves are in accordance with needs. Trees that need more heat, have thin leaves so that they could quickly absorb it. Then there are trees that do not need that much heat and so, have thick leaves. Some leaves have thorns and some ooze out poison, probably as a protection against intruders. Our tea is also leaves. Tobacco leaf absorbs various elements from earth and air and that is why it has a very peculiar shape. According to scientists, diversity of plants is because of diversity of leaves.

In short, each leaf is a complex machine of nature running in billions but unlike man-made machines, without making any noise, rather making food for us. How ungrateful the man is that it has the entire universe in its service but even then, does not care about his responsibilities.

Sunrays reach us from 150 million km [93 million miles], convey water vapors cause lightening, fill earth with life while raindrops bring down invaluable treasure of nitrogen that provides an essential nutrient to plant life. Tree roots absorb water, make various essential elements for plant life and ultimately end up as our food and shelter.

Now let's see what Allah has to say about what we have said above:

> Let man consider his food: How We pour water in showers, then split the earth in clefts, and cause the grain to grow therein, and grapes and green fodder, and olive trees and palm trees, and garden closes of thick foliage, and fruits and grasses: Provision for you and your cattle. A'bas, 24-33.

Stupendous Supervision

It has already been discussed that each seed has two knot-like elements of which one comes out as plant 'stem' while the second anchors into the soil as its root. You press the seed in any manner, bring the root-knot up and the stem-knot down, result would be the same: stem would go up and root, down. Why so? Because nothing is out of sight of Allah, no matter if it is in the deep ravines of the Himalayas, or up in the heights of skies.

Not an atom's weight, or less than that or greater, escapes Him in the heavens or in the earth. Saba, 3.

At yet another instance, Allah says:

He knows that which is in front of them and that which is behind them, while they encompass nothing of His knowledge save what He will. Baqarah, 255.

Passion for Rearing

When a plant matures, a beautiful change occurs in it. Seedlings that were till recently braches and trees, converts into clusters that transform into flowers and flowers into seeds, i.e. eggs. Breeding is the passion that is equally found in man, animals, and plants.

Seeds are the equivalent of eggs. That is why these are wrapped and protected in hard shells. Seeds are also human food, for example, peas, beans, pine seed, etc. Nature has not protected them much so that 'dear' man has no problem in having it. Some useful trees for example, apple, orange, etc., have smaller number of seeds but bitter so that man may not eat it and the generation of these trees could sustain. Some seeds are our daily food, for example, wheat and maize that have been given to us in abundance.

Wheat, rice, and other crops become ready-to-use in four to five months, while mango tree gives fruit in seven or eight years. It appears as if Nature whispers into the 'ears' of all the plants to be alert because the farmer is coming with a sickle in his hand, ready to harvest it. So be quick: grow, bear fruit, spread it on the earth, and get going.

An American tree called Ageva matures in 80 years. Its slow growth is because it has no fear of sickle. Now at certain places, it is used a fuelwood with the result that it now matures even in ten years. Why so? Nature has whispered in its ears that now you have enemies, be quick and grow fast.

A clever gardener when sees that after a wait of eight years, mulberry tree has started giving fruit, he cuts its branches. Fearing death, the tree starts growing fast so that before that happens, it could bear fruit and lay the foundation of coming generation.

There is a lesson for us in the philosophy of plants: to make lazy nations move fast and be of utility, and to convert their weakness into strength, the use of sword is very necessary. Let's keep it in mind that Allah has sent Muslims to ensure discipline in around the world.

You are the best Ummat that has been appointed for the welfare of nations of world. Aal-e-Imran, 110.

It is therefore incumbent on Muslims to wholeheartedly use sword and ensure peace and stability to safeguard human rights in the world.

Duty of Flowers

Flowers have color and fragrance to attract meloids and honey bees. In other words, this color and fragrance is the result of bees hard work. The moment the job is done (pregnancy!), flower withers; because it has done its job and any further stay becomes useless.

Only useful nations have the right to live on earth. And there is no place for useless, worthless, superstitious, and of course for those who find shortcuts to paradise. How aptly the Qur'an has defined a useful nation:

Only useful and well-mannered nations and things are left on earth. Ar-Ra'ad, 17.

Protection of Flowers

Nature has adopted a number of precautionary measures to protect plants from wild animals and birds. For example, Allah made the shells of almond and walnut very hard. Some have been wrapped in bitter cover (for example, orange, pomegranate) that no animal would even touch let alone eat it. Look at the workmanship of Allah that pomegranate has the same branches that convey moisture to it but its bark is very bitter though its seeds are very sweet. It appears as if nature has established two different factories to manufacture the both; one manufactures bitterness and the other, sweetness. Both are in extreme close vicinity but do not ever mix up. Who could have done this, save Allah?

He has loosed the two seas. They meet. There is a barrier between them. They encroach not (one upon the other). Ar-Rahman, 19-20.

Walnut and almond grow on high hills where because of snow and bitter cold, animals of plain cannot reach. There the only danger is from squirrels and mice. And that is why their shells have been made tough to avoid loss to these animals.

Nature also wished that fruit trees are not confined to just one part of the land. That is why a variety of means were used to transport their seeds to distant areas, for example:

1) Winds convey seeds to far-off places, even countries.

2) Seeds flowing in streams and rivers reach other areas.

3) Mice, parrots, mynas, especially migratory birds

transport seeds to far-off lands.

4) Men transport fruit to other countries, even continents.

Fertilization of Figs

Arabian Desert is spread over thousands of kilometers where camel is still used as an effective means of transportation. There was every possibility of the traveler becoming short of food. For this, nature grew oasis at suitable intervals and were made tall so that wild animals may not damage their fruit. Moreover, stems of date trees were made fibrous and hollow to act like a thermos bottle so that internal environment is not affected by the external heat and with that, the fruit may remain fresh and juicy. Man's body needs two things the most: sugar and carbohydrates. Both these things are present in abundance in dates.

Where could look for the preparations to keep fruits from rotting? Banana rots in just a few days. Similar is the case with guava, mulberry, etc. Nature has however kept dates safe with certain preparation that keeps it fresh for months. Date roots suck two types of juices from soil: dense and light. Dense juice helps in the construction of stem and branches while light extract is used for making of fruit. Each fruit piece has a 'cleaner' attached to it that cleans the juices yet further. Date seed is made up of both dense and light juices but basically, it is bitter while its peel is sweet. Between both these, a 'screen' has been established so that bitterness and sweetness do not mix up. What Qur'an has said on one sentence, man has said in numerous paras:

And the earth has He appointed for (His) creatures, wherein are fruit and sheathed Date palm trees. Al-Rahman, 10,11.

Signs of Destination

Trees generally grow along paths. And that is why man eats fruits and throws the seed where more trees grow. If you see trees but no path, you must be sure that people have not passed through this area some for some time. When Arabs invaded Sindh, they brought dates and wherever they passed from, they threw seeds. The result is that today, one can have Arabian dates for hundreds of kilometers.

Evergreen Trees

These trees remain green even in autumn. Reasons:

First: Some trees have oily leafs and a waxy material on it. It keeps the leaf pores sealed with the result that moisture is retained and leafs remain fresh.

Second: Some leafs have a whitish wool that stops transpiration and thus keeps trees green.

Third: Conical, long and narrow surfaced leafs compared to wide leafs are less affected by sun and thus don't loose much moisture. That is why they remain green. Had the leafs of olive and dates been wide, these would have been shedding in autumn.

Benefits of Trees

1) Tree roots absorb extra water from soil and thus do not let the land become waterlogged.

2) Due to transpiration, trees somewhat heat up the immediate environment. It makes the air (relatively) lighter and as a result, clouds near the earth surface become denser causing rain.

3) Because of leaf-shedding in autumn, soil becomes

fertile.

4) Had there been no trees on mountains, areas nearby would have been flooded with rainwater causing erosion and making it unfit for human use.

Some Interesting Trees

Cinchona: Cinchona is a tree found in southern America. Its bark had been used in making quinine. It was first known to some Hispanic immigrants. The wife of Viceroy of Peru, Countess of Cinchona introduced this tree in Europe. After that some missionaries took its bark to Italy and distributed to patients, free of charge. After sometime, the use of its bark was given up. When in seventeenth century, England's King Charles-II fell ill, the royal physician Dr. Robert Tablet cured him with the power of its bark and the King got well. Next year, the doctor treated a few aristocrats of France who also got well. After that, everybody came to know about the usefulness of quinine.

Rubber: Initially, rubber tree was only found in south-central America. In nineteenth century it was planted in Sri Lanka (then Ceylon) and Malaysia (then Malaya). Its juice is used in the manufacture of rubber. Today everyone knows the importance of rubber.

Olive: Its oil is extremely useful that is used in machines, soaps and consumed by human beings. It can live for a thousand years. Its wood is very strong.

Mulberry: Mulberry leaves are browsed by animals that give milk. Bees make honey after sucking its fruit juices while silk is produced by silkworms that eat mulberry leafs. It is widely used in sports-goods and its wood is ideally suited in making of world class hockey sticks.

All the praise for Allah, Who is the best Creator. Mominoon, 14.

Coconut: In extreme hot weather, a traveler reached a hut that had the shadow of coconut trees. The house owner presented the traveler wine, milk and pudding. The traveler asked him as to where these delicious foods came from. All this is because of coconut, he was told. I get water from unripe coconuts, milk from ripe ones, pudding from its leaves, wine from its buds, sugar from its flowers, utensils from its bark, fuel from its wood, make roof of my house from its leafs, ropes from its fiber and light from its oil. When the traveler was leaving, the host stirred a branch from which a dusty material fell down. He used the dust in making ink and wrote a letter to a friend.

This is the Creation of Allah. Now show me that which those (you worship) beside Him have created. Luqman, 11.

Tree-eating Plants

Some climbers do not get food directly from soil; they rather live on juices of other plants and as a result, the hunted trees die. Subjected nations soon 'dry down' because their juices have been sucked by the ruling nations. Has it stirred this sleeping Muslim nation? I doubt!

Animal-eating Plants

There is a plant in America that has its branches spreading over soil like a net. The moment an animal passes over it, the net squeezes the animal and thus becomes its food.

Bee-eating Plants

Sundew flower has a sticky juice. The moment a bee sits

on it, it sticks and flower petals attack it and eats it. The fact is that soil, where this plant grows, has no nitrogen and thus it makes for its deficiency by hunting bees.

Similarly, there is glue on the leaves of Butter warts. The moment an insect sits on it, the leaf closes like a fist. But if a sand particle or a pebble is thrown on it, there is no reaction. In other words, it is intelligent enough to differentiate between its food and non-foods. Who could have done it, except Allah?

Some ponds have bladder warts the braches of which have small bladders. These bladders open like mouse-traps. When water-borne insects enter it for food or rest, they are trapped. Similarly, flowers of Pitcher Plant are hanging like pitchers that have sweet nectar and oblique thorns with its internal walls. When an insect enters for nectar, thorns reduce their speed of exit. It tries and tries and ultimately gets tired and into the trap.

Workmanship

Think over carrot, turnip and onions at one side and fig, dates and mango on the other. Leaves of the former are so designed that when it rains, leafs collect raindrops and direct towards its roots. Leafs of latter plants spread the raindrops and throw it down. The reason is that carrot and other plants have one root and nature has arranged raindrops towards its root. On the contrary, mango and other trees have roots spread far off that need water spread to reach all the roots. What a workmanship!

Carbon and Oxygen

Lives of animals depend on oxygen and of plants, on

carbon. If oxygen reduces, animals would die and if carbon's quantity reduces, plants would die. And then carbon is a very poisonous gas and its abundance can be fatal for animals. Look at the nature's arrangement: carbon is food for plants and oxygen, for animals. Animals produce carbon for plants and plants produce oxygen for mankind. All the animals on earth produce about 200 million tons of pure carbon. Similarly, animals consume about 8 billion cbm oxygen. Now think! What a justice. What a wonderful system on earth for the sustenance of life! How the grace of Divinity appears it its different forms and manifestations.

All the praise for the Protector of Universe (whose Divinity is so awe-inspiring). Al-Fatiha, 1.

Protection of Plants

Nature has arranged for the protection of plants in a number of ways, for example:

1) The initial and lower leafs of Holy plant are thorny and while going up, each leaf has just one thorn. This is so because ordinarily, most of the animals would have access to lower level leafs; where greater protection is needed.

2) Animals are of two types: soft-mouthed like cow, buffalo; and hard-mouthed that can chew even thorns, like sheep, goat, camel, etc. Latter category of animals was weak therefore Nature gave thorns to some trees so that soft-mouthed may not browse them and could only be browsed by hard-mouthed animals.

3) While touching 'Scorpion plant', fire erupts.

4) Similarly, the sting of Devil's Leaf gives pain up to

one whole year. It can sometimes even kill a man.

5) An Australian plant 'Laporticamatioder' is so dangerous that even if a horse touches it, it would die.

6) By touching 'Poison Ivy', can cause swelling of hands and feet and turns eyes red.

7) Some trees produce such a bad-smelling juice that even animals can't dare to be close by.

8) 'Touch-me-not' is so sensitive that even by breathing, it contracts and can even embarrass animals.

9) 'Telegraph Plant' wave even without wind and make the animals fearful.

10) To trap dangerous insects, certain tree stems and branches produce special glue that traps them. This glue can come out only if it is bored. For this purpose, Nature has created birds with long and sharp beaks that drill holes in the tree that is used as protection against insects and is the medicine for the tree wound.

11) Some bunches of flowers excrete sweet juices and to get it, ants go up. They drink juices and also destroy those insects that harm the plants. When these flowers mature into seeds, the juice dries up. This juice is the prize from plants to return favors to ants.

12) On some trees, large ants keep on moving up and down. Their job being watch-n-ward. These ants bite invaders so ferociously that they have no way other than running away.

Now let's ponder! How wonderful a system Nature has established for our food and how equally excellent is the system devised to protect it for us from the invaders. And then how many lessons are there for us in each plant, how much is the diversity in plants, how much difference in the make-up, characteristics, and fruits of each plan, and remember! No mistake anywhere, no disorganization, and indifference to their protection, upkeep, training, and growth. Let's sing in the praise of that Eternal Creator Who made our planet earth the center of beauty and grandeur and decorated trees and plants with flowers of every hue and color and animals for our service. Let's end our discourse with the following poetic verse:

> Praise Allah, the Most High, Who creates, then disposes; Who measures, then guides; and Who brings forth the pasturage.
> A'ala 1 to 4.

Chapter-III

Tour of Skies

Lo! We have adorned the lowest heaven with an ornament, the planets. And verily in the heaven We have set mansions of the stars, and We have beautified it for beholders. Saafaat, 6 and Hijjar, 16.

Like earth, sky is also a gorgeous creation by Allah that has innumerable signs for us. Let's look at the details of those signs:

An Example

Suppose a beautiful woman has ten daughters but all of them are less beautiful than their mother. These girls revolve around their mother. And then each daughter also gets ten daughters who are all less beautiful than their mothers and they too revolve around their mothers. Same is the case of planets. Their first mother was galaxy that is the abode of billions of starts and planets. Each one of the suns has ten daughters that revolve around it. Our sun is the last mother that has given birth to eight daughters, i.e. Neptune, Uranus, Saturn, Jupiter, Mars, Earth, Venus, and Mercury. Our earth has also given birth to a daughter i.e. moon, which is less beautiful than earth and is revolving around its mother.

Seven Skies

Sky is too far away from us and therefore our knowledge about it is very inferior, lacking, and incomplete. But what astronomers have found out is that apparently, we see seven segments of the sky. In first segment there are only four large stars, segment two has 27, segment three, 73, segment four, 199, segment five, 650, segment six, 2,200, and segment seven, more than 3,000. And this number increases till in twentieth segment, we have 606,000,000 stars. Till now, we have seen about 200,000,000 stars.

What Qur'an mentions is probably those skies that we can see without a telescope.

And we created seven paths above you and We are never unmindful to creation. Mominoon, 17.

Latest research about skies has revealed that there are quite a few 'transparent walls' in the atmosphere. There is also a 'wall' that stops cosmic rays containing ca. 10 billion volt electricity. If somehow, these rays pierce through that (incredible) wall, life on earth would immediately cease to exist. There is also another 'wall' that stops ether waves and sends them back to earth. And it is because of this that we can listen to radio. Another 'wall' stops heat emitted by billions of stars. If we go just a hundred miles [162 km] above and we have a glass of water, it will start boiling. How great a bounty of Allah that we have been kept protected from such colossal natural hazards.

Sun

Had we been any closer to the sun, we would have burnt because of heat. Conversely, had we been too far away from the sun, we would have frozen to death. Allah has kept us at an optimum distance from the sun; so that we do not come in harm's way.

وَمَا كُنَّا عَنِ الْخَلْقِ غَافِلِينَ (23:17)

Do not make me of those who are ignorant (of your mercy).

When we look at the sun and the flood lights and then think that it is not just the earth that gets light from the sun and that just a tiny portion of its light - ca. $1/20,000,000^{th}$ - reaches us, we shudder because of the grandeur this globe of light.

Distance of Sun (from Earth)

Sun is 93 million miles [ca. 150 million km] away from earth. To properly understand the true expression of this distance, fix a clock in a room and consider each 'click' as letter. The clock clicks 60 times in a minute, 3,600 times in an hour and 84,400 times in 24 hours. This way, to measure the distance of sun from earth, would take about three years.

A yet another example: If a train runs towards sun with a speed of 40 mph [ca. 65 km/h), it will take it 265 years to reach it.

Revolutions of Sun

Sun revolves around its axis. Unlike earth that completes one revolution in 24 hours, sun completes its revolution in one month. It has been observed through powerful telescopes that sun has certain smudges that keep on changing their locations. Those smudges cannot be seen on 16th and 21st day but reappear on 26th day. Though scientist believe that sun revolves around itself but Qur'an proves it wrong. In this regard, human knowledge is so rudimentary that inspite of great efforts, it could not catch up with knowledge of Divinity. Of all the astronomers, only Herschel has accepted the sun as moving. A day will however come that human endeavors and research would be able to testify the truth of Divinity and say:

And the sun runs on unto a resting-place for him. That is the measuring of the Mighty, the Wise. Yasin, 38.

Western scientist believe that earth moves but in the east, it is considered static. Qur'an has lot many Ayaat about earth, for example:

(1) *(He) Who has appointed the earth as a cradle. Yasin, 53.*

"Mehd" (in Arabic) means cradle that is of two types: one that is established in fun-fare and two, the one that is used in houses for children. Both the cradles have however, motion in common.

(2) And He has cast into the earth firm hills that it quake not with you. Nahl, 15.

To give stability to earth, Nature arranged mountains. Had earth been static, there would not have been the question of 'running away'. The fear of 'running away' (of earth) could have occurred only if it is accepted that earth is moving while passing through different routes. Had its weight been lesser that what it is, it is quite likely that it would have been attracted by some other planet and earth, because of fear, would have run away.

He has created the heavens and the earth with truth. He makes night to succeed day, and He makes day to succeed night, and He constrains the sun and the moon to give service, each running on for an appointed term. Zumar, 5.

How express is the announcement of earth's movement: Earth makes an orbit of 585 million miles [ca. 948 million km] around the sun. Its speed is 64,800 mph [105,000 km/hr]. To have a better understanding of the enormity of earth's speed, suppose you have gone to a cinema and return after three hours. You must know that meanwhile, you have travelled about 200,000 miles [324,000 km].

The Moon

Diameter of moon is 2,160 miles [ca. 3,400 km] and that of earth, 7,980 miles [ca. 12,900 km]. Moon is 13½ times smaller than earth and revolves around the earth with a speed of ca. 3,680 km/hr. The orbit of the Moon around the Earth is completed in approximately 27.3 days. However, it is revolving around the already fast-revolving earth with such an ease that it neither collides with earth nor with any other heavenly object. Earth completes one revolution in 345¼ days (around the sun) while moon does so in just 27 days (around earth).

Solar and Lunar Eclipse

When moon occurs between earth and sun, it causes solar eclipse. Quite frequently, complete solar eclipse occurs in India but in Siberia, it is half eclipse. Reason is clear: we and Siberians look at the sun from different angles. It is quite possible that at the time of complete solar eclipse, moon is not fully stationed between sun and earth. Similarly, lunar eclipse occurs when earth occurs between sun and moon.

Distance of Moon

Moon is some 240,000 miles [ca. 388,000 km] away from us. If a train runs with a speed of 40 miles per hour, it will reach moon in 250 days. In other words, if we take a thread and spread it ten times around the earth at the Equator, and then throw it towards moon, then one end of the thread would be at earth and the other, at moon. Or if we can manufacture a gun whose blast could be heard up to hundreds of thousands of kilometers, such a sound[23] would reach moon in fourteen days.

We have no idea of the internal world of moon. Though

---

[23] Sound travels at a speed of 12 miles [ca. 19.5 km] per second

it is 240,000 miles away from us and can be brought just 240 miles away from earth, but when an eye cannot see something even as close as one mile, it won't see 240 miles [389 km] way. We however know so much that moon has mountains that were volcanic in earlier ages and whose lava has cooled down and frozen. If the lava of Sandwich Island would freeze, they would certainly look like lunar mountains.

Earth is hot from inside. If we heat up two iron balls, one small, the other large, the smaller one would cool up relatively quicker. With the same analogy, moon is a 'child' of earth and was given birth when earth itself was like boiling iron. Because of smaller size, moon has completely cooled down while earth is still very hot from within. Till now, its outer shell has cooled down and a time will come when its interior would also cool down like moon.

Moon has neither air nor water and hence not fit for human habitation. It is just a dry wilderness. Since its volume is 13½ times smaller than earth, its gravitational force is also very small. Things have weight because of gravitational force. Stone is heavy because earth attracts it. When we pick up a stone, earth's gravitational force tries to 'snatch' it from our hands and thus give us the feeling of 'weight'. Astronomers have proved that moon's gravitational force is 6-times lesser than earth's. Therefore, if a man can carry one gunny bagful of grain on earth, he would be able to carry six bags on moon. There cricket ball would go six times farther than on earth while a football would go six time up as on earth. There won't be any feeling if we carry say a pocket watch to moon. But if carry the same watch to another planet that is hundred thousand times larger than earth, the same watch weighing 1.1 oz [ca. 31 gm] would weigh more than 13,000 lbs and will certainly crush us.

It is the beneficence of Allah that our planet earth is neither so heavy that would make even taking a step difficult, nor so light that with a just a small breeze, our houses would fly like cards, trees would be uprooted and our children would be subjected to flying like a tiny piece of wood while just a stroke to cricket ball, would cause it move miles away. And this way, earth would become a problem.

Now let's see what Allah has to say in the Qur'an in this regard:

We created everything according to scale. Qamar, 49.

Scientist have proved that fast speed brings changes to gravitational force. If earth would start moving 70-times faster, weight of all the things would reduce. And if earth would accelerate its speed seventy times, nothing would have weight. If the atmosphere is filled with mercury, that is 1,460 times heavier, we will be crushed to death. These are the lessons about skies and earth that have been advocated many a time.

There are lessons for the believers in the earth and the skies. Jasiah, 3.

Stars

Let's look at what we have in our vicinity:

1) Venus: It is as large as our planet and gets light from our sun. In shape, it is like moon and increases/decrease like moon. It completes one revolution around sun in 255 days.

2) Mercury: It is 37 million miles [ca. 60 million km] away from sun but looks like closer to sun. It also gets light from sun.

3) Mars: It has strange habits. It stops while moving,

comes back and starts again. It completes one revolution in 1,686 days and completes one revolution around its axis in 24 hrs and 37 minutes. Its surface has water and has large white spots at northern and southern sides that reduce in summer and increase in winter. Scientist think that these are not spots but snow that increases in winter and reduces in summer.

4) Jupiter, Neptune, Saturn, and Uranus: These starts are much larger than our earth. Jupiter is 1,300 times larger than earth and completes one revolution around its axis in 9 hrs and 55 minutes, and round around sun, in 12 years. It has occasionally clouds on its surface.

Volumes of Stars

1) Earth's circumference is 40 million meters and radius, 6.378 million meters. Its surface area is 510 million km^2 while its land covers 126 million km^2.

2) Mars' volume is six times lesser than earth and its one year is equivalent to our 687 days.

3) Jupiter is 1,300 times larger than earth. Its one year is equal to our 12 years. Its diameter is 1.04 trillion meters.

4) Saturn: it is 718 times larger than earth and has a diameter of 9.3 billion meters

5) Uranus: it is 29 times larger than earth and 2 billion miles [324 billion km] away from sun and completes one revolution in 24 years.

6) Neptune: its volume is 55 times more than earth and

completes one revolution in 165 years.

7) Moon: its surface is 14 times lesser and volume is one-fiftieth. It has 40 mountains some of which are more than 4,800 m tall.

8) Sun is 1.3 million times larger than earth. The enormity of its light is such that 800,000 complete moons combined cannot emit as much light as sun does in mid-day. And to top it all, there is another sun that is 150 trillion miles away from us. It's lighter by 800,000 times than our sun.

Now let's think over the mind-boggling grandeur of Allah. How infinite in numbers are the suns and moons and then under what a wonderful system they all are moving around their axis and around their suns and never any collision, disarray, or disorganization occurs. How so? Let's see what Allah has to tell us:

1) *Neither sun can create hurdles in the movement of moon nor is there any disorganization in the system of day and night. All these suns and moons are swimming in the atmosphere in great discipline. Yasin, 40.*

2) *Allah has stabilized skies such that they cannot fell on earth without (My) Command. Hajj, 65.*

Look at the railways system in the world. Those changing tracks, signal men, watchmen, etc. all are doing their jobs, but every now and then, we see trains colliding, people die and traffic remains suspended for weeks. On the other hand, billions of great satellites are moving with the speed of electricity and there is not a single signalman, track changer or other people but even then, everything is moving in perfect precision. Why? Because there is an EYE that sees and never makes a mistake.

Everything in universe knows about discipline and duty. Noor, 41.

Point of Day and Month

Dr. Sahbli thinks that there is a concentrated light in the atmosphere around which all the suns revolve and each revolution is completed in 300 million years. In other words, our 300 million year is their one year. Since there is no limit to solar systems in the universe and each sun's movement is different than other suns, therefore the duration of day and month is also different. To us, one day and night is the name of earth's axial revolution and year is earth's revolution around sun. But days and years of other systems are different than ours. For example, Mercury's year is only of 88 days, Venus' 225 days, but in case of Jupiter, it is 12 years Saturn, 29½ years, and Neptune's 165 years. Similarly, some stars complete on revolution in 1,000 years and others in 50,000 years. Therefore, Allah's signal is very appropriate:

Allah's one day is equal to your 1,000 years.

At yet another place, Allah says:

Such a day that is equal to your 50,000 years. Me'araj, 4.

Movement of Stars

If we could manage such a height where there is no wind and no gravitational force, and we throw a stone in a straight line, it will keep on moving till Eternity. This will be so because there would be no air resistance and no gravitational pull to stop it. Same is the case of stars that billions of years back, some flames from the galaxies broke up that are still flying in the universe. Different suns after attracting them, have caused their equilibrium. Had suns not been providing this service, these floating objects would have been, God knows where, how many things on their way they might have collided with and how much destructions they might have wrecked, is hard to imagine. The way a bull of oil-extraction system moves in a circle, the same way the pull of sun has established the routes of Jupiter, Mercury, earth, etc. and all these planets follow these routes in full precision.

A Joke

Hazrat Musa^{AS} asked Allah as to when does He sleep? Allah in response asked Musa to keep these two bottles in his hand. After that, Allah blew cold air. Hazrat Musa^{AS} felt sleepy. His grip on bottles loosened and fell down and what happened to the glass, is not hard to imagine.

What a way to make Hazrat Musa^{AS} understand that even for a moment if Allah would sleep, what will happen in the universe after colliding with each other and creating hell before Hell.

There is just one Allah in this universe that is eternal that does not sleep. And that is because the management of skies and earth is with Him. That high and mighty Allah does not get tired of the protection of earth and skies. Baqarah, 255.

The Point

During all the ages in Europe and Asia, there was a thought that on each day of the week, a particular planet has a special impact on the government of the day. Because of this thought, people called some days as 'fortunate' and others as 'unfortunate' and then kept the names of those days as of the planets, for example:

1) Sunday, i.e., named after sun

2) Monday, i.e. named after moon

3) Tuesday, in fact called Morsday in French i.e. the day of Mars

4) Similarly in French, Wednesday is called Mercredi Day, i.e. Mercury Day

5) Thurs is Jupiter and Fri is Venus in a western dictionary

6) Saturn in fact was given to Saturday

As against these names, Islam was free of such superstition and called days of the week as first day, second day, etc. so that Muslims do not feel afraid of the unknown evil impacts.

Satellites

These are in fact huge suns that are too far away from us that in so many ways, is the mercy of Allah on us:

First: Had these been closer by, we would have been burnt to ashes because of their intense heat.

Second: These huge suns would have attracted our earth and disturbed the entire Solar System.

These satellites are so far away that if we could somehow manage to sit on any one of them and look down, our sun would look like a tiny dot; and of course, there would have been no question of seeing earth. We can see with our bare eyes just 6,000 stars. With telescope, the number could go up to tens of millions.

Photographic plate is a very sensitive material that can take pictures of such stars that cannot be seen even with a telescope. Mr. Isaac Robert (of Liverpool) photographed a thousandth of sky's portion, and caught pictures of 16,000 stars. According to that calculation, the total number of starts should be 160 million. But who else, save Allah knows the actual number?

Sometimes students of physical sciences are heard saying that Day of Judgment is the figment of imagination of mullahs. They contend that end of human life is death and that's it. Did it ever happen that a dead man got life again? Is it is not a joke to infuse life in old bones? These are their questions but these ignorants don't know that in this universe, millions of worlds are moving and there is a breathtaking environment all around. Is it difficult for Allah, who is managing this entire system, to put life in a dead body?

Let's see what Allah has to say in this regard:

Are you the harder to create, or is the heaven that He built? Alnazi'at, 27.

Comets

These are in great numbers in the skies and no one has any idea of their movements. Quite frequently, they move away from the sun but then come closer and start revolving. While in close proximity to sun, their speed could be as high as 200 miles [325 km] per second. These stars are made up of some transparent material. That is why one can see through them other stars that are behind them. Their tails are in fact vapors that come out because of sun heat. The moment they move away from the sun, their tails would disappear.

Meteors

These are very small stars that can be seen only when they die. Their speed is about 12,000 miles [19,000 km] per second, i.e. 100 times faster than a bullet. They can complete one revolution around earth in just 2½ hrs. It is a lightless small star with no potential to get light from sun.

When it comes closer to earth while traveling, the earth attracts it. As a result, it travels fast in the atmosphere and after rubbing with dust particles, first gets heated and then catches fire and converts into gases and scatters in the atmosphere. This is the reality of meteor.

Since its speed is 100 times that of a bullet and bullet also heats up while travelling, so after calculating the heat of bullet and comparing it with meteor, its heat has been calculated to be $10,000°C$, sufficient to melt it and vaporize the material that it is made up of. We got some pieces of steel from the depths of oceans and from uninhibited lands. After testing, we concluded that these were in fact, pieces of meteoroids.

Had the speed of meteor been slower, it would not have melted and as a result, we on earth would have been under their constant bombardment. Be thankful to Allah that He has kept us from harm's way.

Or have you taken security from Him Who is in the heaven that He will not let loose on you a hurricane? But you shall know the manner of His warning. Al-Mulk, 17.

Presence of dust particles in the air is a necessity. First, because sun's heat is conducted only by dust particles. Since air is bad conductor of heat, nothing could live without sun's heat. Two, rain also occurs due to these particles because raindrops would never have formed without dust particles. Since large quantities of dust particles come down with rain causing their reduction in the air, so its deficiency is covered by the dust of meteoroids. What a glorious act of Allah.

Back in 1939, a pilot was flying a plane. When it reached quite a height, all of sudden stones started falling. Afraid, he returned. These were in fact parts of a meteoroid not fully pulverized.

When earth was separated from sun, it was relatively

smaller. It got bigger because of those millions of meteoroids falling on it. On September 21, 1876, a meteor kept on travelling for one thousand miles and burst between Chicago and Saint Louis. From it, small starlets separated and disappeared at some distance. Moreover, a tremendous sound could be heard that reached earth after 15 minutes. Since sound travels with a speed of 12 miles [19.5 km] per minute, this way, the meteoroid was 180 miles [290 km] away from earth when it burst.

Sir Robert Ball says that on the night of November 13, 1866, two meteoroids burst and split in four, then eight, then sixteen and then innumerable pieces. The entire area was lit with dazzling lights and continued for good three hours. This scene appears every 33 years.

On November 13, 1902 such a lot of meteoroids fell that made the people fearful. Then on November 11, 1932, Mr. Kirkwood saw this scene in Africa. He says that at midnight local Africans started making noise saying 'save us', 'we are being killed', 'world has caught fire', etc. I drew my sword and came out and saw as if the whole sky was under fire because of falling meteoroids' debris. This scene repeats every 33 years on the night between 12 and 13 November and seen in 1866; 1899; 1933. It will now be seen in 1965.

Reason for falling meteors is that they revolve around earth such that every 33 years on the night of November 13, earth crosses their path. As a result, all those meteoroids that are closer to earth, are attracted by the gravitational pull of earth and create light after getting lit up. Though earth passes through the same route each year but meteoroids are present only after 33 years, except occasional meteoroids that might come in harm's way, and ignite, is another matter. Let's also keep it in mind that twice a year, earth passes through the routes of meteoroids.

Sometime, meteors can collide even on August 9 and 10.

Birth of Meteoroid

An American inventor invented such a powerful gun that when its ammo was blasted in the air, it went out of earth's gravity and started flying freely. Similarly, sometime volcanic mountain spews lava with such a tremendous force that quite a lot of it goes out of the gravitational pull of earth. Now whenever earth gets a chance, it attracts such wayward children back to its bosom.

Distance of Stars

Our months and years are entirely insufficient to measure the distance between earth and stars. That is why astronomers have coined the term 'light year'. A man can in one second, take at the most, one step while light can travel 186,000 miles [ca. 301,000 km] in one second. If, for example, an average man travels 20 miles [ca. 32 km] a day, he would need 19,300 days to travel the distance that light travels in just one second. In other words, a second of light is equal to our 53 years.

Distance of the nearest Star (from Earth)

Sun is 93 million miles [ca.150 million km] away from us from where light reaches us in ca. eight minutes. The nearest star to us is 2,000,000,000,000 miles [3,240,000,000,000 km] away. Let's appreciate this distance by an example. In Yorkshire, a factory prepared so much cotton thread that could be used to take seven rounds of earth. If we want to manufacture so much thread that will reach the nearest star, it will take 400 years.

Meteor travels with a speed that is 100 times faster than bullet. The speed of light is 10,000 times faster than meteor's. This light reaches us in three years. Since 'seeing' can be done only through light, therefore what status the meteor is in today, was in fact, three years earlier. In other words, if we somehow manage to fly and sit on it, then the things that we would see on earth at that particular moment, would be those that had occurred three years earlier. If this meteor finishes today, we will be able to see it three years later.

Light reaching us from 'Vega' is 100 years old. Again, if we manage to fly and sit on it, we won't be able to see any human being of today rather those of the last race. Some stars are even further away. For example the nearest star of galaxy is 1,000,000 light years and the farthest one is 150,000,000 light years away. If we manage to be there, we should be able to see the pre-Adam age.

Let's suppose that we lay down a railway line to the nearest star and keep one Anna as travel cost per 100 miles. You want to get a ticket from the railway station. Now convert Annas[24] in Rupees and Rupees in Pound Sterling and put the whole amount in a box, pick it up and move towards the railway station. The box is (naturally) very heavy, so you ask a coolie to help. One coolie cannot do it, okay, call 20 coolies. But the box is so heavy that even 20 coolies won't do. Now get a car, but wait, the box cannot be placed in it. Now let's calculate and after a lot of multiplications and additions, we calculated that we would need 7,500 bullock carts to transport the cash. Okay, but what about those stars whose light has not reached us as yet;

~~since the creation of the Universe. Some have even~~

---

[24] One Rupee used to have 16 Annas

disappeared but alas, we are still waiting for its light to reach us.

Some stars are white, some golden, others green, still others are blue and red. All these stars have been created from the same material that our earth has been. Some are 1.6 million times brighter than the sun, having a diameter of 400 million miles [650 million km].

How enormous are the worlds in skies, how in perfect equilibrium are these heavenly bodies revolving and how breathtaking speed are they moving with. And when we put a quick glance at all this, and compare our world and then ourselves, we get the right feeling of our being so infinitely minuscule and so helpless and so very powerless. And with that comes the feeling as to why Allah had to be so 'concerned' about our welfare that he had to send prophets from time to time to keep us on the right path; that we are so 'fond' of deviating from. And then our pride of being the dear ones of Allah but never bother to act as commanded. On the contrary, we wear rags and having parasites on all of our bodies and claiming to be the 'Ummat' of that greatest personality, the most dearly of Allah of all the mankind - Mohammad.

Earth and skies are telling the stories of grandeur and might of Allah Who is the highest, the wisest. Jasiatah, 27.

Match

Our planet earth is a small sphere. There are millions of spheres that are in motion for millions of years. If we suppose that there is no life on these spheres, is wrong. Compared to these, our planet is just a toy. Only Jupiter is 12 times larger than earth. Now a question arise: have all these heavenly bodies been created just as decoration pieces? Or just for fun? With no other purpose? May be, but our knowledge is still rudimentary. To understand even a fraction of the whole Godly system and its immense mysteries, we would need to spend millions of years and only then, may be, repeat, may be, we are able to understand a fraction of it.

And We created not the heavens and the earth, and all that is between them, just for fun. Dukhan, 38.

Till now, man has written ca. 80 million books on civilization, history, governments, geography, ethics, etc. Had we access to the knowledge of other planets as we have of earth, we would have written books on them also. Since such heavenly bodies are at least 100 million, it would have caused a hundred million times increase in our knowledge.

If we wish to keep all such books in a library, and each room of the library had the capacity of 10,000 books, we would need 80 billion rooms. And if we assume 300,000 houses in Lahore, we would need 266,667 cities as big as Lahore just to accommodate all those books. If a man were fast enough to read one book each day, he would need 2.2 trillion years.

Are we still not impressed by the greatness and vastness and infiniteness of Allah? Have I succeeded in causing a stir in your hearts - the purpose of all these details?

He makes the night to pass into the day and the day to pass into the night. He has subdued the sun and moon to service. Each runs unto an appointed term. Such is Allah, your Lord; His is the Sovereignty; and those unto whom you pray instead of Him own not so much as the white spot on a date-stone. Fatir, 13.

Chapter-IV

World of Animals

See they not that it is We Who have created for them -- among the things which Our hands have fashioned -- cattle, which are under their dominion? And that We have subjected them to their (use)? And they have (other) profits from them (besides), and they get (milk) to drink. Will they not then be grateful? Yasin, 71-73.

Catch a mouse and it bites. Go near a wasp and it stings. Deer runs away if it sees man even at a distance of one kilometer. It is hard to sit on a lion or rhino. If a camel becomes rebellious, it will kill its owner under its knees. And if an ox gets defiant and out of control, it will in no time destroy a house. How great a Divine bounty that large animals like he-buffalo, horse, camel, even elephant, act as commanded. They bear the burden that we want them to carry and cross deserts but never complain.

And then each cow and buffalo is like a machine that provides us the best food like milk, butter, yoghurt, etc. Had the color of milk been red, we would have hated it. We get fresh white milk coming out of their udders that we relish. Milkman takes out all the milk from buffalo and cow but they do not object. This is because a cow prefers our brought-up over its child's. Impressed by its sacrifice, Hindus started worshipping cow. The fact is that the universe is so full of such interesting scenes that one wonders.

When he saw the moon rising in splendor, He said: "This is my Lord." Al-An'am, 77.

Sabiyen acknowledge sun as their god. Zarathustra and Musa saw the Glory of Allah. Saints found a whole panoramic scene of garden in each flower. In short, there are such a lot of wonderful scenes in this world that it appears that each one of it points to the "BEING" of Allah.

A son goes to the bazaar with his father. Whatever shoes he sees first, wishes to purchase. But father is along and purchases the best shoes for his son. Had we not been guided by the Prophet, we too would have been worshipping whatever came our way. All the prophets had been saying loud and clear: Lo! Never be confused by these scenes. The one to be worshiped is the one who has created all these things. All these things are your servants and in your service, not to be worshipped.

Types of Animals

Animals are of different types. Some are such that they only have the sense of touch, for example sea shells, internal insects of animals, bacteria of marsh, etc. Others have esthete and touch, for example insects rearing on flowers and fruits. Still some have three senses: touch, esthete, and count, for example those animals that live in deep seas or dark places. And then we have animals that have four senses, for example animals living in dark caves who, because of the non-existence of light, have lost sight. As for the animal that has five senses, all of us know – is man. And look at the wonder of Nature that each one of them is complete in itself.

Protozoa

These animals are made up of just one cell and were the first to have been created. Today, shells of such animals can be found in mountains that remained submerged in oceans for millions of years. Most of the stones, especially lime stones are made up of these animals. Then one can observe thick layers of these animals on pyramids. Even Malaria is caused by such animals. These microscopic organisms protect themselves through various means; the most important being that they reproduce in millions in an hour time. Most of the times, they remain hidden under vegetables and in ponds. The enormity of reproduction of cholera organisms for example, can be gauged from the fact that just in one hour they can multiply to a mind boggling number: 5,000,000,000,000,000,000,000,000 [5×10^{20}] so that even if most of them are destroyed by medication, still millions would be left to propagate.

Animal Diversity

Some living organisms run rather than walk, for example snow worms, others crawl. Some creep through their bellies, for example snakes. Some walk like rats, some fly with two wings while others use four wings, for example locust. And then some have two, some four and others have six legs while still others have tens of legs, like centipede.

And Allah has created every animal from water: of them there are some that creep on their bellies; some that walk on two legs; and some that walk on four. Allah creates what He wills: for verily Allah has power over all the things. Noor, 45.

Allah created millions of animal types and created millions of each category and each one of them has different appearance. Some of the insects on flowers and vegetables are so minute that if picked in fingers, they will burst. But look at the workmanship of Nature that each one of them has body system complete with bones, lungs, stomach, heart, legs, wings, even brain. All of them perform all the conceivable function expected of a large animal. To know about the craftsmanship of Nature, better look at these animals and insects, rather than the Himalayas.

Self Confidence

Wild animals protect themselves from calamities and that is why they are quick, cunning, agile, fast, healthy and above all, great pretenders. As against that, cows, goats, donkeys, etc. are protected by man. That is why they are lazy, ugly-looking, and easy going. A nation that does not use their body parts, Allah takes backs those parts. Being followers, instead of leaders, as they should have been, Muslims have given on the use of mental faculties. Therefore, Allah has snatched from them all such faculties; and that is why they are treated like domestic animals (and rightly).

Movement of Animals

Movement of animals is for food. Since trees get food from soil, they don't need to travel in search of food. If for example, trees too would have been walking in search of food, there would have been great disorganization in the world. Every day, thousands of trees would have been moving on roads, like cows in India, causing massive traffic jams. A tree of the farmland of Zaid would have moved to Bakar's and there would have been fist fights. Some might have ended on mountains; never to come down.

But since animal feed is spread through and through, it has to move around. Allah has given special characteristics to every being in line with their requirements. For example, sponge is such an animal that it stays where it is and gets its food there. Then we have Sea Squirt that when needs food, just extends its neck from the shell and gets its food.

Different animals have different actions according to the circumstances. Some sleep in the day and come out in the night and vice versa. Some animals hibernate for months in extreme summers and winters in holes and caves. Frog sticks to pond's clay after it dries and comes out again in monsoon. To live without food for months, even years is a stupendous miracle of Allah's infinite qualities. Animals that have access to abundant food, get heavy and ugly, like elephant, rhino, buffalo, even frog; the reason being that they need not work hard in search of food and have almost no enemies, nor competitors. As against them, deer too has abundant food but since it has so many enemies, that is why just a faint sound is sufficient to make it run very fast; and for miles. That is why a deer is very agile and quick on its heels. And finally, let's look at the last Abbasid Caliphs and Mogul Emperors who had become extremely lazy and easy-going. And that is why Allah felt their disutility and sent them packing.

Frogs have lesser enemies on land and so has a slower speed on land than in water. It has just one enemy on land – snake. To protect it from the excesses of crawling snake, Allah has given it the quality of jumping. Then there is a hydroid that lives on bacteria that is abundantly available in sea water. It just drinks water and gets what it needs – (bacterial) food.

Female Mosquito

After laying eggs, female mosquito becomes weak. To regain strength, it needs quick and nutritious food - human blood. To suck blood, Allah has given it a lancet. Male mosquito lives on food in ponds. Since mosquito lays eggs in summer that is why it needs human blood in summer. It also needs human blood to sustain and be able to propagate its breed.

Ages of Animals

Tortoise can live up to hundred years, some fishes, 150 years, falcon, 118 years, dog, 35 years, horse and cat, 40, cow 25, hen 30 years, duck 75 years and crocodile can live up to 40 years.

Some Strange Animals

1) Hamster sleeps for six months.

2) Some oceans have a (sort of) donkey that brings out a sinking human on its back and on the coast.

3) Pearl is such an animal that sits in the boat of shell. It first swims on water surface and then goes down in depths. It has gauze that filters food. There are a number of mouths behind the gauze and each mouth has four lips. Creation of pearl is the mixture of microscopic animals and sand. These animals discharge a sticky material that glues sand and ultimately, becomes what we know as pearl.

4) Chameleon has a big head, small neck and snake-like tail. While on a tree, its color is green and sometimes yellow. In case of stimulation, oblique lines appear that slowly spread on the entire body and its color gets yellow because of anger.

5) A doctor once treated a female elephant. After fifteen years, she met the doctor just by chance. Running towards him, she turned her trunk around

him and started exhibiting love as if they were close friends and had met after a long time.

6) Another doctor once administered injection to a child under a tree. Some monkeys up in the tree were observing him. He left his kit and went for some urgency. When back, he saw a large monkey administering injection to a youngster.

7) Female frog lays eggs in water and male spreads its sperms on eggs that are wrapped in bad-tasting membrane so that water animals may not eat the eggs. In it certain microscopic organisms enter that discharge nitrogen so that eggs could keep on maturing. This membrane also breathes and because of that, eggs come on the surface of water. One frog lays 1,000 to 2,000 eggs. When toddlers are born, they swim with the help of their tails. But when its claws (ores) appear, its tail disappears. Besides nostrils, a frog can breathe with its skin as well.

Oddities of a Camel

1) Allah has gifted camel with round feet so that it could easily travel in desert.

2) Long legs to complete journey quickly.

3) Long neck so that it could get food both from trees and ground.

4) Accumulated so much fats and water that it could live for up to four weeks.

5) If its driver has no food, he drinks its milk.

6) Allah made all the plants its food; even those plants

that other browsers would not even go closer to.

7) Gave it tough mouth so that it may even browse acacia leaves.

8) Gave it the strength to bear even a very heavy load and made a special seat near to hump so that its driver can easily be seated.

9) Made it obedient so that proper use could be made of it.

10) If it sees a route once, it can remember it for years, even if all the previous signs have gone.

Because of these oddities of camels, Allah has asked for our attention:

Don't you see how We have created the camel? Ghashiatah, 17.

Chapter-V

The World of Birds

These quadruped and birds are ummats like you (human beings). An'am, 38.

These ummats do not suffer from diseases and have hardly signs of old age. They remain quick and fast till the end. They do not suffer from flu and malaria, nor do they contact pneumonia and cough. This is so because these ummats follow a special system of living. They eat suitable food, take proper exercises and don't cross the limits of eating for the purpose of taste. Lion goes to his female once a year, but man ....? Birds generally change with environment but man generally does not. Taking shelter behind religion, demeanor, traditions, man stays at one point with the result that nations that go along the era and time, subdue the nations that remain reluctant like Gul Mohammad[25], in their thoughts, and do not budge even an inch. There are thousands of lessons for us in birds. They are Ummat like us but stick to what the Nature has ordained for them and thus keep on chirping for life.

See you not that it is Allah Who is praised by all beings in the heavens and on earth, and the birds with wings outspread? Each one knows its own (mode of) prayer and praise. And Allah knows well all that they do. Noor, 41.

Unfortunate are those birds and quadruped that live in the vicinity of mankind, for example cow, buffalo, donkey, horse, hen, pigeon, etc. Man happens to be quite dirty. He spits here and vomits there and urinates, especially where it

---

[25] It is a Persian adage – *zameen jumbad, na jumbad Gul Muhammad* – that means that even if the earth moves, Gul Muhammad would not.

is prohibited (e.g., in the vicinity of a mosque) and leaves dirt everywhere. Because of such a dirty environment, birds and quadruped get sick. On the other side, look at the nests of birds and see how clean they are kept. Cat digs a pit and covers its refuse into it. In other words, man is daily given a lesson by cat, but alas, he never bothers. And when the wrath of Allah befalls on him, he asks for some more time to improve; though he never will.

O man! Keep away from dirt. Mudassir, 1-5.

But how this unfortunate man, who does not listen to the prophet and does not care about the commands of Allah, would learn from a cat? After all, he is the best of the creatures.

Living nations, where have other qualities, there they also care about cleanliness. They are very neat and clean, like cleanliness, and have good habits.

A Joke

Back in 1920, Ross Keppel, Chief Commissioner of Frontier Province called a Jirga[26] of the maliks of Waziristan. After the Jirga, a Waziri Malik[27] said to him, "Sir! We are very happy with you. But there is one deficiency in you: how good it would have been, had you been a Muslim".

Ross Keppel asked him what was the benefit of being Muslim? The Pathan said, "You would not be thrown into Hell". "A good man like you would look better in the Paradise", he concluded. Ross Keppel said, "What a reply.

---

[26] A tribal assembly of elders that takes decisions by consensus, particularly among the Pathan

[27] A tribal chieftain who is paid a token amount of money to keep calm in his area and to act as an intermediary between his people and the government

You know when we will go Hell, we will keep it clean and make it a Paradise. You dirty people, when you will go to Paradise, you will throw *naswar* [28] everywhere, cough, and spit, wear dirty clothes, shit all around, throw banana peels and other garbage and soon, would convert Paradise into Hell".

Besides bad habits, slave nations are bereft of niceties, delicateness, and cleanliness. They don't have the cleanliness of bird, alertness of deer, chastity of lion, quickness of falcon, and majesty of eagle. They are clumsy like buffalos, dirty like vultures and messy like an owls.

Since it was the will of Allah to make the Arabians, the rulers of world, because of the prophet Mohammad, that is why there were special instructions given about cleanliness: O you wrapped up (in a mantle)! Arise and deliver His warning! And your Lord do you magnify! And your garments keep free from stain! And all abomination shun! Mudassir, 1-5.

Though all the Commands of Qur'an are obligatory but mullah says that only five are so, i.e., Kalma Tayyabah, prayers, fast, charity, and Hajj. Of the rest of six thousand Divine Commands, just a few are considered virtuous [mustahab], some are desirable [mustahsin] and others, unnecessary. If Allah's Command is binding then how could *"wa sibabaka fatahhiro, war-rujza fahjur"* [29] be excluded from the list of incumbency? See what has become of Muslims because of living in dirty houses the like of a dungeon and unclean environment and what has happened to their health, and how much dignity they have lost because of wearing stinking dirty clothes?

---

[28] Snuff made up of tobacco, lime, and wood-ash placed in mouth as a stimulant

[29] *And your* garments *keep free from stain! And all abomination shun!*

All the rest of religions consider it a private affair and personal belief, limited only to some worships and some other rituals. And that's it. On the other side, Islam is a complete code of life. Right from the outset, enemies of Islam had been striving to make Islam limited to a few beliefs and to disfigure the real Islamic identity of social life and of its enormity in the realm of cultural and political influence. To meet their nefarious designs, they concocted such Ahadeeth that confined Islam to just five obligations mentioned earlier, taking all the rest of its facet out of its ambit.

Just consider cleanliness that takes into account the cleanliness of clothes, of house, of household effects, of domestic waste, of bacteria, avoiding food that makes one weak, dirty environment, avoiding houses with no proper ventilation and natural light, insects, dirty teeth and body, etc. To avoid all these things are exactly the Commands of Islam and like the five fore-mentioned obligations, these too are the (religious) obligations of Muslims. Are we listening? Hardly!

Just think how big is the punishment to disobey even one Divine Command and how horribly we are suffering because of such insubordination. Look at the heaps of dirt in and around our houses. Our mouths emit foul smell and our teeth are yellow. How much dirt our bodies have accumulated and how badly our children suffer because of fatal diseases. How pale we are because of excessive carbon, malnutrition, and deficiency of clean air. And how miserable, spreading hordes of diseases, these ugly-looking Muslims are in the eyes of developed nations? Be honest and say who is acting upon the Qur'anic Ayaat. We or the English? Mr. Brain goes to our villages and tells them about cleanliness while we right in the mosque, right in the presence of tens of persons, blow our nose and no one cares. We make urinals in the vicinity of mosques that spread stink all around and don't feel ashamed.

A son of Hazrat Adam killed his other son and then had no sense where to dispose it off. And then Allah sent a bird that directed him so:

Then Allah sent a raven, who scratched the ground, to show him how to hide the shame of his brother. Ma'eda, 31.

This story is in fact a sort of instruction: to bury all the dirty and stinging material under the earth. The Prophet Mohammad was sent to salvation of Muslims of bodily and spiritual impurity. But today, our mullah considers it his disgrace to even speak about cleanliness. All the Ayaat that refer to cleanliness are interpreted as spiritual cleanliness. Okay but then could a person who stinks be authorized to say anything related to morals? And who has hundreds of lice crawling on his body and has mounds of contaminant all around? Remember! The Prophet was sent to teach us how to be neat and clean, both physically and spiritually. Let's see what Allah says in this regard:

A Book that We have revealed unto you, in order that you might lead mankind out of the depths of darkness into light – with the permission of Allah - to the Way of (Him) Exalted in Power, Worthy of all Praise! Ibrahim, 1.

How beautiful is the land of Allah? How beautiful are the flowers? And this greenery! How heavenly! What lessons do we get? That Allah is Beautiful and likes only those nations that love cleanliness, neatness, and delicateness. The Prophet repeatedly said that I love fragrance. Why not? And we, ...?

Allah is Himself beautiful and loves beauty and has called 'dress' a Divine bounty.

O you children of Adam! We have bestowed raiment upon you to cover your shame, as well as to be an adornment to you, but the raiment of righteousness, that is the best. Such are among the signs of Allah, that they may receive admonition! A'araaf, 26.

Does 'raiment' mean the one that has not been washed even once? The one that stinks or the one that is clean like a bird and neat like a flower?

In summers certain people coming to the mosque have clothes that stink but mullah would never mention it. Why? Because to him the Divine Command "*War-rujza Fahjur*" is unnecessary.

People migrating in winter from Kashmir to the plains, come with raiment that is dirty to the very core and stink like a wild boar. How beautiful are the uplands of Kashmir and how ugly are its people. While looking at such people, I wonder that if a man cannot keep his dress clean how on earth could he keep his soul clean?

Wonders of Nature

Following are some interesting facts pertaining to nature:

1) Some birds fly with a speed of 60 miles an hour (ca. 100km).

2) Tit is a bird that prepared its nest from exactly 2,379 feathers.

3) Sea Swift is a bird of Masjid-e-Aqsa[30] that prepares its nest with the help of its spit.

---

[30] Al-Aqsa Mosque or Bayt al-Muqaddas is the third holiest site in Islam. It is located in the Old City of Jerusalem. The site on which the silver domed mosque sits, along with the Dome of the Rock, is the holiest site in Judaism, the place where the Temple is generally accepted to have stood. Muslims believe that

See next page

4) Hazrat Suleiman said that certain things were beyond his understanding. One of them was that how a large vulture can glide in the air for hours, without moving its wings. This doesn't mean that he did not know it. It rather means that his knowledge about such things was so much that he was wonderstruck; the limit of knowledge is heart.

A Joke

Someone asked Allama Iqbal: What is the threshold of knowledge? Allama said, how very strange. And then asked him, "What is the extreme end of love"? Allama said love is limitless. The person immediately objected and asked him the meaning of a verse[31]:

Tere ishq ki intiha chahta houn [I ask for the extremity of your love]
Iqbal said that unfurls my stupidity:

Meri saadgi dekh kia chahta houn [Look at my simplicity as to what I am asking for]

Coleridge, an English philosopher, says, "Knowledge in wonder".

A Hadeeth says, "O Allah! May I be ever increasingly amazed about You".

Mohammad was transported from the Sacred Mosque in Mecca to al-Aqsa during his journey to heavens. Islamic tradition holds that Mohammad led prayers towards this site until the seventeenth month after the emigration to Madina, when Allah directed him to turn towards the Ka'aba.

[31] Various types of poems are marked by particular patterns of rhyme and syllabic pulse. Each line is divided into two half-lines (called *misra*); the second of the two ends with a rhyming syllable that is used throughout the poem.

5) C.T. Hudson says that in winter, I saw a pair of partridges that male flies and comes closer to the female, makes out some angry voices and alludes female to fly too. It is a question of thousands of miles journey, a worry to lose companion. The female would however not budge. To know the reason behind all this, I saw that female's wing was broken and male was getting mad in her love.

6) A water bird (Stormy Petrol) keeps on flying over water waves, though sometimes it comes to the land in search of food.

7) Cuckoo picks its eggs in its beak and places it in some other bird's nest and leaves. That 'other bird' keeps the eggs warm and takes care.

8) A scientist provided suitable heat to hen eggs but no chicken came out. He tried a lot of times but failed. Incidentally, he spoke to a villager about his dilemma. The farmer said you might not be turning the eggs from time to time as done by the hens. The scientist did so and succeeded.

9) If a bird's tail is cut, it will have difficulty in flying. This is so because it will not be able to keep a balance. Birds with small tails spread their legs backwards like tail so that they could fly easily.

10) Ostrich lays 20 to 30 eggs and then divides the clutch into three parts: it buries one part in the soil; keeps second part in the sun; and it self warms the third part. When chicks hatch, it breaks the eggs left in sun and gives to the chicks. When done with those eggs, it brings out the buried eggs, makes a hole in to them to which insects come to eat. The ostrich

catches those insects and throws in front of the chicks. When their stomachs become strong enough, they can eat even pebbles.

11) Both males and females of pigeon, house sparrows, doves, etc. rear their chicks together, though there are just two chicks. As against these birds, a hen looks after so many chicks but the fowl does not help her in any way. In case of former, the reason is that chicks of house sparrow and dove are very weak that warrant the look after of both male and female. As against these, the moment poultry chicks are out of the egg shell, they start running, can find food for themselves and are full of feathers; as if Nature has already taken care of them before hand. And that's why fowl does not extend any help to his fellow hens.

12) A type of bat first throws air with its wings to a sleeping person. When he gets fully besotted, it drills a hole in his body and starts drinking blood, till the man dies.

13) While flying, owl creates no noise. That is why it can attack a bird unawares. Its food is six times that of a cat. A farmer grows foodstuff but does not have the capacity to control insects and pests. Allah has deputed some birds in the day and some in the nights that take care of pests. Owl and bat are two such creatures.

14) Crow is our sweeper. Same is the case with vulture and black kite.

15) While seeing an approaching prey, a water bird throws a black material that makes water black. It

dives-in to keep itself hidden and when the prey approaches, it comes out and gets the prey.

16) Another water bird lays eggs on sea shore and sprays salt on it; so that sea shore and the place where it has laid eggs, look alike and thus eggs are saved from predators.

17) There are two birds on sea shore: one eats fish but cannot swim and other eats greenery but can swim. It catches fish and puts it in the mouth of the former that in turn keeps some greenery in its mouth and gives to the latter.

18) A bird of Brazil can fly with a speed of 815 miles an hour, i.e., 14 miles per minute and 1,200 ft [ca. 333 m] per second. A bullet travels with a speed of 2,700 ft [ca. 82 m] per second. The bird moves its wings thousands of time in a second. As against this, airplane's fans revolve 333 times per second. If a man would travel with the speed of that bird, it will complete a journey around the world in just 17 hours.

These are some of the strange things about birds.

Chapter VI

Performance of Insects

In the past pages it has been said that some verses of the
Qur'an are about insects for example, Nahal [honey bee],
Namal [ant], Ankaboot [spider], etc. From these verses, it
appears that Allah wished that after going through the
"wonderful deeds" of man, to sing in His praise. Had He
wished to be praised just because of food, then the very
first Ayat of the Qur'an would have been:
*All praise for the Rabb Who gave us food and water and the
luxury of children.*
But proclaiming *"all the praise for the Rabb of all the worlds"*,
turned our attention towards other worlds. It is therefore
our responsibility that we turn all the pages of the book of
Nature such that our brains become the abodes of
Bounties of Allah.

Ant

Hazrat Suleiman was once passing through the burrow
of ants. One ant said:
O you ants, get into your habitations, lest Solomon and his
hosts crush you (under foot) without knowing it. Namal, 18.
Allah has drawn our attention towards ants but with a
purpose. Let's see what:
Because of its physical strength, lion is considered the
King of Jungle. But had the selection of king been based on
intelligence, ant would certainly have been the king. Ants
are very intelligent. They make groups, arrange food
storage, go for masonry, guarding, infantry, practice

farming, even slavery. Let's see how.

Each burrow has four types of ants: king, queen, soldiers, and laborers. Soldiers are more agile and have greater size while laborers are more in numbers. Both king and queen have wings while the queen is fat.

Besides the five senses, each ant has four jaws, intestines, tail with a sting and a nearby pouch of poison, and two holes to its sides to breathe. After entering through these two holes, air goes in to innumerable ducts spreading in the ant the way there are veins in a plant leave.

Its burrow is 15 to 20 feet [ca. 4.5 – 6.1 m] deep where one can see a wonderful scene of workmanship. At the deepest point are a few rooms, mirador (in the upper portion), galleries, and meeting halls can be seen standing on clay pillars. Getting impressed by the craftsmanship of ants, Hazrat Suleiman once said:

Go to the ants, consider their ways and be wise.

Goethe once said:

Hard work, patience, and steadfastness lead to the perfection of humanity. All these three qualities are found in ants, in abundance.

Birth and Look after

Queen lays eggs in the burrow here and there. Laborers pick these eggs and place them in a safe place. Matrons are deputed to look after the eggs. When children come out, in the beginning they are given digested food. Matron keeps them in a row according to their ages. She pats, lick and gives them bath. If an enemy attacks the burrow, she takes them to a safer place. If they get wet due to rain, she takes them out in the sun to dry up.

Farming

Ants plough some corn nearby and when it matures, they pick it and in to the burrows.

Sometimes they get juices from plants. They drink some and store the rest in the dead bodies of ants to be used sometime later.

Parasites

Both queen and king are lazy and lewd. If other ants won't bring them food, they would prefer to die than try to get food. Laborer ants keep themselves up by hunting. Their habits are like the African wild people, always ready to fight and don't like to be subservient to others for the sake of food.

Cow: Ants get hold of an ufs and bring it up through some chemical action, till it starts giving milk. Ants relish that milk. When ufs lays eggs, they take care of them as well.

Some insects are seen moving around the ant burrows. Ants play with them as we play with a cat.

Bizarres

1) There are more than one thousand types of ants.

2) Their average age is seven years.

3) If ants from different burrows are caught in a flood, then ants of each burrow will recognize its fellows from their smell and will pick them up to their burrows.

4) Ants sometimes catch other insects. After due process of consultation, they let the elders go and

keep the kids. This is because kids can be molded in any manner while elders can't be.

5) Sometime ants would bring tree leaves and then after saturating them in water, use them as floor in their burrows.

6) Ants can pick a load three hundred times heavier than their weight. If man would do so, he can hold 450 maunds[32] weight.

7) If an ant gets a wound, another ant would quickly convert its spit through some chemical action, in to a thread and sew the wound.

8) If an ant dies, first its funeral is picked and then buried with full customs.

9) An eye of an ant is in fact a combination of two hundred eyes. There are certain insects whose eyes are a complex of 2,700 sub-eyes.

Spider

Spider makes its house (nest) from threads. Each thread is a combination of four minute threads. And each minute thread is made up of still minute 1,000 threads. In other words, each thread of the nest is composed of 4,000 threads. Then there are 4,000 minute ducts in spider's body. Each duct manufactures a thread and a little ahead, there are four ducts. In each cavity 1,000 threads enter to transform into one thread. Then at the tail-end, there is just one duct through which these four threads pass to make one thread. It extracts glue from wood and applies to the threads and then weaves such a strong house with the help of these

---

[32] One maund is ca. 40 kg

threads that even if it is the oldest one, it can withstand storms and rains.

It weaves a hexagonal web each side of which is equal to the radius. Man learnt about hexagon from the same geometrician (spider). While making the web, spider goes and comes over each string five times and keeps on adding one thin thread to it. This way each thread of the net becomes so strong that it can withstand 8-times the weight of spider.

When an insect fly's by and sticks in the web, the spider administers a poison that renders it unconscious; so that it may not break the web while pulsating.

A spider can remain hungry for up to six months. It has eight eyes. It gives up to 2,000 eggs in one go that she keeps in tender and golden threads. Though it is just one but can produce threads of different colors. Each thread that it produces is 90-times thinner than the silk thread (produced by silkworm).

Till now, we have not been able to find the use of its threads. Once Japanese made socks and gloves from it but were not durable. Till now, just one use of the thread has been tested: it can controls bleeding.

Types of Spiders

A type of spider makes a white domed house under pond water and peeps out of water from time to time. For the purpose of breathing, it fills air in a pouch and then goes underwater. Another type of spider makes web over flowers. Its job is that it does not allow insects any closer. It is like a watchman that remains in the tent, performing duty day and night.

Then there is another type of spider called Mygale that

has a house 8-10 in [20 – 25 cm] deep and one inch [2.54 cm] dia and fixes a mud door to it so that it meshes with the surrounding soil. And then it cultivates seeds around the house so that it remains in shade. The door has holes where the spider puts its claws to open it. If attacked, it shuts the door. A long-beaked bird lies in its wait. The moment it comes out of its house, the bird puts its beak in to find siblings. Since spider knows all this, she prepares another room to the side of the house and keeps its kids there where the bird's beak cannot reach.

Impressed by the intelligence of these insects, a western intellectual says:

In these things, so minute, what wisdom is displayed, what power and what unfathomable perfection.

In fact it is not possible to even guess about the workmanship of Allah. A European philosopher says:

In contemplation of things by steps we may ascend to God.

After the mention of spider in the Qur'an, there is an Ayat:

And these similitudes We put forward for mankind, but none will understand them except those who have knowledge (of Allah and His Signs, etc.). Ankabut, 43.

Have you thought that Allah has called it "knowledge" while mentioning spider. This is that 'knowledge' the absence of which is causing the Muslims embarrassment.

Say: Behold all that is in the heavens and the earth, but neither Ayat nor warnings benefit those who believe not. Younas, 101.

In this Ayat, those who do not concentrate, have been called dishonest. How apt a European thinker:

He who casts himself on nature's fair full bossom, draws food and drinks from a fountain that never dries.

Those who are oblivious to the miracles of creation, have no idea of the exact nature of Allah's greatness. A small inducement is sufficient to send such men away from the true path. Such people become instruments in free environment and are bent on worshiping wealth and rulers. They remain busy, day and night, in achieving even the meanest objectives. They just prey like spiders but do not have the wisdom of spider.

The likeness of those who take Auliya' (protectors and helpers) other than Allah is as the likeness of a spider, who builds (for itself) a house, but verily, the frailest (weakest) of houses is the spider's house; if they but knew. Ankaboot, 41.

Honey Bee

Honey bee is very greedy: steals honey from every shop and every flower. Sometimes, it spoils the sweets during its preparation at the sweet shop. At others, it picks so much load that it dies before reaching the destination. Each beehive has a Queen that gracefully strolls over the hive accompanied by a few maidservants and sees each hive if it has been completed or not. When satisfied, it starts laying eggs of three types: one type gives birth to Queen, second type, King, while the third type of eggs are laid to produce workers. How very strange! One bee and three types of eggs.

If due to some accident, the Queen dies and there is no Princess in the hive, the bees depute a she-worker as Queen and start training her. If there is no egg in a chamber, bees get disheartened, stop eating and drinking, hive destroys and bees die. Workers have both males and females. Male goes to bring nectar and female looks after the house [hive]. Death of Queen causes great disturbance in bees and can be seen as if whispering in disquiet.

A beehive has two types of chambers – large and small.

Large chambers are reserved for royal family and small for workers. When Queen lays eggs in a chamber, the matron bee takes its extreme care. When the youngster grows, the matron opens the mouth of chamber, the kid comes out, she trains it how to walk and fly. When sufficiently trained, she accompanies it to the flowers and brings it back.

Royal eggs are looked after with extreme care. If at some moment, a princess is born but is not needed, the Queen immediately stings and kills her. If a Queen gets too old and remains of no use, another Queen is appointed and the elderly queen is pushed out of the hive. Because of the maltreatment of workers, the ex-queen wails that can be heard upto several meters. Her wailing is so ardent that each and every bee becomes dumb quiet and motionless. The moment this ritual of wailing stops, all the bees gathers around the ex-queen and start stinging her till she dies a humiliating death.

This is exactly the type of end that incapable and incompetent nations are sure to face. Till the time Muslims had the capabilities, they rules most of the Europe, almost the entire Asia, even islands in the Pacific Ocean. And when they lost those traits and were reduced to rituals and pointless wazaif [33], shirked hard work, stopped enquiry and attainment of honor and dignity, Allah shook their very foundations. They were thrown out of their beautiful lands and on the ground from the throne. But we still have it in mind that we are the best of nations. May Allah give them eyes to see and to observe their real worth and status.

Then what is wrong with them (the disbelievers) that they turn away from (receiving) admonition; as if they were frightened (wild) donkeys. Fleeing from a hunter, or a lion, or a beast of prey. Mudassir, 49-51.

---

[33] A (so-called) Sufi practice of reciting and meditating on some or all of the 99 names of Allah

Back to the Purpose

Sometimes a redundant princess is kept alive so that in case a new hive is established, she could be nominated as its Queen.

Different Types of Honey

Generally the people know of yellow honey but botanists say that honey in green, red, and light pink colors may also be seen. When a western philosopher, Kate Lovell, saw this Ayat of Qur'an:

And Allah inspired the bee, saying: "Take your habitations in the mountains and in the trees and in what they erect. "Then, eat of all fruits, and follow the ways of your Allah made easy (for you)." There comes forth from their bellies, a drink of varying colour wherein is healing for men. Verily, in this is indeed a sign for people who think. Nahal, 68-69.

He was amazed that how big a scholar an uneducated Arab was, he wrote:

Mohammad was a great king, a mighty conqueror and very clever and learned man. From the Qur'an we learn that he was a lover of Nature and he knew something of bees and the value of honey. He speaks of bees building nests for themselves and producing honey of various colors. These things could not have been possible without certain amount of enquiry and observation.

The way the prophet Mohammad has been presented by this western thinker, is hard for us to even think. To us, his being is so much that he would get forgiveness for us from our sins and by reciting *Darud Sharif* even once, we can get ten beneficences.

Search for Honey

Lower lip of honey bee is long. It remains contracted but while sucking nectar it spreads and extracts juice even from the innermost layers of flowers. Bee consumes some of the juice, some is kept in a pouch near its food duct and after some chemical reactions over there, outpours it in the hive chambers.

During juice extraction, pollen of flowers sticks to the legs and wings of bees. This becomes the food for those bees that do not leave the hive. These 'domestic bees' don't have food pouches like the worker bees. It is because that they can get readymade food.

When in winters, flowers desquamate and bees are left with no food except what is stored in the hive, infelicity draws on non-worker bees and are killed by the worker bees.

But as for him whose balance (of good deeds) will be light, he will have his home in Hell. Qari'ah, 8, 9.

Wax

Bees extract a sort of wax from fresh clods and use it in the manufacture of hive compartments. If the incoming quantity of honey is more than the capacity of compartments, the wax-making bees have to work extra hard. A dozen bees clamp one another's wings in their forelegs and remain hanging for 24 hours. Meanwhile a chemical process occurs and the pouches under their bellies become full of wax. This way is then made available for chamber making.

Such are the works of honey bees that by a rule in Nature, teach the act of order to the kingdom of people.

Wings

Bee has four large wings. While flying, the front wings are attached to the rear wings through a special mechanism. Wings have soft fur so that when it rains, it can easily glide down and the wings remain dry. Air is filled in tubes under the wings so that a bee could fly with ease.

In summer, a beehive gets warm and there is danger of honey flowing out. To stop over-pouring, bees blow air with their wings to keep the hive cold.

Eyes

Honey bee has five eyes - three on top of head and two to left and right of head. Each eye is a complex of 3,500 eyes, i.e. each eye can snap 3,500 photographs of objects. Unlike our eyes, bees cannot move their eyes. It may be because of the extremely large number of eyes, movement is not needed.

Eyes over the head have some linkage with flight as well. It's flight rule is that first, it flies up and then makes a straight line flight. Once a naturalist spread color on the heads of a few bees so that eyes on their heads could be made redundant. This resulted in an upward flight; no flight in straight line. What happened to those bees, only heaven knows.

Sting

When a bee pierces its sting in a body, the sting is left there, the bee flies and dies. Why so? Because it becomes defenseless and according to the Law of Nature, dies; like a nation that cannot protect itself, is swept from the surface of earth.

A western scientist kept on thinking over the acts of bees. Just see what he had to say:

How mighty and how majestic are thy works and with what a pleasant dread they swell the soul.

His thoughts seem to be the translation of what Allah says:

It is only those who have knowledge among His subjects that fear Allah. Fatir, 28.

Remembering Allah

Qur'an has repeatedly ordained to remember Allah. To us, its explanation is to get hold of a long paternoster and daily say Allah, Allah, Allah for thousands of times, and get rid of all the sins and have a confirmed ticket to Paradise. Any benefit of this mirthless and tasteless ritual? No!

It is very strange that when there are innumerable colorful, intuitive and enrapturing poems, a man could just move ahead, unimpressed and then goes into seclusion. And what are those special things that impress a man that make him go for such pointless rituals. Allah's wonders are spread everywhere, over the whole Universe, but we try to find it out in a dark corner of a secluded room. What a parody!

To me, remembrance of Allah is synonymous with majesty, command, and ecstatic state that are the result of acts and deeds rather than rituals.

And remember Allah by your tongue and within yourself, humbly and with fear without loudness in words in the mornings, and in the afternoons and be not of those who are neglectful. A'araf, 205.

It is the remembrance of Allah that strikes the hearts, not loud repetitions.

The believers are only those who, when Allah is mentioned, feel a fear in their hearts. Anfaal, 2.

And these are the Ayaat that enhances Eimaan and strengthen a man's soul:

And they said: "Why is not a sign sent down to him from his Allah? Say: "Allah is certainly Able to send down a sign, but most of them know not. There is not a moving creature on earth, nor a bird that flies with its two wings, but are communities like you. We have neglected nothing in the Book then unto their Allah they (all) shall be gathered. An'am, 37,38.

Are these birds and animals less than a miracle? But alas! There is no cure for (internal) blindness and ignorance.

And how many a sign in the heavens and the earth they pass by, while they are averse therefrom? Yousaf, 105.

Mosquito

Right in front of its mouth, a mosquito has a syringe-like duct through which it drills holes in body and enters poison. Its eggs feed on microscopic life. To get air, eggs come over the water surface keeping their mouth in water and tail outside. There is a hole for breathing in its tail. When half of the mosquito comes out of egg, it gets a hole in its back. At the time of birth, eggs come on water surface and due to heat, burst and there goes the mosquito. And when their wings get dried in heat, they fly.

At the time of birth, each egg opens to one side. If a mosquito would move even a little, water will fill in the shell and the mosquito would die. Since mosquito knows all this, it remains motionless in the shell and remains there in absolute tranquility. If sometime storm occurs, these shells drown in water. It has the advantage that each day, millions of mosquito eggs drown in water, otherwise they would have made human lives far more miserable than what they are, right now.

A creature like man with such a knowledge and wisdom, and subdued by a mosquito, is nothing but a gorgeous charisma of Allah. It makes the life of all the beings miserable and reigns over all the habitations. Even kings tremble from mosquitoes. Why? Because they have a very potent weapon: a poisonous pump. A mosquito is a reminder to nations that if they want to rule they must have appropriate weaponry. Look at the USA! It has weapons and it is virtually ruling the world. Back in early twentieth Century, it was Britain that ruled the world. In that regard, an adage was frequently referred to: Sun never sets on Great Britain.

Momin is very hard to those who disobey Allah and soft to those who are with Him. Fatah, 29.

It is possible for a sculpture to carve out an elephant, a horse, or camel from marble. It is however not possible for him to carve the figurine of a mosquito. To make its trunk, eyes, head, legs, veins, wings and hair, is beyond his skills and the art of his workmanship. To the other side, look at the superb skills of the Supreme Sculptor – Allah - who has crafted perfect creatures that are millions of times smaller than a mosquito that can walk, run, and fly. If you want to know the extent of his prowess, see those microscopic creatures. And honestly, if Qur'an mentions such superb masterpieces of the minutest creatures, would it be something unique?

Verily, Allah is not ashamed to set forth a parable even of a mosquito or so much more when it is bigger (or less when it is smaller) than it. And as for those who believe, they know that it is the Truth from Allah, but as for those who disbelieve, they say, "What did Allah intend by this parable?" By it He misleads many, and many He guides thereby. And He misleads thereby only those who are rebellious and disobedient (to Allah).Baqarah, 26.

House Fly [34]

Fly has so many advantages. It has been deputed for the cleanliness of world. We the human beings make the earth dirty and it cleans it by licking: the greater the dirt, the greater will the number of flies. Clean houses do not need their services as no need is felt for these sweepers. The way a sweeper is not dirty by himself, rather it is the job that he performs that is dirty, similarly fly by itself is not dirty but because of human-made dirt, its legs and wings get dirty. Just look at the corpse-eating white worms that are generated by fly eggs.

Some animals keep their eggs warm under their bodies. Since a fly does not have the luxury of so much time, it just lays eggs and, gone while nature manages the rest. It can fly 18,000 feet [ca. 5,450m] in an hour. If it gets afraid, it may fly with a speed of 20 miles [ca. 34 km] an hour.

---

[34] Latest studies have shown some additional interesting information about flies. Here is what it is:
There are 120,000 species of flies, ranging in size from 1/20th of an inch to 3 inches [7.62 cm]. Flies are the only insect to have 2 wings - all others have 4. After studying 300,000 flies, researchers Dr Yao and Dr Yuan of China concluded that an average house fly carries 2 million bacteria on its body. House flies' feet are 10 million times more sensitive to the taste of sugar than the human tongue. House flies walk upside down using glue-oozing toe pads. To land upside down on the ceiling, flies grab it with their front legs and then somersault the rest of their body over. A fly beats its wings 200 times a second, 3 times faster than a hummingbird and travels by thus my perseveres in its belly for breathing and are

covered with hair so that dust may not enter the ducts. It has great ability of smelling however it is not yet known as to where from it smells.

How does a housefly manage to land on the ceiling upside down, remained a mystery. Some scientist think that it has minute hooks that it puts in the minute wooden pores while others say that a sticky material comes out of its legs that helps it remain suspended[35].

A fly has five eyes and each eye is made up of four thousand microscopic eyes.

When a fly maggot matures in the egg, it hits the egg shell with its head and breaks it open and comes out. Its wings are wet that it dries with its front legs and then flies. A fly lives for about a month and meanwhile lays innumerable eggs. Scientists have estimated that in just one season, a fly's breed reaches two million.

Man eats clean things created by Nature. What man rejects become food for flies and other scavengers. Flies are eaten by other animals and birds as well. Animals become our food and we will become food of small insects. To avoid such a dreadful end, we need to break all the barriers of time and become eternal.

Man can make planes but a tree cannot stick a fallen leaf onto itself. A man cannot make even a fly. It is the prerogative of Allah where man has no nose to poke in.

---

[35] Scientists using "freeze frames" from high-speed cameras have proved that unlike previously though, flies do not flip, but flop, as they land upon the ceiling. Prior to impact, the fly extends its forward legs over its head, makes contact, and uses the momentum it has gathered in flight to hoist the remainder of its body to the ceiling. Thus, the fly proves to be more of an acrobat, than of a fighter pilot practicing in maneuvers.

Fly has wings and thousands of eyes but a powerless insect like spider can control it. On the other end of the spectrum, fly teases us the whole day; neither lets us sleep properly nor allows us to work freely. It snatches cleanliness and delicacy from our food and we can't do anything about it. If man is so helpless to fly, how could his opposition to Divine Laws save him from the wrath of Allah?

See what Allah has to say in this regard:

O mankind! A similitude has been coined, so listen to it (carefully): Verily! Those on whom you call besides Allah, cannot create (even) a fly, even though they combine together for the purpose. And if the fly snatched away a thing from them, they would have no power to release it from the fly. So weak are (both) the seeker and the sought. They have not estimated Allah His Rightful Estimate; Verily, Allah is All-Strong, All-Mighty. Hajj, 73,74.

Black Wasp

It makes house from mud and brings insects to feed its children. It first stuns the insect so much that it may not run away; if they die, they will create bad odor in the house.

Chrysis

It is a beautiful insect. Its tail is golden and wings are green. It changes its color according to season. It lays eggs in another insect's house. When the owner of house sees a stranger in its house, it immediately stings and kills the visitor who lays its life happily. When the dead insect's children come out of the eggs, simultaneously, owner insect's off springs also come out. To revenge their mother's death, the children of Chrysis quickly eat all the available food with the result that children of owner insect die of hunger.

Black Beetle

When female intends to lay eggs, it takes out a juice from its body and makes a cap-like housing having sixteen small chambers where she keeps one egg each and seals the chamber. When children are ready, it softens the cover with its spit. It explodes and the children come out. These kids take four years to mature and meanwhile, change their skins seven times. Though they are black but after changing the skin, they are white for a few days. They eat bed bugs but themselves become prey of mice, cats and sometimes, even birds. There are yellow-colored parasites that during their entire lives are sitting on their backs and suck their blood.

Crane Fly

It digs its tails into the earth and lays two eggs and dies after laying 100 eggs.

Cricket

This gray colored mustached insect is the enemy of our silk clothes. Listen to it in the evening that is given by male cricket that sings for the female. Its brain is to the back of neck and some of its types can even fly. Some have their ears near their legs and breathing holes to its sides. Insect are generally deaf but it can listen. The proof is that when it sings and someone nearby speaks, it stops singing. If it involves in a fight with another insect, it cuts the throat of its adversary eats it and then starts singing again.

A Kind of Termite

These ants are found in southern Africa and parts of America. They make a house that is 15 to 20 ft [4.5 to 6.0 m] tall. From a distance, these tall conical houses look like huts of farmers. Each house is raised on arches. Their roofs are so strong that they can bear the weight of several men. In the center of each house, a King and a Queen live while laborers live in the chambers all around. Then are the chambers of matrons and then stores. Queen remains confined to the room because its door is made so small that she cannot come out. She is made her food available in the room by the workers. These houses have no doors, nor the ants have eyes and that is why they live underground so that predators may not hunt them. If they plan a journey, they make a tunnel and keep on moving. Some of their types get eyesight if they venture to go out. Since the entire breed is blind and fears for the Queen, she is confined to her room. Due to easy life, she can be as thick as a human thumb. The Queen daily lays about 80,000 eggs.

Teeth of male termites are so strong that they can turn a piece of wood into smithereens in matter of seconds.

If they are made as large and powerful as humans, they will be able to make a tower as high as 2,800 ft [ca. 870 m].

Glowworm

Female worm emits more light than male, is larger than male and has no wings. Male has larger eyes so as to see the female from a distance. Female can frighten predators with her light. Since male does not have this safety gear, it has been given wings to fly.

Female makes three uses of its tail light: (i) protection from enemies; (ii) search of food in light; and (iii) be able to be seen by male from a distance.

If Allah would wish to punish man for his misdeeds, nothing living would be seen on earth. Fatir, 45.

Flea

The people of Syria used to joke about Socrates that he measures the jump of flea the whole day. This is no joke but a point to wonder: how a small insect could jump so high? Compared to its length, it can jump 200-times. Had a man been able to do so, he would have been able to go up to 1,100 ft [ca. 330 m].

A flea of southern America makes a hole in human body and hides in it, causing extreme pain. It is said that if a plant called Warm Wood is kept in a room, fleas would run away.

Black Wasp

You might have seen them on cow dung making balls of it and moving it in different directions. If a hurdle comes its way and the ball goes down, it goes after the ball, picks it up and keeps on trying till it succeeds. There is an egg in the ball and this dung ball is the food of that kid.

Getting impressed by its hard work, ancient Egyptians used to worship it. They used to make its pictures on stones, jewelry, buildings, even coins and considered it a reflection of day and night, month and year and of sun and earth.

It has five plumes on its head and Egyptians used to relate them to sunrays. Their making of dung balls was equated with god making the earth. Its six legs and head were considered seven days of a week. Its each leg has five comb-like indents and when multiplied by six legs, was equated to 30 days of a month. This insect does two useful jobs: first, it cleans the earth surface; and second, it makes the soil fertile by burying the balls under the soil.

The poor chap has neither a sting nor sharp teeth however it has a pretence up its sleeve: the moment it is disturbed, it immediately draws breath and becomes motionless as if dead. Considering it dead, the invader gets going. Besides that, it lays motionless with its legs up and the stink of its legs (for obvious reasons) forces the attacker to beg its leave.

Cochineal

In Eastern Spain people get a red color from an insect. Somewhat similar insect cuts tree branches, even trunk. The tree discharges a juice that is used as food by the worms while human beings use it as "lakh". Their mother dies before their birth and the kids grow in the belly of the dead mother and when mature, come out.

Bull's Fly

This fly bits the bull and lays eggs inside the wound. When the off-springs come out they make sure that their tails remain inside so that the wound doesn't heal. When they get semi-mature, they come down of bull's body and hide under soil. When fully mature, they come out.

One type of these worms lays eggs in the nose of sheep. The offsprings go to the brain for food. Meanwhile, sheep sneezes a lot and remains in great pain. After some time, they drop on soil and at maturity, fly.

Trees' Fly

This fly injects a poisonous sting in tree branch and lays just one egg. The poison causes that part of the branch to swell and later, the same swollen portion is used as food by the kids.

These were some lessons of the world of *Entomophilies* that we unfortunately, pass by with our eyes shut. Let's look at this Godly warning:

See they not what is before them and what is behind them, the miracles of the heaven and the earth? If We will, We shall sink the earth with them, or cause a piece of the heaven to fall upon them. Verily, in this is a sign for every faithful believer that [believes in the Oneness of Allah], and turns to Allah (in all affairs with humility and in repentance). Saba, 9.

Chapter-VII

Water World

The Qur'an says:
And the two seas are not alike, this fresh sweet, and pleasant to drink, and that saltish and bitter. And from them both you eat fresh tender meat, and derive the ornaments that you wear. And you see the ships sailing, that you may seek of His Bounty, and that you may be thankful. Fatir, 12.

There is a saltish ocean above the earth and sweet water below. Look at Allah's bounty that this sweet water is not impacted by the saltish water. Though seawater is saltish but if we dig a well on shore, its water would generally be sweet. There is a (sort of) wall between the two waters; to keep both the waters separated.

And Allah has placed firm mountains therein, and has set a barrier between the two seas (of salt and sweet water). Is there anyone, save Allah, who could do it? Namal, 61.

Clouds form from seawater, which is saltish but clouds are of sweet-water. Billions of tons of water 'swim' in the air. Water on earth is saltish and in air, sweet. There is a 'screen' that stops saltish water from intruding in sweet water.

To the east is Pacific Ocean and to the west, Atlantic. Both the oceans meet in north and south and there is piece of land between the two. These oceans are miles deep and if today, earth's surface is flattened, its entire surface will submerge in water to the extent of 10,000 ft [ca.3,000 m]. A lot of large cities of the world are located on seashore but are safe. Why so? Because everything is subservient to Allah's Command. Unless ocean is commanded to invade land, it cannot dare to do so.

He has let loosed the two seas (the salt water and the sweet) meeting together. Between them is a barrier which, none of them can transgress. Rahman, 19, 20.

If we put water in a cup and leave it open, aerial bacteria and dust particles will adulterate it, thus rendering it unfit for consumption. That is why water of open wells and ponds is unsafe. Allah has been too benevolent to us by keeping water hidden under the layers of earth. If we collect pond water, filter it and boil it, would cause us a lot of botheration, time, costs, and energy. Allah has let clean mineral water under earth's layers such that we have access to freshwater, anywhere.

And We sent down from the sky water (rain) in (due) measure, and We gave it lodging in the earth, and verily, We are Able to take it away. Mominun, 18.

Ocean

Five-sevenths of earth is water and two-sevenths land. At the time of evolution when earth came out of the sun, it was extremely hot (for obvious reasons). There was smoke in the atmosphere all around. This smoke (electrons!) had all the ingredients of becoming earth and skies and water and air. As such, sun and stars were created and earth separated from the sun. When earth became somewhat cold, the surrounding smoke (water vapors) came down on earth in the form of water and formed oceans. The internal material of earth oozed out and made mounds of soil and mountains. To top it all, frequent earthquakes made the earth surface uneven such that water accumulated in lowlands while the highlands stood to welcome the life. And so the life started from ocean.

And then Allah willed to create skies and there was smoke in the entire atmosphere. Ha Meem, 10.

This world would once again perish and convert in to electrons and the atmosphere will be filled with smoke. Then wait you for the Day when the sky will bring forth a visible smoke. Dukhan, 10.

The universe has seen a time when it was water all around and Allah reigned over water.

And His Throne was on the water. Hud, 7.

Rag Veda, Chapter 10, Mantra 121 says:

Earth was created from golden eggs (truth). First water was created and then male was created. And then male was divided in to two parts and from that came the female.

Modern research has established that in the beginning a body [amoeba[36]] was born that after division and sub-division, ended up in male and female.

O mankind! Be dutiful to Allah Who created you from a single person (Adam), and from him He created his wife [Eve], and from them both He created many men and women. Nisa, 1.

The way sometimes a male and sometimes female is created from the sperms the same way male and female were created from the original life [amoeba]. Gradually there was rush of fishes, hydroids, leeches, etc., followed by life on earth that took different shapes in different environments. The way differences occurred in the looks of an African and a European, similarly, life took different forms in different parts of the world. Somewhere it crawled and somewhere it flew and at others, it walked.

We can not only see differences in physical appearances but find differences in sounds and words in different

---

[36] A single-celled organism found in water and in damp soil on land, and as a parasite of other organisms. Lacking a fixed form and supporting structures, an amoeba consists of a protoplasmic mass in a thin membrane, and forms temporary projections pseudopodia, in order to move.

locations. For example, an Arab cannot pronounce 'che' [چ[, 'gaf' [گ], 'dal' [ڈ], 'de' [ڑ], and 'pe' [پ] while Brits cannot pronounce 'te' [ت] and 'dal' [د]. Indians have problem pronouncing 'khe' [خ] and Punjabis, 'zhe' [ژ]; calling it 'ye'[37] [ے]. In fact, environment is a very powerful factor that can change language, sound, even physiques. It may therefore be expected that animals swimming in water, may one day start running on land, even flying.

We have found such animals from mountains that remained under water for millions of years. They are 30 to 40 ft [9-12 m] long. Its face was like crocodile, body like fish, two arms to swim, and one foot, 12 in [30 cm] wide eyes. Still, skeletons of some animals have been found that were 45 ft [ca. 14 m] tall and would cut even big fish into two. Environment of both land and sea did not suit it and thus became extinct; the way a worthless Pir[38] of today is getting extinct, God willing.

Neither Ayat (proofs, evidences, verses, lessons, signs, revelations, etc.) nor warners benefit those who believe not. Younas, 101.

Sea Waves

And when a wave covers them like shades, they invoke Allah. Luqman, 32.

At yet another instance, grandeur and might of the ocean waves have been described in these words:

---

[37] They call 'Zhob' as 'Yob". Honest.

[38] Pir, literally "old person" is a title for a Sufi master, are also referred to as a Hazrat or Sheikh, which is Arabic for Old Man. The title is often translated into English as "saint" and could be interpreted as "Elder". In Sufism a Pir's role is to guide and instruct his disciples on the Sufi path. After their death, people bow their head on their tombs; as a mark of respect.

So it (the Noah's ship) sailed with the people amidst the waves like mountains. Hud, 42.

The distinctive feature of the style of Qur'an is that there is no overdraw and no aberration from fact. Each fact has been described in absolutely measured words and one is left with no choice but to praise the style and sobriety of narration.

The Qur'an descended when human world was cut off from the world of Allah and wandered in the valleys of abject degradation and misery. Nothing of Eiman and Gnosticism could be observed anywhere. Such a wayward human nature demanded that a book be sent having poetry, hyperbole, grandeur and mythical narrations. Instead the Book given to us had all that we need, except poetic exaggeration and imaginativeness. In the Ayat narrated earlier, 'ocean waves' have been called 'mountain-like (colossal waves)'. Let's see how!

Ocean surface is never calm but rather has waves because of winds. Since waves move faster than air, they generally appear 24 hrs on the shore before the windstorm. Such waves are not very obvious in deep water but take horrendous shape near the coast.

One can frequently come across waves in Indian Ocean that are 29 to 37 ft [ca. 9 to 11 m] high, 770 to 1,000 ft [ca. 230 to 390 m] wide and having a speed of 25 to 32 miles [40 to 50 km] per hr. Their might can be gauged from the fact that once a large vessel was caught by the waves and within no time, was torn to pieces.

Sometimes these waves are created by quake. In 1922 on Chilean Coast and around Yapp Island, such huge waves were seen that were up to 50 ft [ca. 15 m] high. People of the Chilean port of Coquimbo got so much terrified that they climbed over mountain. One of these waves was 180 ft [ca. 55 m] that picked ships like straws and threw them 1,500 ft [ca. 444 m] away on the coast. Its impact was also felt some 5,000 miles [8,100 km] away in Hawaii.

In 1872, a wave to the south of Cape Lapataka raised to the height of 210 ft [ca. 64 m].

Water Vapors

Hydro scientists estimate that each year 14 ft [427 cm] thick water layer evaporates from all the oceans combined and transforms into clouds.

Living-ware

Ocean's water always goes up and down. Warm water comes up and cold goes down. This is because the upper water should get oxygen from air and give it to water animals that stay at the bottom of ocean.

And so many a moving creature there is that carries not its own provision! Ankabut, 60.

Destructions of Oceans

How much death and destruction have oceans wrecked on earth, let's see:

1) The English city of Ravenspur, that used to elect two members of Parliament, does not exist anymore.

2) Cornwall[39] used to have an area of 1.5 million acres [ca. 600,000 ha]. Because of intrusions by the ocean, its area has been reduced to about 830,000 acres [ca. 335,000 ha].

---

[39] A county in the extreme southwest of England, bordered on three sides by the ocean.

3) Portion between Cicely Island and Italy is called Lyoness. It had 140 churches and as many towns. Today, it is under water.

4) Mountains Bay was a dryland. Proof? From its bottom trees and skeletons of animals have been found. This area was submerged in fourteenth Century.

5) North Wales was submerged by water some six hundred years back inundating fourteen villages.

6) Back in the past, Dunwich was the capital of Eastern Anglia. It had a mint, 52 churches and 226 schools. It had been part of Roman Empire. During the reign of Edward-II, 400 houses were washed by water. Then in 1538 and 1600 A.D., six churches submerged. In 1702, Peter's Church went down and in 1712, the entire city came under water.

7) Ecles, Wimperell, Shipden, and Norfolk were large towns that have been engulfed by water since long.

8) Where there used to be Auburn, Hartburn, and Hyde, now are sand dunes.

9) Two-thirds of Friesland has disappeared in the Ocean

10) Islands of Heligoland that used to be known during WW-II, and according to Adam Bremsy was 400 miles [ca. 650 km] long, is now just one mile [1.6 km] long.

11) Water destructions in Holland are phenomenal where Lake Dallart appeared that caused loss of a lot of land area. In 1280, River Zeider flooded and 80,000 people lost their lives. There used to be 23

large islands in sixth century A.D. Now these are just spots that can better be called mounds of sand.

12) Island Wangerooge, that was once a very lively island, is now just a heap of sand.

English stars are on climax everywhere. During the last one thousand years, Holland, Germany, Italy, and other countries have lost a lot of land to rivers and oceans, but England has been in the benefit. Just a few years back, the Government appointed a committee to develop a report on the status of various islands. Summary:

Name	Area taken by river	Area came out of river	Net Gain	
	acres		acres	ha
1. England and Wales	4,692	35,444	30,752	12,445
2. Scotland	815	4,707	3,892	1,575
3. Ireland	1,132	7,853	6,721	2720
Total	6,639	48,004	41,365	16,740

One can conclude that each year, UK had been adding 1,125 acres [ca. 455 ha] of land to its territory.

A terrific English orator Edmund Burke had once said: Even gods cannot annihilate space and time.

Had he been alive and seen the death and destruction wrecked by waters, he would have reconsidered his views.

Depth of Ocean

Atlantic Ocean between England and USA is at places as deep as 12,000 ft [ca. 3,600 m] and reaches a depth of up to 21,000 ft [ca. 6,400 m]. Earlier, these portions were lands and some of the mountains were up to 20,000 ft [ca. 6,000 m] high one of which was called Lara. Its mention can be seen in old manuscripts of Egypt. Today, ships cruise over its top. Similarly, another mountain called Chaucer, was 10,000 ft high [ca. 3,000 m] but today, is submerged under 6,000 ft [ca. 1,800 m] deep water.

To the south of Newfoundland, depth of ocean is 21,000 ft [ca. 6,400 m] and at two locations in East-Indies [Malaysia], it is 20,000 ft [ca. 6,000 m]. At a depth of less than 2,000 ft [ca. 600 m], one can find sand and pebbles, at 12,000 ft [ca. 3,600 m], while lime, between 12 and 14 thousand ft [ca. 3,600 and 4,200 m], grey chalk while at still deeper sites, volcanic lava can be seen.

At a location to the north of Newzealand, ocean's depth is 28,878 ft [ca, 8,750 m] while at a location to the northeast of the Philippines, ocean is 32,100 ft [9,700 m] and probably the deepest potion of any ocean. If the topmost summit of Himalayas is placed over there, one would need to dive 3,000 ft [ca. 909 m] to reach the summit.

Ocean between Japan and USA is about 5 miles deep [ca. 8.1 km]. In other words, Japan is located at the mouth a very deadly cave and no one knows when a quake may pick it up and throw it in that deep cave.

Almost all the large cities of the world are located right next to such deep caves. To destroy these cities, just a little quake and the rest should be left to the waiting gaping hole. How very strange that the nearer they are to death, the farther they are from Allah.

Light Towers in Oceans

To facilitate sea transport, light towers are installed at suitable locations.

And landmarks and by the stars (during the night), they (mankind) guide themselves. Nahal, 16.

At present, there are about 12,000 lighthouses in the world. There are three hundred around the UK while on the coasts of USA, 3,000 lighthouses have been established. Some are established right within the oceans on solid rocks and others, on coasts.

The world's largest tower was established at Alexandria some 2,200 years ago. After a century, Romans established lighthouses at different locations. In 1800 A.D., there were just 25 towers in the UK. The very first tower in ocean was constructed in 1696 that was destroyed in 1703. In the beginning of eighteenth century, towers were made of wood. John Semeaton was the first engineer who used stones in the construction of towers. In 1807, Robert Stevenson constructed a gigantic tower at Bell Rock that took four years and 600,000 Pound Sterling to build.

Till the end of nineteenth century, lard-oil was used in the towers. After that, electricity was used to keep the towers lighted. Most of the towers have radio sets as well so that the watchmen, usually three in number, could be kept in good stead.

Some towers still use oil for lighting, for example Tower at Eclipse Island in Western Australia. Its tower has 1,160,000 candlelight[40] power. Then there is a tower in France, located at Cape de Hover, is lit with electricity. Its light is equivalent to 22,500,000 candles.

Boats and Ships

Verily! In the creation of the heavens and the earth, and in the alternation of night and day, and the ships which sail through the sea with that which is of use to mankind, and the water which Allah sends down from the sky and makes the earth alive therewith after its death, and the moving creatures of all

---

[40] An obsolete unit of luminous intensity, originally defined in terms of a wax candle with standard composition and equal to 1.02 candelas. Also called *international candle*.

kinds that He has scattered therein, and in the veering of winds and clouds which are held between the sky and the earth, are indeed Ayat for people of understanding. Baqarah, 164.

And then Allah says:

Then We saved him (Noah) and those with him in the ship, and made it a warning for everyone. Ankabut, 15.

Both these Ayaat prove that boats have great role to play in the ascendancy of nations. And it is the duty of scholars to inform the people of shipping. This would lead to the implementation of Ayaat.

The Beginning of Oceanography

In the beginning, people considered ocean as the other end of world and were afraid of putting their feet in it. Homer's writings say that till 12th even 13th century B.C., people were afraid of ocean. As such, we can concur that the very first boats might have been put in some lake. Before that, wood and grasses were used to cross waters. Such vegetational means are still used at certain places along the River Nile. After that, hollowed tree trunks were used a means of transportation. Such means are still used in some African lakes, British Columbia, and Solomon Islands. Robinson Crusoe wanted to use a hollowed stem as boat but could not drag it to water. In 1904, a group of people from British Columbia prepared a boat that was used by Capt. Voss and traveled around the world in three years. In River Tigris, people wrap hides around a large basket and use it as boat. It can accommodate up to 20 persons in one go.

Ancient Sailors

The largest boat of ancient times was constructed by

Hazrat Noah. It was 450 ft [ca. 136 m] long, 75 ft [ca. 23 m] wide, and 45 ft [ca. 14 m] tall. It weighed cool 15,000 tons.

In 700 B.C., the Finnish constructed such boats that were used for coastal business along the Mediterranean Sea, to the south, up to the coast of Africa and in the North, up to Canaveral.

Before the Finnish, Crete Island was the center of sea-based activities. And before that, the people of Atlantis were experts in shipping. After the Finnish, Carthiegie sailors reined the seas. Aristotle said that they were ship-makers, each with eight oars.

Graves of ancient Egypt have pictures of boats. In 1906, Prof. Flenders Petrie got a picture of such a boat that he snapped at a grave in Rifah. Boats of similar shape were seen on the shores of Malaya and were also used in some parts of River Nile. These boats could travel with a speed of about 9 miles [ca. 15 km] per hour. Almost similar boat was made by Napoleon-III in 1861 that was 120 ft [ca. 36 m] long and 70 ft [ca. 21 m] wide. Its model is available in the Museum Lourvre in Paris.

Evolution

After some time, use of iron was started in some parts of boats. Such boats were first used in a war between Iranians and Peeloponnesslans. And then in the war of Acrium, Antony used boats that had 20 oars while the boat used by the Admiral or the Emperor had colored ropes and oars. Antiquities of such boats were found in Lake Nami some parts of which were made up of brass and lead. One such boat/ship was 90 ft [ca. 27 m] and the other was 450 ft [ca. 136 m]. Long. Both were commercial ships with a storage capacity of 150 tons of grains. War boats used to be relatively smaller.

When the Roman Emperor, Julius Cether attacked Gaul he saw some ships on the English Coast and said, "These are stronger ships than ours". The surface of Atlantic Ocean is more disturbed than the Mediterranean Sea and there only strong ships could work. The British ships were made up of hollowed tree stems. Just 50 years back, another ship was found at Briggs near Lincolnshire. It was made up of a tree trunk that had a circumference of 18 ft [ca. 5.5 m] and belonged to 2000 B.C. How those people could have felled such a tree with just stones and how did they hollow it, is still a riddle.

When in 5 B.C., Cether attacked Veneti and saw huge ships tied with chains, he said, "Compared to these ships, ours are just toys".

Norsemen used to dispose off their dead chieftains in two ways: they would put the dead on fire, place it in a boat and send it to ocean, or would bury the boast along with the dead one on the coast. In 1880 A.D. such a boat was found near Sander Jard that was 79⅓ ft [ca.24 m] long, 16½ ft [5m] wide and weighed 560 maunds.

Once Danes conquered England with the help of their ships. Alfred, the King of England, prepared a fleet of ships and defeated the Danes, confiscated six of their ships and drowned 18. Alfred is considered the father of British ship industry.

Back in 1170, England made a ship that has the capacity of four hundred persons. Richard was the first king who developed SOPs[41] for the ships. He had 203 ships. King John introduced the salaries of sailors. And when Edward-II besieged Gaul, his fleet had 700 ships and 14,000 sailors. Each ship weighed between 700 and 1000 tons.

---

[41] Standard **O**perating **P**rocedures

Initially, ships used to have Perriers and in 15th Century A.D. cannons were introduced. Henry-V made ships that had 225 cannons. During his tenure, a famous ship Santa Maria was made that was used by Columbus who found a new world. During the reign of Queen Elizabeth, Ark Royal was made. It had three compasses and 400 sailors. Towards the end of 17th Century, the combined tonnage of European countries was 2 million tons[42], of which Holland had 900,00 tons, England, 500,00 tons and France, just 100,00 tons.

In other words, England was a very weak country. Brave and hardworking Brits laid the foundations of a gigantic empire. To the other side, just a few years back, we were the most gorgeous nation. But unfortunately, our incompetent, lazy and lecher leaders and wazaif-sayers destroyed us.

There was a time when we reigned supreme over lands and seas. Kings and emperors used to tremble hearing our names and used to pay homage to us. Wherever we looked, we changed the destinies of people. The stroke of our swords used to make nations tremble. But today, we are just the most wretched ones, are intoxicated with the promise of paradise and the hangover of intercession, and our hubris of bead-revolvers have left us worth nothing. O Muslim! Think, wake-up, see, come up, get up and move that Allah's bounties are still waiting for you. Gather courage because weakness is death. Discover yourself, give up enervation because foolery has robbed you of all that you once had.

Back to Purpose

In 1492, France attacked England and destroyed its naval force however the courageous English nation manufactured

---

[42] Today, England alone has a fleet of 150 million tons.

3,281 ships in just nine years. To the other side, Muslims are ruling Iran for more than 1,300 years but during this entire period, they could not make even a single boat, let alone warships.

Steamships

The very first steamship was manufactured by Jonathan Bulls in 1736 but could not fully succeed; some defects still needed to be rectified. In 1806, Robert Fulton, an American inventor, made a steamboat that could attain a speed of 4½ miles [ca. 7 km] an hr. In 1817, he developed a 500-ton steamship costing 22,000 Pound Sterling. After that, in 1836 alone, there were 13,000 steamships of the total number of ships that anchored at various English ports. Be at ease that not a single ship belonged to any Muslim country. This was because the Muslims were either busy in religious rituals or worshipping their loved ones. Where could these "extremely busy" poor chaps find time to go for the "luxury" of making ships? And then who could dare attack *the most loved ones* of Allah? The same Allah, who sent martins to save Muslims from the onslaught of renegades, and blasted them to rags. What would Allah do to those who would dare attack Iran and Arabia, is anybody's guess. Be contented and be sure that nothing could ever happen to Muslims; after all they are the ones who are always busy in rituals, beading and praising Allah and asking for His forgiveness and His bounties; of course without doing anything practical.

How apt Allah had been when He said:
And We shall leave them in their transgression to wander in distraction. In'am, 111.

Alas! After getting so much beating (at the hands of renegades) the Muslims could not understand that Allah has been indifferent to thoroughly corrupt and degraded nations and had no hesitation in annihilating them.

And whoever disbelieves, let him remember that Allah is surely independent of all creatures. Aal-e-Imran, 97.

Back to Purpose

The English manufactured a 4,000-ton ship that could traverse Atlantic Ocean in just 17 hrs. In 1933, France manufactured a 68,000-tonner. The same year, English made another ship that was 73,000 tons with 80,000 Horsepower[43]. Another ship, Olympic was 852 ft [ca. 258 m] long, 92 ft [ca. 28 m] wide and 175 ft [ca. 53 m] high. It had an engine with 90,000 HP and had 800 sailors.

This is that POWER by virtue of which, nations could live and these are the Ayaat because of which, the Eiman of living nations perpetuates:

Those gigantic ships on seas are the signs of Allah. Shura, 32.

The unfortunate Muslim is oblivious to Allah's signs. King Ibne Sa'ud has a port but not a single boat could be seen there. Not even a broken ship could be seen in the Persian Gulf. Be honest and say that if a nation cannot break a tooth for a tooth, it has no right to live.

Allah has been teaching us time and again about strength and dreadfulness:

1. *Be in this world such that people could feel your quickness. Taubah, 123.*

---

[43] Horsepower (hp) is the rate at which work is done (per unit of time). Earlier it was measured in terms of a horse's power which James Watt, a Scottish Engineer calculated to be ca. 33,000 ft-lb/minute. Today, the most common conversion factor, is watt and 1 hp = 746 watts. The term was adopted to compare the output of steam engines with the power of draft horses.

2. *Be stern with disobedient to Allah. Fatah, 29.*
3. *We sent iron that is a dreadful metal. Use it and be pompous. Hadid, 25.*
4. *Ships are the signs of Allah. Shura, 32.*
5. *And make ready against them all you can of power, including steeds of war to threaten the enemy of Allah and your enemy. Anfal, 60.*

Unfortunately, we have forgotten these lessons and have rather understood that the biggest"A'mal" is to offer two "Nafal" and the biggest "Struggle" is to sit in a dark corner of a mosque and keep on repeating "Allah" for umpteen times and that worldly pursuits are neither compulsory nor desirable, rather against the basic tenets of Islam. See how the avoidance of these "worldly pursuits" has led us to destruction and how our past grandeur has become a forgotten story.

This is the Day of the final decision which you used to deny. As-Saffat, 21.

Salt in the Ocean

Why there is salt in the ocean? This has been the question under discussion of scientists since centuries. Recently a western scientist has described an interesting reason for it. Salt has the quality that keeps meat from rotting. Ancient Egyptians used to apply salt to their dead ones to keep them from rotting. We in our houses apply salt to meat to keep it fresh and be cooked the next day. Since each day, millions of sea animals die and during wars, hundreds of thousands of people are killed, that is why Allah included great quantity of salt to sea water.

If a carcass is thrown in sweet water, it will decay but in seas and oceans, it does not happen and remains fresh. Allah has turned our attention to this phenomenon in the following Ayat:

And from seas you eat fresh meat. Fatir,12.

Fishery

Man of the earliest days lived near the coasts and lived on fish. From past tradition it appears that Hazrat Adam was kept in a garden in Yemen. When he was removed from there, he might have been shifted to what we now know as Jeddah and possibly Mecca. History of Mecca has it that the first thing that Hazrat Adam did was that he constructed Ka'abah. Whether true or wrong, historians can hardly be of help, though we are told by travelers that the grave of Eve is in Jeddah. In Arabic, word "Jeddah" means "valley". Since it has the grave of men's grandmother, therefore it was given the name Jeddah. Sociologists believe that Hazrat Adam generally relied on fish for food.

In early days, people used to hunt fish with arrows. After that, net and later, angle was invented. People of Rome and Greece had excelled in the conservation of fish and traded with even far-off countries. Gradually, England excelled in fishing. In 1578, 450 English ships were involved in fishing that used to venture into seas for upto 600 miles [ca. 1,000 km] and earned about 2 million Pounds. Canada and the USA fought a lot of wars over fishing. Finally in 1817, the "Agreement of Washington" was signed according to which both the countries got the permission to fish in each other's sea territories.

Since Canadian fish was better in taste, another war broke out. In 1877 Britain got 12,500,000 Pounds from the USA and allowed it to fish in Canadian waters. But again in 1898, a conflict arose and because of that, the USA lost the right to fish in Canadian waters.

Fishermen had made the British Fleet the largest in the

world. These fishermen used to venture into open seas in small boats and knew every nook and corner of the Atlantic Ocean. They knew where rocks and other dangerous spots were located. Today, these people are working as sailors in the British fleet.

Each year, 200 million pound [90 million kg] fish is caught worldwide. At the rate of Rs. 15 per pound, this will come to three billion rupees – twice the total receipts of Indian Government.

Boats used for fishing are called troller and could catch upto 80 times more fish compared to ordinary boats with sails. Britain has about 1,000 such trollers, Germany, 5,000, France, 3,000 and Denmark, Holland, and Belgium have 400 each. In 1913, Britain alone caught 812,500 maund fish.

It will not be out of the context to mention that there were Islamic states as well, all located along the coasts. None of these countries ever caught fish. What these helpless Muslims can do: fish do not let be caught; they swim away.

Whale

While swimming, whale keeps its mouth open. When tens of animals enter that 'tunnel', it shuts its mouth; rest is history. One type of whale has so much fat that if extracted, it could be 5,000 kg. In 1895, a ship in the Arctic caught ten whales that had 14 maund [500 kg] bones and sold for 14,000 Pounds. Its fat was used to make 252 maunds [10,000 kg] oil.

Whale can remain underwater for an hour. When hunters locate a whale, they come closer and when it comes out to breathe, they fire cannon ball that is attached to the ship with steel wires and goes straight into whale's body. Embarrassed, it runs and so the hunters and keep on firing till it gives in. Today, South Africa daily catches 16 whales and because of the unsustainable catching, their numbers are decreasing.

A whale gives birth to one cub at a time. It matures in 50 years. Each whale is at least 80 ft [ca. 24 m] long and 60 ft [18 m] thick.

Whale's skin is used in making machine stripes while its skeleton is used as fertilizer. On the other hand, Muslims don't need whales because they don't have machines, nor they have such farmlands that need fertilizer.

Sea Serpent

In 1848, the captain of ship Deadalus saw a 60 ft [ca. 18 m] long sea serpent. In 1872, captain of Osborne ship saw a serpent that was 15 to 20 ft [ca. 4.5 to 6 m] wide and part of the body that could be seen was about 50 ft [ca. 15 m]. In 1870, sailors of an American ship 'Drift' saw a serpent near Cape Cod that came out of water and stood 40 ft [12 m].

Nature's Wonders

1) British Star Fish gives 200 million eggs in a year

2) A tooth of male whale is 6 ft [1.8 m] long

3) Tortoise can live upto 100 years

4) A 20-ft long snake lives in coastal mountains. Each year in October it comes down to shore, grips a rock and spreads its tail over water. Because of waves, its tail breaks down that is full of eggs that then become snakes. Meanwhile its tail heals reappears and again starts its business.

5) A fish of China Sea has the quality that if someone eats it, he would keep on laughing till he dies. Its sale

is prohibited. In ancient times, when chieftain would be punished, he would be given this fish to eat. What would happen next, is not difficult to fathom.

6) There is also a fish whose tail burns like a candle. It has a whooping light of 500 candles.

7) There is a pump in the body of fish. When it inhales air, it gets lighter than water and comes on surface. And when it exhales air, it becomes heavier and goes down in water. Making boat, Hazrat Noah taught the lesson of "life" to his nation in particular and to Muslims in general.

We gave you the same Deen that We gave to Noah. Shura, 13.

But no one paid any heed and Allah annihilated that nation, the way Muslims are on their way to destruction.

So We inspired him (saying): "Construct the ship under Our Eyes and under Our Revelation. Then, when Our Command comes, and the ocean gushes forth water, take on board of each kind two (male and female), and your family, except those thereof against whom the Word has already gone forth. And address Me not in favour of those who have done wrong. Verily, they are to be drowned. And when you have embarked on the ship, you and whoever is with you, then say: "All be praised and thanks to Allah, Who has saved us from the people who are oppressors. And say: "Allah! Cause me to land at a blessed landing-place, for You are the Best of those who bring to land." Verily, in this, there are indeed evidences, for sure We are ever putting (men) to the test. Then, after them, We created another generation. Mominum, 27-31.

Chapter-VIII

Some Pages from Nature's Manuscript

The Beginning of Evolution

Allah has commanded us:

Say: "Travel in the land and see how (Allah) originated creation. Ankabut, 20.

Scientists believe that in the beginning, it was smoke all around. This smoke is in fact the elements that became the reason for the creation of universe. After the creation of sun and other stars, a very large star passed by, closer to sun. Because of its gravitational force, far in the vast emptiness, a part of the sun was tore and thrown 93 million miles [151 million km] away. That piece is today known as earth. In the beginning, it was hot like molten iron. After millions of years, its crust became cold enough but its core remained as hot as it was in the beginning.

If we start going down the earth, then after every 30 m descend, temperature would increase by one degree. This increase would be 100 degrees at a depth of 3,000 m and at 30,000 m, it will be 1,000 degrees. When separated from earth, earth's temperature was more than 10,000 degrees. After two million years, earth's crust to the depth of 994 m cooled down. And first of all, it was all smoke, later storms came and because of quakes, mountains were created. This was followed by plants and finally, life took form.

Rain of Gold and Silver

When earth separated from sun, it was too hot. As a result, metals used to be blown up towards sky. Reaching the dry atmosphere, these would come down again and again would be transformed into gases and go up. For millions of years, clouds used to rain gold and silver. When the earth's crust started to cool down, these metals also solidified. First, it was gold followed by copper and then lead solidified, till quakes took them down the earth crust.

Six Stages

Crux of the above details is that universe passed through six stages of evolution:

1) Elements appeared in the form of smoke

2) These elements gave birth to heavenly bodies

3) Earth came out from the sun

4) Earth cooled, vapors became water and started raining while quakes created mountains

5) Then plants appeared

6) And finally, animals were created, whose evolutionary shape is human being

ADAM was the first civilised person send down to earth (with EVE) which was now ready to receive start of new creation. Adam was taught names (KNOWLEDGE) while Angles were not taught. The children of Adam used this GOD given knowledge to research and treat diseases like malaria, TB, Cancers, Heart and Liver transplants and so on. Now these people of knowledge have reached Moon and stars.

Conclusion is that skies were created in two stages and earth in four stages. These conclusions were drawn by the scientists after hundreds of years of research. The Qur'an said it some 1362 years earlier:

Say: 'Do you really disbelieve in Him Who created the earth in two days? And do you set up equals to Him?' That is the

Lord of the worlds. He placed therein firm mountains rising above its surface, and blessed it with abundance, and provided therein its foods in proper measure in four days — alike for all-seekers. Then He turned to the heaven while it was something like smoke, and said to it and to the earth: 'Come ye both of you, willingly or unwillingly.' They said, 'We come willingly.' So He completed them into seven heavens in two days, and He revealed to each heaven its function. Ha-mim As-Sajda.

This means that Allah created earth, mountains, plants and animals in four days and the skies in two days. Qur'an is testimony to the fact that skies' exaltation and equation and day and night was done first, followed by the creation of earth.

Are you harder to create or the heaven that He has built? He has raised the height thereof and made it perfect. And He has made its night dark, and has brought forth the morn thereof; And the earth, along with it, He spread forth. He produced therefrom its water and its pasture. And the mountains, He made them firm. All this is a provision for you and for your cattle. Naz-e-A'at, 27,33.

Six

There are three types of figures: (i) Extra; (ii) Inferior; and (iii) Perfect. In case of 'extra', the total of multipliers is more than the actual, for example 12. Its multipliers are 6,4,3,2,1 that total to 16. 'Inferior' have the total of multipliers less than the actual for example, 8. Its multipliers are 4,2,1 that come to 7. As for the 'Perfect', the total of multipliers is equal to the actual figure, for example, 6. Its multipliers are 3,2,1 that again come to 6.

Till 2,100,000, 'Perfect' figures are only 6; i.e. it reached 2,100,000 in just six jumps. Similarly, when the universe passed through six ages, more or less, 2,100,000 plants, animals, and flowers were created. And this diversity was complete in all respects.

Number of Earths

Astrologists believe that there are about 300 million earths orbiting in the universe. This theory is based on the observation that there are 100 million suns and there are more or less three earths orbiting around each sun.
And none knows the soldiers of Allah except Him. Mudassir, 31.

Hell

Some Ahadeeth mention that hell in beneath the earth. Modern scholars have proved that the inner-most core of earth has fire as hot as 1,300°C. Lava that comes out of volcanic mountains is melted by the internal fire. We can imagine hell because of a severe quake, the inner-most core of earth comes out and there is fire all around with full might and fury.
O mankind, fear Allah. Indeed, the convulsion of the [final] Hour is a terrible thing. Hajj, 1.

It is estimated that if the inner-most core of earth comes out, all the oceans would immediately start boiling and the entire environment would glow like ambers.

It is also possible that on the day of Resurrection, Allah brings out another earth from a sun that might be extremely hot and it is also possible that on that day the sun reaches so close to the earth that it may become oven of an iron smith.

However, no one knows the actual status at that time. This is so because:
Indeed, Allah [alone] has knowledge of the Hour [the Day of Judgment]. Luqman, 34.

Age of Earth

At some ancient sites in Egypt, about 4,000 years old houses have been excavated. On the wall of one such house, these worlds were written:

Julia, my dear Julia, is a beautiful pig.

The following words were written at a grave:

She had no other shortcoming except that she left me.

From these sentences it appears that the mindset at that time was not different than ours. Since man needed hundreds of thousands of years to pass through various stages of barbarism, therefore, age of the earliest man was 6,000 years as indicated in the Bible. It however does not seem correct[44].

According to Lord Cloven, age of earth is 20 million years. This concept is based on various forms of the outer core of earth and internal temperature. According to him, earth's external crust might have cooled down in 2 million years.

Some geologists opine that inner layers of earth have tremendous quantities of Radium. Since radium produces heat, therefore internal parts of earth are very hot however Lord Cloven does not agree to this theory. Therefore, he wrote a letter that was published in 1906 in "British Weekly":

This is absolutely unbelievable that sun and earth are emitting heat and light because of Radium.

Professor Jolie's Assumption

In the beginning when oceans first came in to existence,

---

[44] What I mean to say is considering Biblical year to have 365 days is not correct. Allah's days and years are far too long, otherwise to call it wrong is not the purpose (Burq).

their waters were sweet. But then when hill torrents and rivers kept on bringing Sodium along, oceans gradually became saltish.

After years of research, Professor Jolie declared that each year, world rivers and streams add 160 million tons of salt to oceans. At present, total quantity of salt in the oceans is estimated to be 14,000 billion tons.

Evolution of Life

After microscopic inspection of animals and plants, it has been determined that all of them were made up of cells. These cells were developed from a membranous matter that is available on sea shore. The first thing that developed from this matter was amoeba, a single-cell organism that lives in mud. After that, animals composed of one, two, even millions of cells, came into being.

O mankind, fear Allah who created you from one soul and created from it its mate and dispersed from both of them many men and women. Nisa, 1.

Chemical composition of amoeba is carbon, nitrogen, and hydrogen and the same are our composition as human beings. This proves that animal life started from water.

In Torah's Chapter on Birth is written:

And then We commanded waters to create living creatures.

Qur'an says:

Have those who disbelieved not considered that the heavens and the earth were a joined entity, and We separated them and made from water every living thing? Then will they not believe? Anbia, 30.

After passing through different stages, this single-cell creature ended in the creation of man:

1) First plants were created.

2) Then animal-plants appeared, i.e., such plants that had stomach and could move but could not see and smell.

3) Then crawling animals came into being.

4) After that, shells and leeches came.

5) And then sea-scorpions were created and scorpions appeared on the coasts.

6) After that, fishes, crocodiles, and other water animals prevailed.

7) Then life stepped on dryland and insects, birds, and quadruped and finally man came into being.

8) ADAM was the first civilized person send down to earth (with EVE) which was now ready to receive the start of new creation.

Womb

Womb contains exactly the same elements as in oceans where temperature is also the same. After experimentations and observations, evolution experts concluded that the way the life originated through different stages culminating in the creation of human beings, similarly a wonderful sequence is working is mother's womb. Sperm is first a cell and after passing through certain stages, it transforms into a leech, then frog, then a beak like bird appears and then quadruped. In the fourth month, along with head and arms, a small tail appears that disappears in fifth month. In sixth month, it is either a male or a female. In eights month, it opens its eyes and hair appear on its head.

In short, human child passes through all the stages the way life had to pass through various stages. Some of these stages have been described in the Qur'an:

> And certainly did We create man from an extract of clay. Then We placed him as a sperm-drop in a firm lodging. Then We made the sperm-drop into a clinging clot, and We made the clot into a lump [of flesh], and We made [from] the lump, bones, and We covered the bones with flesh; then We developed him into another creation. So blessed is Allah, the best of creators. Mominun, 12-14.

In these Ayaat, four words need special attention:

1) *Salat*, offspring i.e. child, essence i.e. extract

2) *A'laq*: leech

3) *Mufgha*: of all of its extracts, there is a word that means "horse's arms". It has been earlier said that in a stage in mother's womb, child is a quadruped.

4) *Kahlqa akhar*: child is first like a leech, then bird and quadruped. In the end, when it takes the form of a human being, it is in fact, a new creation.

English Rendering of Ayat

Scientists believe that man's creation began on the ocean near Equator. Human womb not only conserved that heat but all those elements were also present that are available in the ocean.

Allah be praised! Look anywhere at the creation and perfection and we see it everywhere. The time has come man unfurls this mystery.

Building Blocks of Universe

All the scenes of universe are composed of electrons. If we observe water through a microscope, we will see small particles each one of which will have a dia of $1/50,000,000^{th}$ of an inch. Look at microbe that is too small compared to dust particle but in fact is composed of thousands of atoms. And then each atom is made up of electrons and neutrons. These thousands of times smaller than microbes are those "bricks" that were used in the construction of universe. Each and every scene of this gorgeous universe originated from these (almost) weightless particles. This scientific discovery is the greatest argument in favor of the Oneness of Allah.

Suppose that a man tears down the earth and brings out a new metal. And then he dives down in the Pacific Ocean to the depth of seven miles and brings out a shell. After that, he goes up in the universe for billions of miles and brings a piece of a dim star. He then observes each of the three materials. He will be extremely bewildered to see that composition of all the three things is the same - electron. It can be seen in a flower, a water drop, moon, or sun. This, in a nutshell, is the irrefutable declaration of the Oneness of Creator.

There are so many forms of atom. For example water molecules, oxygen, carbon, etc. The smallest drop of water is made up of one atom of oxygen and two atoms of hydrogen that when combined, is called a molecule. Molecules of certain matters are composed of atoms that run into hundreds and up to a thousand. In water, one atom of oxygen can contact two atoms of hydrogen while in salt, one atom of sodium can contain one atom of chlorine but the chloride of gold's one atom can contain three atoms of chlorine.

There were times when scholars had a lot of reservations about the existence of Allah. Then, knowledge was so deficient and inferior that the limits of ignorance and wisdom were conjoined. Today, western scientists have unfurled a lot of mysteries and want to reach the ultimate Truth - sometime, someday.

Atomic Fusion

Atoms constitute different things while in different quantities. This fusion is the result of some natural and chemical compositions for which there is no definite knowledge. General theory claims that some have positive and others have negative electricity. Since positive electricity attracts negative electricity, atoms combine. If two atoms have the same electricity, negative or positive, they will repel each other. Allah has ordained positive electricity in hydrogen atom and negative in oxygen atom that make them attract each other. And we know that water is a pre-requisite for all the living beings.

Mutual grip of atoms is so strong that if we plan to break just $\frac{1}{4}^{th}$ of an inch thick iron rod, we will need a force of 100 tons. If we keep two broken pieces of iron rod side by side, they will not reconnect. This is so because for complete fusion, atoms need to come extremely close; something not possible without fire and hammer.

Oscillation of Atoms

All the atoms are in a perpetual state of oscillation that creates some heat. When a train runs over railway lines, the rails get warm because of oscillation of particles. Some materials, for example wood, has little propensity to oscillation. Such materials are called 'cold bodies'. Oscillation in fact is the consequence of motion. And motion can happen only when atoms are separate even if they are in cohesion.

After constant observations, scientist have declared that in spite of cohesion of all the atoms, there is also disconnection and motion. If we keep iron over fire then because of oscillation and disturbance, atoms would reduce their grip, iron would spread and after further heating, these atoms will separate from each other, taking the form of liquid iron. If the temperature reaches 6,000°C, liquid iron would turn to gases. Needless to say that each material body has pores otherwise it would never have been possible for atoms to move.

Motion in steel is like clock's pendulum but in certain other bodies, this is periodic motion and elsewhere, it is interfusion. After putting milk in tea, atoms of tea mix up with that of milk. Similarly, atoms of flower's fragrance mix up with atoms of air and reach our sense of smell.

An electron travels with a speed of 5,000 miles [8,100 km] per hour. If air pressure is reduced and the speed of electron is enhanced with electric current, its speed can reach 60,000 miles [97,200 km] per hr. To put it plainly, an electron would be able to cross Atlantic Ocean 20-times in a matter of just one second and will take four seconds to reach moon. The volume of an electron is 1,800 times less than water atom while each molecule has 100,000 electrons.

Life in Everything

As has been said earlier, atoms are made up of electrons. There is a space between any two electrons where it can move. Because of fast speed, this open space is filled in the example of a burning wooden stick when revolved, gives the look of a fire circle. Universe is the combination of these living and fast particles. That is why the Qur'an has set the mountains in motion:

You consider mountains to be static? Though they are running like clouds. Namal, 88.

This movement of mountains is first, because of earth's motion and second, because of electrons that are used in their composition.

Diversity in Universe (A Question)

Question: If the composition of gold and soil is the same then how gold became gold and why soil lagged behind?

Answer: because of increase/decrease in electrons and because of the differences in system and diversity has been created in the universe. In some atoms, electrons are in center while in others these are at the outer sides. And then there is difference in numbers as well. This difference in system, location, and quantities results in the diversity of material and the 'scenes' that they present.

These are the building blocks of universe. A western scientist while observing the breathtaking mechanism, yelled:

This is wonder that man's brain reels before the infinitely great things of the universe on the one hand and the infinitely small things of nature on the other.

Qur'an has asked for our attention to these microscopic bodies in these words:

And not an atom's weight in the earth or in the sky escapes Allah, nor what is less than that or greater than that, but it is (written) in a clear Book. Younas, 61.

In this Book if small and large are not considered as electron and molecule, the entire Ayat would be rendered crypto-logic. Since Allah knew it all too well that scientists of 20th Century would be able to find out various forms of particles, therefore to ensure the loftiness of this Great Book acknowledged through Revelation, Allah also mentioned the types of particles – large and small. What else could render greater proof of the Divinity of Qur'an that it has a mention of one thing the knowledge of which cannot be attained without the aid of microscope?

I have myself passed through a period of *irreligiosity* (1925-30) when (God forbid) I used to call religion a farce and joking about Allah (may Allah forgive me for taking such a liberty), was my pet hobby. But now, my eyes have opened. Now each particle of the universe and each page of Allah's Book, is a treasure trove (of knowledge, of understanding; of greatness, vastness, and infiniteness of Allah).

After studying these microscopic particles, Lord Cloven used to say loud:

This is impossible to conceive either the beginning or the continuance of life without an overruling creative power. Overpowering strong proofs of benevolent and intelligent design are to be found around us that all living things depend on the everlasting greater ruler.

His conclusions and thinking reach quite effectively to the Divine Though:

Worthy of worship is the one Who created earth and skies and Who neither sleeps nor slumbers. Baqarah, 255.

Why is there no collision among those billions of spheres? Its simple answer is that Allah is awake:

Allah has gripped the reins of defiant spheres of earth and skies lest they leave their pre-determined course and run away. If that happens by chance, there will not be anyone to control its aftermath. Fatir, 41.

Allah further says:

And He holds back the heaven from falling on the earth unless by His leave. Hajj, 65.

Electricity

Where did electricity come in to these particles? We don't know. All that we know is just that there are two types of electricity: positive and negative. If a glass rod is rubbed with a silk cloth, a lot of negative electricity will be transferred to the rod and just about all the positive electricity would be left behind. If an ebonite rod is rubbed against the same cloth, the negatives will shift to the rod and the negative electricity would increase. When negatives increase in a body, it throws out the extra negatives. Scientifically, this 'throwing' of negatives is called 'discharge'. This (discharge of) negatively charged body is always towards the positively charged body. Since copper wire is very solid, and its atoms are too closely knit, therefore these atoms can very quickly throw negative charge towards each other. It can be illustrated through an example that 50 active boys are standing in a row of whom first transfers a thing to second and second to third. Same is the condition of copper wire: the first atom transfers negative electricity to the next atom. And this is what we call Electric Current.

When we bring brass closer to zinc, the electrons of zinc intrude in brass. If we dip zinc in a solution where it can dissolve, all the electrons of zinc will mix in the solution. And then if we put a piece of brass in that solution, and connect both zinc and brass piece to a brass wire, then because of the excess of electrons, electric current in the wire would be very powerful. On this principal, batteries are manufactured.

Some bodies move electrons quick while others are slow. The first one is called 'conductor' and the latter, non-conductor. Compared to iron wire, a copper wire conducts electricity six times faster. Glass is lower level conductor and wood, non-conductor. If you sit on a wooden bed and touch electric wire, you will not be shocked. This is because electricity cannot move through wood and onto the earth.

Look towards the Himalayas in monsoon. A dreadful black cloud advances towards the plains. Heart sinks, pounding high lest electricity may not roast us to death. How much grace is there in the speed of these clouds? It is because in its wake, is the storm of electricity. And how lifeless are the clouds of winters that don't have the treasure of electricity and no firework. From these narratives, we conclude that only those nations in the world are called honorable and dignified that own electricity and whose comrades are hurricanes and storms and whose stupendous speed would create awe and terror in the hearts.

He it is Who shows you the lightning, a fear and a hope, and raises the heavy clouds. Ra'ad, 12.

During the last 800 years, our (so called) sophists and preachers have conveyed such a lot of sheepish language to Muslims – a nation whose name was sufficient to strike terror in the hearts of opponents. By doing so, they instead destroyed their moral fiber, making them stoop to the lowly status that all their fast and stormy determinations were transformed to the silence of (moral) death.

Nations around the world are dominating the universe, conquering unknown worlds and because of their hideousness, earth and skies are trembling, and equally the nations of world. And we? Well, this unfortunate Muslim nation has been consigned to the dustbin of history where it is busy offering prayers and nawafil and asking for godly assistance as if they are without brain, eyes, ears, arms and legs and are just a heap of flesh that can hardly breathe and is at the mercy of Allah.

If they want redemption, they must return to Allah:

Lo! Allah! Unto Him belongs the sovereignty of the heavens and the earth. He quickens and He gives death. And you have, instead of Allah, no protecting friend nor helper. Taubah, 116.

The Problem of Ether

Though Ether is present in the universe since its inception but scientists have recently discovered it. Radio and then television are the miracles of Ether. To explain this, let's go for a small experiment.

Throw a stone in a calm pond. Waves would be created. Water would stay where it was but waves would reach the brink of the pond. In other words, water is a source of transfer of waves. Similarly, ether also serves us in a number of ways. It transfers our messages thousands of miles away. Our eyesight is also occurring because of ether.

This is the law of nature that one body cannot act upon another body without a medium. A sailor sees a lighthouse in the dark night. There is a 'means' between the sailor and the lighthouse that causes the light reach the sailor. This in-between (means) distance is called ether. Light of the tower creates waves in ether. These waves strike the eyes of sailor and his brain sees the light. Let's keep it in mind that this 'act of seeing' is done by the brain while eyes are just an instrument of sight.

Similarly sun stimulates ether. And this stimulation, after reaching our brains, gives us the sense of light and heat. A magnet attracts a needle from a distance. We need to accept that there is a 'means' between the magnet and the needle. It is called ether.

If somehow we manage to extract air from a water container and keep a bell in and leave to ring continuously, we won't be able to listen the bell. Why? Because the means of communication – in this case, air – between us and the bell is absent. If in the same container, we light an electric bulb, we will see light. This is because the medium of sight is present in the container.

A Russian scientist Mendeleev thinks that ether is something different even from gases whose particles can enter any body. But till now this theory has not been confirmed.

Ether waves travel with a speed of 186,000 miles per second. Sunlight also reaches us with the same speed. From this, scientist have concluded that it is not the light that travels, it is rather ether waves that travel.

Who discovered Radio

Christiaan Huygens[45], a Dutch Professor declared some 200 years back the existence of ether. After some time, when a British scientist Dr. Thomson further elaborated the theory, no one paid any attention to it. Rather an article was written in Edinburgh Review (Vol. 5 of 1804, page 97) but just a single copy of the journal could be sold. After some time, researchers paid attention to the theory and today, results are in front of us.

Ether Waves

Study the waves generated by throwing pebbles in standing water and see the distance between two consecutive waves. And then throw 20 pebbles in one second and you will see the in-between distance of two

---

[45] Christiaan Huygens, (14 April 1629 – 8 July 1695) was a prominent Dutch mathematician and natural philosopher. He is known particularly as an astronomer, physicist, probabilist and horologist.

waves has decreased to 1/20th of the earlier two waves. Same is the case with ether waves. If interval between two is large these would be long waves, otherwise short. Each radio wave travels 186,000 miles [291,000 km] per second. If in a radio wave movement is created 100 times, the distance between any two waves would reduce to 1,860 miles [2,913 km]. Radio experts have seen waves that are 1/15,000th of an inch apart. These radio waves are created because of the motion of electrons and under different conditions, create different colors; like orange, yellow, green, etc.

Positive electricity, gravitation, earth, spirit, and radio are the secrets that man has not yet fully grasped. Till now only this much has been known that radio is present everywhere. This is a sort of extremely light cloud spreading from Godly Throne to the extreme depths of universe. It has neither vacuum nor weight nor could these be created. Probably the following Ayat points to radio:

Have they not looked at the heaven above them - how We structured it and adorned it and [how] it has no rifts? Q, 6.

Light and Sight

Light is the name of 'feeling' of those waves that are created due to the 400 million revolutions per second. Waves created from sun have 30% light and 70% heat waves. The tail of glowworm has only light waves. If (somehow) it would tell its secret, we might lighten up the tail of a joker in a circus.

When radio waves strike a body, it creates disturbance in the electrons. The 'feeling' of this disturbance is called eyesight. Let's remember that electrons of light, after striking the body, become motionless and create disturbance in the electrons of that body. There are certain bodies that can be pierced through by these waves without creating any disturbance in electrons, or very less. This means that if electrons of a particular body are strong, they will resist and as a result ether gets agitated. And if weak, then ether would give way and radio waves would pass through. Such bodies are called transparent. Since each body's electrons resist even somewhat, therefore nothing can be called as absolutely transparent so much so that certain scientists do not consider even air to be perfectly transparent.

The Sense of Color

Since there are seven colors therefore in ether, electrons create seven types of waves. If all these waves absorb in something, it will look black. If all the ethers reflect and reach our eyes, the thing will look white. If six waves are absorbed and those creating the feel of blue color are not absorbed, the thing would look blue. Let's remember that each wave will agitate its own electrons. Waves that create the feel of a yellow color, all the rest will absorb, without hesitation. If today, red color is removed from the sun, nothing would look 'red' in the world. And that is why if we see a red flower under the light of mercury-vapor lamp, it will appear 'black'; because the lamp does not have the waves that create red color.

There is a depression in the center of retina that has minute promontories that have the potential to sense different colors. And the interesting thing is that for each color, there is a separate promontory.

Ozone Layer

At a height of 25 miles above earth, there is Ozone layer

that stops certain deadly radiations of sun. And then there is another layer that is 25 miles thick that reflects ether waves towards earth. In the absence of this layer, we would not have been able to send and receive wireless messages.

Creation of earth and skies, ... Rum, 22.

Did you see that to Allah, only those people are scholars who think over earth and skies?

What is dialogue? Aerial waves, i.e. 'knotting' the air. This is the source that created thousands of knowledges, speeches and poems. The same undulation [waves] is the name of music. And the same undulation brought hundreds of political and moral revolutions. If undulation is excluded from the air, the chirping of birds, cuckoo's songs and bulbuls' melodies will disappear. The way 4,000 languages were created, was because of air undulation. Similarly, different scenes of universe came into existence just because of undulation.

Arabic has 28 letters of which 14 are used in certain parts of verses. This points to the fact that half of universe' beauty is because of letters and half because of elements.

The way different combinations for example, of praise, of satire and of agony are created, similarly, ancient elements gave rise to different scenes. Gardens and meadows are the scenes of nature. And then those gorgeous mountains, roaring oceans, and thundering clouds are the elements of war while noise of earth, bitter water and plants are the elements of parodies.

Permanent element of composition[46] is ether. The way no reduction or increase occurs due to our speaking, similarly the creation of universe has had no impact on the source of ether. Elements are like letters. From letters came the knowledge and the same letters resulted in the writing of

---

[46] Hydrogen, nitrogen, oxygen, chromium, Uranium, and sodium, etc. that have reached 92

innumerable essays and poems.

Say, "If the sea were ink for [writing] the words of Allah, the sea would be exhausted before the words of Allah were exhausted, even if We brought the like of it as a supplement." Kahaf, 109.

In this Ayat *"Ikhtilaf-ul-Suntakum"* calls for the study of nature while *"Ikhtif-ul-wanukum"* invites to the study of elements.

Because of the former, tremendous progress was made and such a lot of literature was created in different languages that universe had to, once again, acknowledge the glory of man.

There are two major languages: Aryan and Semitic

Different branches of Aryan are English, Greek, Latin, Swedish, Danish, German, Dutch, Armenian, Bulgarian, Bohemian, Russian, Hindi, Persian, and Sanskrit.

Similarly, Sami has Hebrew, Arabic, Aramaic, Maltese, Amharic, Babylonian, Assyrian, etc.

Today, about 4,000 languages are spoken worldwide. Europe has 787, Asia, 937, Africa, 276, Americas, 1,624, and in India, about 400 languages are spoken.

Different languages not only cause progress and development, but man's respect and dignity also enhances if he speaks so many languages. A man after studying different languages becomes expert in various fields and ultimately becomes scholar of universe. The Ayat *"Inna fi zalika la Aayatin-lila'alamin"* points to the fact that the study of universe starts after the attainment of knowledge.

Chromogens [47]

Color is a pre-historic invention. We have got archaic pictures that are colored and prepared thousands of years

---

[47] Color-making Agents

back.

Red color is extracted from the roots of a plant called Madder. It was first done by the Turks. In 18th Century, Europeans also learnt this skill. In 1894, Picric acid was used in making yellow color. This was prepared by Wolfe using Indigo Nitric acid. In 1865, experimenting on quinine, Vigoin got the material for making red color and called it Magenta. Sometime earlier, color used to be extracted from leafs and roots and later, through chemical methods. In 1850, Peter Grace found that in Ammonia compounds, one atom of nitrogen can substitute three atoms of hydrogen and the compound can be mixed with Carbonic Acid and Aniline to make different colors. These could be used to color silk, wood and leather. Before 1884, using these materials aluminum and other compounds could also be made use of. But in 1884, Batiger discovered a matter that could be used to color various items without the help of any other compound. Orange color is the compound of Indigo and Bromine.

In the days of Hazrat Musa^{AS}, colors were obtained from sea shells. Till now, more than 2,000 colors have been invented.

Why Does Cloth Accept Color?

There are different theories about it. More logical one is that in coloring material and in cloth components, positive and negative electricity exist. That is how the cloth attracts color. Compared to cotton cloth, affinity to color attraction is 15 times more in woolen cloth. That is why color of woolen cloth is permanent while cotton cloth looses luster with the passage of time.

Finesse in the Colors of Animals

Jackal, fox, deer, rabbit, partridge, quail, etc. have earth-like colors that keep them from their hunters. Had a rabbit been of red or yellow color, hunters would have been able to see it from quite a distance and soon would have ended up in his stomach. Since protection of domestic rabbits is the responsibility of the household, that is why they could even have white color. And then there are certain animals of prey that too are grayish so that their prey may not be able to see them while attacking and thus may sustain.

Allah is responsible for food of all the living things. Hud, 6.

African forests have a lot of lions and zebras. Owing to their contrasting (black-n-white) stripped bodies, zebras can be seen by the lions even from a far-off place and are thus chased. What happens next, is not difficult to imagine.

Colors of cows, bulls, horses, dogs and cats are diverse because they live under the protection of man. And because of diversity in their colors, it also satisfies man's esthete and penchant for colors.

What we can conclude is that animals that remain under the protection of man, Allah has deprived them of the most important source of protection. To the other side, deer has been give grayish color so that it may not be seen from a distance. It has been given fast legs to be out of danger in seconds and a sleek body to avoid gasping for oxygen. In fact, Allah belongs to those who have none else to look after them, or those that cannot self-protect. Those living under the tutelage of man are hulky like a camel, clumsy like a buffalo, lazy like an ox, fallen like a donkey and greedy like a cat. To the other side, a free nation is dreadful like a lion, quick like a deer, beautiful like a cheetah, and speedy like a falcon.

Black Color

Black color is a nature's bounty. The way green goggles keep eyes from bright light, similarly, black skin stops body cells from burning. It is because it quickly absorbs sun heat and equally quickly sends it out. And this way, no harm occurs to the body. Nature turns a man's color black while working in open farms so that their body cells are not damaged. Make it this way that black color is a body armor that protects human body from the onslaught of fiery arrows.

Naturalists believe that all the black animals (cuckoo, crow, black sheep) were created around the Equator while their colors were meant to protect them from intense heat. From there, these animals migrated to other parts of the world and there too, their colors remained black.

Hair Color

There is a coloring agent in the roots of hair that diminishes with the advent of old age. The space thus occupied by the color, is instead, taken by air. Because of old age, man looses the strength to walk and is thus confined to shade. Compared to that, a young man works in the sun and has black hair so that it could protect his head from sun-related damages. Those working in offices and others working under the shade, get their hair white rather sooner; because nature does not feel the need for their hair being black.

Based on skin colors, there are two types of human beings: white and non-white. White man's skin has red-coloring material called "Chromogen" while other men have black matter called "Ferment". Zebra's body has ferment at some parts and air at others. That is why it becomes mottled. Mixing hydrogen peroxide with ferment can be converted to yellow and brown. This chemical reaction perpetuates in animals. That is why color of some animals keeps on changing according to age.

Color-giving material can be created only in light. For example, Proteus lives in such caves, where there is no way for light and heat to enter, its color remains white.

Some colored animals have been seen in depths of oceans, though there is no possibility of sunlight to penetrate. After great efforts, it was found that certain fishes that live in the depth of seas have lights on their heads. Moreover light from corals and other hydroids is also available in the depths of seas, sufficient to create coloring matter.

Chameleon

Besides chameleon, there are other animals and fishes that generally change colors. This is because of some specific incident, for example fear, shame, grief, and happiness. These states create disturbance in the color-giving matter in these animals. Because of these, such a rush of color appears on the skin that changes the earlier color.

This universe is a grand studio for the miracles of creation whose every scene makes one wonder. Or this is an academy where practical lessons are taught of the signs of Allah. How degraded and shamed are those nations that are unaware or unconcerned about the mysteries and signs of Allah. Just think over the warning of Surah Jathiah:

> Indeed, within the heavens and earth are signs for the believers. And in the creation of yourselves and what He disperses of moving creatures are signs for people who are certain [in faith]. And [in] the alternation of night and day and

[in] what Allah sends down from the sky of provision and gives life thereby to the earth after its lifelessness and [in His] directing of the winds are signs for a people who reason. These are the verses of Allah which We recite to you in truth. Then in what statement after Allah and His verses will they believe? Woe to every sinful liar Who hears the verses of Allah recited to him, then persists arrogantly as if he had not heard them. So give him tidings of a painful punishment. Ayaat 3-8.

Did you see that seekers of the treasures of earth and skies have been addressed as those having wisdom and Eimaan. And those, denying their strength and dreadfulness, have been given the (bad) news of great agony. Both of these scenes are in front of us. Europeans gave due thought to earth and skies and the whole world testifies to their glory. To the other end of the spectrum, we the Muslims have turned our faces from knowledge and the whole world is testifying to our abasement, ignorance, and foolishness.

Chapter-IX

Miracles of Mountains

Then do they not look at the camels - how they are created? And at the sky - how it is raised? And at the mountains - how they are erected? And at the earth - how it is spread out? So remind, [O Muhammad]; you are only a reminder. Ghasiatah, 17-21.

Value of Mountains

Mountains are our wealth, help, reason for our existence, and means of our livelihood. Of these mountain, mineral springs irrigate our farmlands and on its heights are valuable trees of chir and deodar. The same mountains when spewing fire (volcanoes) bring out treasures for our use. And then, coal, lime, copper, gold, iron, and other metals are available from foothills. Their value is because of these services without which man can hardly sustain.

Mountains remained under water for millions of years and after maturity, came out for our service. In fact mountains are under the burden of water.

Have those who disbelieved not considered that the heavens and the earth were a joined entity, and We separated them and made from water every living thing? Then will they not believe? Anbia, 30.

Layers of Mountains

After careful study of the material oozing out of earth through volcanic lavas, proves that there are numerous types of stones down there for example, Granite, Rhyiolite,

Phulsate, Trakite, Andesite, Dialadge, Diorite, Graphite, Limestone, Coal, etc. Of the last one, diamond is its real brother. The difference in the colors is because coal is made up of trees while diamond developed from wood resin.

Do you not see that Allah sends down rain from the sky, and We produce thereby fruits of varying colors? And in the mountains are tracts, white and red of varying shades and [some] extremely black. And among people and moving creatures and grazing livestock are various colors similarly. Only those fear Allah, from among His servants, who have knowledge. Indeed, Allah is Exalted in Might and Forgiving. Fatir, 27, 28.

Sons of Oceans

We get the following things from mountains:

1) Such shells that can only be found in oceans

2) Innumerable skeletons of water-based animals

3) Marks of insects crawling over bog millions of years back leaving a line behind.

From the above facts, we can safely conclude that mountains were submerged under oceans millions of years from hence and in fact, are the 'sons of oceans'.

Formation of Mountains

Mountains cropped out of oceans through two possible ways:

One: Internal material of earth came out because of quakes and kept on accumulating under water and taking the shapes of mountains.

Two: streams, nullahs, and rivers used to bring down millions of tons of stones to oceans that kept on breaking rocks with its furious waves. Water has certain soluble in it for example, lime, iron, silica, etc. that binds stones like glue. And this way, hundreds of miles long and thousands of feet high mountains are formed. To ensure solidification of these stone layers, water pressure played a very crucial role. Then the clay brought down by rivers, also work as a binder. This state remains in action for centuries and when Allah sees that most of the mountains on land have become useless because of the helping material that had been going down to oceans, while mountains in the oceans have been brimming with gold and other precious minerals, then His Nature becomes 'restless'. As a consequence, shakes the earth so intensely that heights are converted into lowlands and lowlands become highlands, and from below the oceans, comes out mountains, full of treasures.

I look at a hen that has laid eggs and sits on it and when chicks are ready, hen leaves the site and chicks (mountains) come out. That Wisest of the Wise does not do anything without a purpose. So long as the existing mountains have the treasures of minerals, no strong quake would come. And when the wealth of existing mountains would exhaust, then for the well-being of human race, new mountains would come out of oceans; as in the past.

And We bring forth [one] better than it or similar to it. Baqarah, 106.

Land that we tread today, was way back under the ocean and my eyes (of imagination) see that sometime, it will once again go under water.

Each and every act of Allah has deep wisdom. What is this world? A grand chemical house! Mountains are created and destroyed, airs are blowing, deserts are burning and the Chemist of Universe is sitting and conducting new experiments, making an array of flowers and fruits with a variety of colors and tastes. Think over this gigantic diversity and honestly tell as who could imagine the enormity of this fabulous creation.

O' Rabb! Tell what substitute is there for this wonder and grandeur that transpires on us when we look deeply into this awesome system that you have so immensely and so delicately developed? This characteristic cannot be reduced even if we bow our heads in your Court for umpteen times. This is a soothing restlessness, heart-rendering impatience, and yes, it is an insurmountable erythrism that wants to see You the way You are. I saw Your Light in the twinkling stars. And I saw Your glimpse as a semi-apparent reflection in a flower. Your grandeur is cascading from mountains while singing the songs of your Loftiness. I feel embarrassed. I am sweating. O my Beautiful Lord! Now I understand as to why Hazrat Musa[AS] fainted. When a helpless man like me can feel terrorized by just the imagination of your pomp and show while looking at all that You have created, then why not a man like Musa should get intoxicated by just a glimpse of Your spine-chilling Grandness?

But when Allah appeared to the mountain, He rendered it level, and Moses fell unconscious. A'araaf, 143.

Types of Quakes

There are two types of quakes: one that comes out of the interior of earth and the other, the epicenter of which is human brain. Earthly quakes bring the treasures of earth out while human quakes bare the human quintessence naked. In Arabic, the word for farming is *"flaha"*, the derivative of *"falah"*, i.e. bring the earth's layers out through ploughing. The way a farmer brings the living forces of earth out, similarly hard work (human quake) puts all of man's internal powers into use. That is why Allah has called hardworking and successful people and nations as *"Muflih"* – apparent.

"Wa olaika hum-ul-fulihun" [and their latent powers are

becoming bare].

In the 'Code' of Allah, the greatest crime is inanimateness and laziness. And today, Muslims are getting dribbled because of laziness. The basic reason for all the moral degradations and lowliness and indignity is ignorance while ignorance is because of laziness. In this regard, it is generally said, "What can we do, the government is of foreigners. Had it been our own government, we would have done everything." These lame excuses are absolutely unacceptable because one, the government has created opportunities in seeking knowledge not hurdles, two, what special progress have you shown in countries where Muslims are ruling (Arabia, Iran, Afghanistan, etc.)? Dark clouds of ignorance are hovering over there also. And there too lack of political and economic progress prevails. They too import even ordinary products like pencils and pens from Europe. Have you seen any product with the mark 'Made in Arabia' or 'Iran'? Never! And for that to happen, we would need to wait for a few hundred years more; if at all. The basic reason is that in Islamic countries the very idea of knowledge has been totally disfigured. We call the jurisprudence-related problems and irrational and unrealistic logic as the pinnacle of knowledge. Each Friday, in millions of mosques, rivers of speeches flow and now it is all in our veins and mind (if still we think we have it) that saying Allah-o-Akbar in mosques is the height of piety and reading a few books in Deoband[48] is the zenith of knowledge. And the knowledge of planes and ships,

---

[48] Deoband is a city in Saharanpur district (Uttar Pradesh, India), about 150 km from Delhi. It used to be surrounded by dense forests, and got its name, from *Devi Van*, or "Forest of Goddess". It is best known for Darul Uloom of Deoband, one of the most important and influential schools of Islamic Studies and the presence of the Jamia Tibbiya Deoband college of Unani Medicine, imparting the qualifications of B.U.M.S. and M.D.

minerals and their preparations, guns, cars, etc. is just materialistic and worldly luxuries and the Muslims have nothing to do with them.

This fatal division and this un-Islamic un-Qur'anic, unnatural, and un-Godly thinking have done irreparable damage to Muslim community. His Deen as well as his world are doomed. And going further deeper in the quagmire of his own doings, he sometimes finds solace under Stalin, sometimes in the lap of American President while at other times he prays and prays and prays by reciting *"Fansurna A'alal qaumul kafirin"*. When you see that for the last two hundred years, Allah has not been positively responding to the prayers of lazy people, then why don't you give up this practice of self deception? Why don't instead you use your brain and why don't you look at the ultimate destination of lazy people and learn lessons?

To conclude, only those nations are called powerful and successful that use the latent powers (quakes) of brains and brings out the treasures of earth for the benefit of mankind. When the earth is shaken with its [final] earthquake, and the earth discharges its burdens, and man says, "What is [wrong] with it?" That Day, it will report its news because Allah has commanded it. That Day, the people will depart separated [into categories] to be shown [the result of] their deeds. So whoever does an atom's weight of good will see it, and whoever does an atom's weight of evil will see it. Az-Zalzalah.

Reasons of Quakes

As said earlier, earth's inner core is an inferno like a furnace that also requires a chimney. Volcanic mountains are a sort of chimneys for the furnace through which internal material spews out. If due to excess of lave or any other reason, the outlet closes, lava would find any other way out and wherever it can find a weak crust or soft spot, it will just tear it open with such a force that earthquake will result.

When smoke from a volcanic mountain stops coming out, it must be understood that earthquake has occurred. In 1633, the mouth of a Kaberia's small volcanic mountain closed. It instantly created tremendous tremors. In 1799 in Indies Island, Mount Lipsto stopped spewing smoke. The result was such an earthquake that 40,000 person of Reumbia lost their lives.

Mr. Malt has prepared a list of earthquakes that occurred between 1606 B.C. and 1860 A.D. After that, a French researcher Dezon recorded quakes till 1850. During this period of 3,448 years, 6,831 quakes had occurred that have been documented, however a large number of quakes have been missed because then there was no formal system of record keeping, except dependence of human memory. These could not be historically documented and those that were, could not be saved, though quakes between 1800 and 1850 were carefully and methodically documented. If in just 50 years, 3,500 quakes occurred, then in 3,448 years, this number could be as high as 2,113,000. Unfortunately, that could not be recorded.

Categories of Quakes

Mr. Malt categorized quakes in to three major segments:

1) Large quakes, i.e., those that were felt between 1,000 to 2,000 miles [1,600 to 32,000 km].

2) Medium quakes, i.e., that were felt from 400 to 600 miles [650 to 1,000 km].

3) Small quakes that has impact of up to 100 to 150 miles [160 to 240 km].

During the period of 3,448 years, we know only of 216 quakes. On the other hand, between 1800 and 1850 A.D., there were 3,500 quakes. From these figures, one can deduce that at any given point in time, each year, a large quake occurred. And if we include small quakes, the number may go up to eight per month.

Strength of Quakes

The epicenter of quakes is 35 miles deep in the earth where its intensity is extremely severe. When it comes up by tearing through, its intensity keeps on reducing because of earth's resistance and consequently, just a fraction of the original force appears. Still, it is so powerful that the earthquake of Rio Bamba threw people up in the air upto 100 ft. The quake of Pompeii (Italy) threw rocks weighing up to 32,000 kg by up to 12,000 ft [3,600 m] up in the air. After these facts, one sees no exaggeration in the couplet of Hazrat Amir Minai (translation):

I am that discarded man who is afraid that earth may not threw me up to the sky

Impact of Quakes on Earth

Because of quakes, sometimes earth's surface goes up or comes down. For example:

1) In 1835 in Southern America, a severe earthquake had its impact on 600,000 square miles [1.575 million km^2] and its surface went up by 207 ft [63 m] and because of slope, the speed of some streams increased.

2) In 1822 an earthquake in USA the surface of Santa Maria Island increased by upto 9 ft. There even

today, one can come across the skeletons of animals that died during the quake.

3) There is an area near Attock called Machh where an earthquake occurred in 1819. It completely destroyed the city of Bhoj and 2,000 square miles [5,250 km^2] area of land drowned in the water. There is also an area to its north that was 50 miles [81 km] long and 16 miles [26 km] wide, raised by 10 ft [3 m].

4) A 25 miles [41 km] piece of 135 mile [219 km] long coast of Kandia island rose while its eastern corner submerged in water.

5) Darwin writes about the earthquake that occurred in 1835 in Wold Yuya:
"During the quake, the condition of earth was like a small boat getting beating from the extremely dangerous ocean waves"

6) Depth of sea near a coastal city of Greece was 1,400 ft [425 m] that is now just 100 ft [30 m].

7) Mediterranean Sea was originally a river that had no link with Atlantic Ocean. Now it is a sea.

8) In ancient times, the Great African Desert was submerged. Some of its parts are even today below the sea surface and can be irrigated by digging a canal from Atlantic Ocean. But who will do it?

9) Previously, Africa and Brazil was one chunk of land. Even today, if both the pieces are (somehow) dragged and brought together, they will so perfectly fit in like a broken piece of a cup. Similarly, North America was united with Greenland and Greenland was jointed with Europe. Likewise, Australia was connected to India and India to Africa. Even today

ocean between these countries is very shallow.

10) Poles were first warm where remains of certain trees and animals have been found that could live only in warm climates. These areas were initially near the Equator but now have gone to north and south. Icebergs as tall as 5,000 ft [1,515 m] have drifted towards Europe making it colder.

In short, no one depends on the reliability of this earth. And no one knows when it may slide under the oceans and that is why, it keeps on rattling.

O mankind, fear Allah. Indeed, the convulsion of the [final] Hour is a terrible thing. Hajj, 1.

Chapter-X

Miracles of Human Body

Man's structure is a wonderful achievement of Allah's creation that makes a man down in reverence. After going through various stages of man's creation, geneticists have brought the fact out that human body is made up of cells that was just one cell in the beginning that keeps on merging till man's body comes into its present shape. Some cells start making ears, noses and all the rest of human body parts. It has not happened till today that cells meant to transform into nose, made an ear, or stick a tail behind a man. This orderly creation is all because of that Supreme Power in front of which the entire universe bows in reverence.

And while to Him have submitted [all] those within the heavens and earth. Al-e-Imran, 83.

Today, knowledge has excelled so much that it is bent on unfurling the mysteries of Nature. To the other end of the spectrum, there might be two percent people who do not feel the need for Allah and who think that this entire system is in place without a creator. One may just ask them a simple question: if all this is happening on its own, then why did your mother's womb make you a man and not a donkey? And why not head of a donkey and body of a monkey? Why don't we get a hen out of a goat's womb? Is there any answer to these questions with these non-believers? If yes, bring it, if no, be and say like us:

It is He who forms you in the wombs however He wills. Al-e-Imran, 6.

Elemental Composition of Human Body

1) Four states: heat, frigidity, *yabost*, and juices

2) Four elements of body: fire, air, mud, and water

3) Four interfuses: bile duct, blood, phlegm, and hypochondria

4) Nine stages: head, mouth, neck, chest, back, waist, thigh, ankles, and feet

5) Pillars: 248 bones

6) Ropes: 750 muscles

7) Treasures: brain, myeloid, lungs, heart, liver, spleen, stomach, intestines

8) Sects and expounders: 360 essences

9) Canals: 360 blood vessels

10) Doors: eyes, nose, chests, mouth, and pudendum

Marvelous City

Consider human body a city that is performing different acts, for example:

1) Cook: stomach makes food like a cook

2) Perfume: Some perfumes brings out the essence of food making it part of the body

3) Physician: Liver like a physician mixes acid with food

4) Refuse's removal: Intestines, skin, kidneys and lungs take out dirt from the body

5) Juggler: Some expert is converting blood into flesh

6) Furnace: Bones like bricks are being baked

7) Cloth maker: some cloth maker is knitting nerves and membranes

8) Tailor: A tailor is sewing human wounds

9) Farmer: like the bulls of a farmer is growing hair on the farm of human body

10) Painter: Some expert is making teeth white, hair black and blood red

11) Sculptor: Some sculptor is carving a beautiful child in mother's womb

A Mini Universe

Go to some large factory. Engine will be in one room and everywhere else different parts would be performing different functions. Somewhere swords would be made and elsewhere, oil will be extracted. To one side, tins would be manufactured and to the other, iron would be melted. By analogy, similar is the state of universe. Just look at the various functions that it performs: rivers are flowing, winds are blowing, sun is throwing light, trees are growing, and clouds are raining. This way, different components of the universe are performing different functions. But there is just one engine: Allah!

Look at the human body: hair is growing, tears are dropping, heart is beating, breathe is running, ears are listening, eyes are seeing and brain is thinking. The engine of this factory is called 'spirit'. Where does the spirit live in a body? Its answer is: in every hair, in every color and in every drop of blood. But if you want to see the spirit by scratching any part of the body, you will not succeed. Exactly the same way, Allah is there in each and every particle of the universe but like spirit, cannot be seen. Human body is in fact a miniature universe where the spirit is working the same way as Allah does in the universe.

There is a Hadeeth that says, *"I created man like myself"*.

Care

No noise can wake us up from slumber but a small sound of a child can do so the mother. Dog doesn't wake up by the noise of inmates and of cars and motor cycles but a faint noise of stranger's feet wakes him up. We keep on sleeping in a plane but the moment some malfunctioning occurs in the engine, all the passengers wake up. Why so? Because a part of man's minds remains alert and keeps on observing all the incidents and dangers. Or put it this way that nature has deputed some guards to us and the moment some danger befalls us, they at once wake us up.

In every moment and at every place, Allah is with you. Hadid,4.

Yawning

When a man wakes up, he yawns; by drawing breathe in for some moments and then draws out. This is because a great quantity of blood accumulates in the lungs to keep the heart beating. Since after waking up, other parts of the body also need to work, lungs contract when man yawns and the blood thus accumulated in lungs comes out and spreads in the entire body and color of the face brightens. Pandiculation helps in spreading blood all around.

Eye

Pupil is a hole through which light passes. If light is more, the pupil shrinks and if less, the pupil expands. Camera is the copy of eye. If we intend to take a nap in the evening, we keep its light hole open for longer time. In more light, it is just kept open for a shorter time.

Tears are prepared in glands that are located in close proximity to eye but towards ears. Since some small conduits connect eye and nose, therefore while weeping, some tears enter the nose and so while weeping, nose also starts running.

Tears keep the eyes clean and that is why eye blinks so frequently so that moisture should reach all parts of the eye. Each part of an eye is like camera plate and to protect it, a hard skin is attached around it. From this very point, nerves reach the brain. When something reflects on it, then through these nerves, a resonance is created in the brain and thus one sees things. It is in fact the brain that does the job of seeing; eye just works as an instrument of seeing. If due to some shock or malfunctioning, these nerves are lost, eye stops seeing.

An eye has several screens, cornea, iris, ocular muscles, vitreous humor, retina, and optic nerves, a net of sensory nerves that conveys feelings to the brain. Lashes control dust and light and eyelids act like a handkerchief and a sweeping brush.

Eye lens is transparent like glass. While passing through it, the light refracts the way a stick looks while in water. If due to some disease, eyes stop working properly, then rays move out of the center of seeing and this way, eye suffers from myopia or hyperopia.

For such deficiencies, glasses are prescribed that neither allow the rays to strike ahead or fall short of the center of seeing (the focus!).

In the last section of eye, there are 3 million layers and 30 million pillars. See how complicated is the machinery of an eye and how intense is its system. That is why the Qur'an has repeatedly mentioned 'hearing' and 'seeing' as evidence of the Divine Workmanship.

We created man from compound semen and gave him the power to see how he uses these Divine bounties. Dahar 2.

Ear

Interior walls of an ear produce a foul-smelling and bitter wax so that dust and insects are caught then and there. If during sleep, some insect enters the ear, man life becomes miserable. Allah created this bitter wax so that an insect may instantly die the moment it enters the ear.

Just a little ahead of wax is a screen and after that, there are three bones interconnected like a chain. The way car's springs absorb shocks similarly, they defuse high and shrill sound making it soft. After these bones is the diaphragm and behind that is water. Water is in fact a bunch of strings. When sound strikes the diaphragm, it creates resonance in the strings and the brain does the bidding of hearing. Radio set is a fine example of ear.

There are 3,000 strings in the ear. Each string conveys a unique sound to the brain through a special channel, That is how we can at a time, listen 3,000 sounds.

Besides smelling and breathing, nose also acts like a spy. When bacteria in the air cannot be traced through any other means, it is the nose that informs the brain of their existence. The brain immediately instructs the hand to reach out to handkerchief so that harmful bacteria may not enter the body.

There is a screen of cyrtostyle, a bone between nose and mouth. This bone ultimately becomes a flesh lump in the form of Adam's apple[49]. When we take something down the

---

[49] Technically, Adam's apple is called *prominentia laryngea*. It is composed of cartilage which surrounds the larynx. As the larynx grows during puberty, the cartilage enlarges to accommodate it, creating a bump.

throat, Adam apple stops the way to nose so that no morsel of food may enter the nose.

There are certain locations around the nose that can rightly be termed as drums. While speaking, sound passes through drums and creates echo. In case of flu or abundance of phlegm, these drums just shut down. That is why man's sound becomes callous.

While breathing, food duct closes because of a nerve and the food going down the throat duct of breathing shuts. That is why neither food enters the breathing duct nor air enters the food duct. Otherwise great discomfort is created.

Sound

There are two strings at the mouth of air duct that have a diaphragm around. When we speak, the air passing through these strings, is transformed into sound. Its structure is such that faint breathe does not create sound. For example if you take a whistle in your mouth and inhale or exhale air slowly, no sound would be created. But if you blow the air with force, sound would be created. Same is the case with those strings.

If strings of a guitar are loose, sound would be thick and blowzy. But if stretched, sound would be clear and melodious. Similarly while generating harsh sound, these strings sag and during clear sound, they get tight. If a singer sings, just touch his throat and it will be strained.

Skin

Sense of feeling is in the skin. Each part of the skin conveys message to the brain through touch receptors and the brain in response, delivers orders accordingly.

In summers, ducts of sweat and blood wide open. This is

because body needs water to keep it safe from heat. Body temperature converts water into vapors and so becomes cool enough. Same is the purpose of tubes around the engine of a motor so that air passing through radiator could keep the engine cool.

In summers one perspires profusely due to which body temperature in consumed by evaporation and skin gets cold. Due to this, blood gets colder in the veins. This way, body temperature remains moderate.

In winters, there is no need for sweats. That is why the doors of sweat and blood close down. It is because of this phenomenon that in winters, man's face is comparatively dull but shines in spring.

Teeth

Teeth enamel is necessary for their protection. It keeps the outer surface of teeth very hard and soft inside. If a bacterium somehow makes a way in a tooth, it immediately destroys the interior. The bacterium breeds innumerable black colored off-springs that discharge a poison that goes into the stomach with food and adulterates the blood.

Birth

Man is made up of cells. Each cell even if divided remains complete. This cell is in fact a small granule containing a black spot. Even after sub-division, the black spot is present in each part of the cell. It is present in the womb but cannot have the potential to divide and sub-divide without man's semen. The moment semen comes in contact with it, it starts dividing and sub-dividing and gets involved in the construction of genes. Some cells make ears, some heart, and other human parts. Since an ever-seeing eye is up there, therefore it has never happened that instead of heart, an ear appears and in place of an eye, a mouth.

Man's semen is made up of ten elements: oxygen, hydrogen, carbon, ozone, nitrogen, sulphur, phosphorus, potassium, lime, and iron. These elements have no brains and senses. But look at the nature's workmanship that parts prepared from these elements, have brain and senses.

We created man from compound semen and gave him the power to see how he uses these Divine bounties. Dahar 2.

A man while relaxing in a room, consumes about 25 cubic centimeter oxygen in an hour. After eating, the consumption increases to 36,000 cubic cm and during exercise, it reaches up to 80,000 cubic cm. In winter, human body needs more oxygen to keep it warm, and that is why one feels hunger more than in summer.

We get five things in our food: water, fats, salts, hydrogenated oxygen and carbon compounds, and nitrogenated compounds. Compound No. 4 is called carbohydrate and the fifth one is called proteins. Carbon and hydrogen of fatty foods when mixed with oxygen create greater quantity of energy. Because of excessive water content, proteins have lesser energy.

Milk is a very good food from all the aspects. A man daily needs about three pounds [ca. 1.36 kg] of food. All the people of world daily consume about 6 billion pounds [2.722 million tons] of food. Some quantity of nitrogen of our body is consumed in the growth of our nails and hair and the rest is discharged through urine and sweats. Hair daily consumes 0.029 gm and nails, 0.7 gm of nitrogen. A cyclist discharges 2.55 kg sweat in just four hrs of which, 0.065 gm is nitrogen and 1.67 gm salt.

During menstruation, a woman daily discharges 0.84 gm nitrogen. In case of hunger, both nitrogen and fats are burnt. During work, only fats are burnt. Carbohydrates burn, both while resting and while working. They do not burn outside but in human body, it burns fast. Fats melt outside but after becoming part of body, it hardly dissolves. Heat in the body is in accordance with the area of body. That is why, a tall man feels hungrier compared to small man.

Vitamins

Vitamins are an important element of the living system. Till now, we know about five types of vitamins: Vitamin A, Vitamin B, Vitamin C, Vitamin D and Vitamin E.

1) In the absence of Vitamin A, body growth stops and eyelids get a disease. This vitamin is present in fish oil, butter and eggs.

2) Absence of Vitamin B results in weak legs.

3) Absence of Vitamin C may result in scurvy.

4) Rest of the Vitamin Bs are necessary for growth. These are found in fruits, eggs and grains.

5) Vitamin C is abundantly found in fruits and vegetables and very useful for blood cleansing, freshness of brain and luxuriance.

6) Deficiency of Vitamin E causes neuromuscular problems. This deficiency can be compensated by using vegetables, oils and leaves.

Food Digestion

After just passing through the throat, food goes into

stomach the walls of which secrete a juice. This juice is very sour and helps in the digestion of food that ultimately becomes body part. Even human spit also helps in the process of digestion.

Question: How could this juice accumulate in the stomach before hand?

Answer: Suppose food is cooking and its fragrance reaches us. Nose immediately informs the brain that in turn directs both stomach and mouth to develop juices for digestion. This way, mouth starts watering and stomach starts producing juice. Sometimes even the mere sound of plates can cause water in the mouth.

A Joke

An English boy told his friends that a platoon of army is coming towards us. I will do one such thing that their drums and flutes would stop giving music. When the platoon came close by, the boy started sucking a lemon. With just the imagination of sourness, their mouths watered and so were not able to blow their instruments.

Liver

Liver is the treasure and sends energy where ever is required. When body parts and nerves are working they need sugar that is provided by the liver and through blood, it reaches the place where it is needed.

When food reaches the stomach, three types of juices mix in it: one is secreted by the walls of stomach; second comes from liver; and third juice is produced by pancreas.

If a liver gets infected, it releases bile, the body, eyes and face gets pale. This disease is called jaundice.

Kidney's Gland Juice

There is a gland near kidneys that secretes such a juice that increases blood pressure. It does not allow reduction in blood circulation and the pulse rate becomes normal. Its composition includes carbon (59), hydrogen (7.1), oxygen (26.2), and nitrogen (7.7). In fear, this gland secretes more juices that increase the blood circulation.

Thyroid Gland

This gland secretes a very useful fluid. If due to some reason, this juice is not able to reach all the body parts, the gland swells to secrete more juices. This effort of gland leads to permanent appearance of glands, prevalent in those areas where water is iodine-deficient. Iodine is a very important part of our body system. If it is absent from water, its deficiency is covered by thyroid gland and that is why it swells.

If in ten million drops of water, just one drop of this juice is added, and if the water has toddlers, they will very quickly become adults.

Think how Allah has managed various means for the development of human body and how "health clinic" has been established within the human body that has bottles of antidotes arranged with great care.

And what bounties of Allah would you falsify. Ar-Rahman.

Essence of Food

After digestion, food passes through a duct and to the large intestine and on its way, keeps on leaving behind fats, sugar, carbohydrates, and other parts of food. All these elements after absorption by the interior of intestine, go into the blood while excrete goes out of the orifice.

Carbohydrates are like coal for human engine while proteins repair the damaged parts of the engine.

Breath

When we breathe air, after passing through the main duct and into two smaller ducts goes straight into the lungs. There is a nerve between the lungs and the stomach that is under pressure while breathing makes the stomach swell time and again. There is air and blood in the lungs but both have separate compartments. There are two advantages of air in the lungs: one, right from here, fresh air mixes with the blood, and two, when we yawn, lungs are stressed. The air present in the lungs make the pressure the way springs of a mattress absorbs shocks. Many a time in the day, we feel the need to contract lungs to send blood to other parts of the body. For example in dark night, when we suddenly hear an unusual sound at an unexpected time, we at once stop breathing and send blood in the lungs to brain and ears so that we may know the truth behind the sound. Body needs to work more while in open sun, more dirt is created that is extracted by the lungs by breathing in shorter intervals. This is called panting.

Heart has two parts: right and left. Right side sends blood to the lungs where it is purified and enters the left side and on to rest of the body.

On all the orifices of veins, there are a few muscles that when required, shuts the mouths of blood vessels. Suppose a student is studying. At that time, his brain needs more blood while his stomach needs lesser. That is why the orifices of vessels of stomach shut down and the blood is directed towards brain. Blood would come to the stomach after eating and the mouths of blood vessels would automatically shut down.

Blood Circulation

With the help of air pressure, heart's pump sends blood to the entire body. Two things send blood to the lungs: one, the flow of blood coming to lungs that makes the slow moving blood as fast moving, and two, when we stiff up, all the veins get tight that causes blood to move forward.

Blood from all parts of the body goes back straight in the heart however blood in the intestines along with the stock of sugar first enters the liver and from there, into the heart. Speed of blood in thin veins is slow to collect impurities from each part of the vein and convey the required food properly.

Carbon and Breathing

Carbon is a pre-requisite for the system of breathing. There must be 5.6% carbon under the lungs, failing which the system of breathing will be disturbed. While breathing, more carbon is discharged and that is why a patient breathes slowly so that the required quantity of carbon is retained in the body. If greater quantity of carbon is accumulated in the lungs, a patient breathes in quick successions to breathe the carbon out.

War and Breathing

In ancient times, wild people used to bring their enemies out of caves by making smoke. The people of Greece used sulphur smoke for that purpose. In Crimean War, Lord Donald suggested using sulphur against the enemy, but sentiments of mercy came in the way. In April 1915, white clouds of Chlorine gas emerged from German trenches and moved towards the French. Their throats clogged, they stopped breathing and lost sight. In September of the same year, British forces responded the Germans with the same coin.

In WW-I (1914-18), twenty five types of poisonous gases were used affecting 80,000 people of whom, 16,000 died and the rest bore the agony for the rest of their lives.

Blood

Blood has two types of cells: red and white. Red cells are called hemoglobin that contain greater quantity of iron and absorb oxygen. If these are put to air pressure, they would at once absorb oxygen. And if pressure is released, oxygen would be released.

When blood enters lungs it accepts oxygen due to air pressure and when it reaches such parts of the body that lack oxygen, air pressure reduces and oxygen is automatically released.

When blood goes back towards lungs, a large quantity of sodium mixes with it on its way back. According to the principle, red blood cells and sodium absorb carbon and on its way back to the lungs, blood sweeps carbon and conveys to the lungs where through a chemical reaction, carbon is separated and exhaled while blood goes back along with sodium. Sodium stops on its way and the blood moves into veins.

Red blood cells are prepared in the marrow of large bones. Each red cell works just for ten days after which it looses its utility, goes in the spleen which serves as the dust bin.

Blood circulation in winters is slow and that is why body color becomes bluish. This in fact is impurity that adds to the blood on its way back.

White blood cells are of different shapes: round, long, flat, etc. The reason is that human body gets different types of injuries. While reaching the location of wound, these cells block the outlet of veins and like bricks, makes layers till the wound heals. These cells fight with diseases. Pus that comes out of an abscess is in fact dead bodies of white blood cells.

Brain

Our brain 'swims' in the strong 'castle' of skull. Benefit of the fluid is that brain does not hit the skull bones while moving up or down. Backbone comes out of the brain and up to the back. Hundreds of its vessels spread into the entire human body. The way there are two wires of telephone (receivers and transmitters) similarly, to convey and receive messages from all the body part, we have nerves. For example, if an insect crawls on our leg, one such wire at once informs the brain and the other wire orders the hand to shoo the insect.

Since some of the times some body parts need more blood. That is why brain can order nerves and body parts to get or stop blood. Suppose a man intends to attack us, brain would at once command different parts of the body, our eyebrows would stifle, nostrils would expand, eyes would bulge and go red, hand would take the form of a fist, while heart would start beating faster so that it can deliver sufficient quantity of blood to various parts of the body that are to be put to use during defense.

Bodily agony is a blessing of Allah. This in fact is a message to the brain to be cautious about the impending danger. Had there been no bodily agonies, millions of people would die before death. Suppose a abscess appears in the brain. Or a man pierces a knife in our heart. If brain is not informed, we will obviously die without a cure.

We are walking in a dark night and suddenly, the hissing sound of a snake reaches our ears. Ears inform the brain and the brain immediately orders to jump and we jump; and out of harm's way.

When we listen some extremely horrible news, the entire blood of heart goes up to brain so that it can think of a remedial measure. This way, even death may occur. While seeing a snake, all blood of small birds goes in to the brain, they become numb and are thus 'a piece of cake' for the snake. Some of the nerves can be damaged by Uric Acid and at the time of danger, orders of brain cannot reach the desired destination; to adopt precautionary measures. That is why such people get senseless.

Since there is an elaborate system of nerves going out of brain to the entire body therefore if during a war, these nerves are severed by a bullet around the back, the lower body would become motionless; paralyzed rather. And if these nerves get damaged that reach the eyes and ears, a man would go blind and won't be able to hear.

Brain has two parts: one, internal that is white; and two external that is grey. Both are interconnected. External part of the brain has a lot of bumps that are in fact the central system of feeling, inclusive and cogent. Some bumps relate to shim, some to imagination, some to academics, and some to maths, for example. If due to shock, any of these bumps is damaged, that human sense would be impaired or lost altogether. That is why some students are weak in maths while others are weak in English. Even the smallest brain is 16 oz [ca. 454 gm] and the largest is 64 oz [ca 1,814 gm].

Hands and Feet

Our hands and feet have 106 bones of which, only hand have 54 bones. Be sure that first 58 bones were made and then after placing them systematically, a net of vessels was spread and then covered with skin. Now be honest and tell that this work is more difficult or blowing spirit in readymade bones?

Does man think that We will not assemble his bones? Yes. [We are] Able [even] to proportion his fingertips. Qayamatah, 3,4.

To cut it short, human body is a wonderful machine, each part of which is a description of Allah's supreme workmanship. Let's sing in honor of that supreme Creator:

Who created you, proportioned you, and balanced you? In whatever form He willed has He assembled you. Anfataar, 7,8.

Chapter-XI

Explanation of Various Physical Signs

As mentioned in the beginning of this book, that the number of Ayaat Kuniya reaches 756, the explanation of some of which has been given earlier; some more Ayaat would be explained but precisely.

$$(1)$$

الْحَمْدُ لِلّهِ رَبِّ الْعٰلَمِيْنَ ۟

This Ayat has been mentioned at different occasions. Here it is just said that there used to be great influence of praise and criticism on mutual relationships of various Arab tribes. Those tribes that were praised by poets remained intoxicated with pride and those that were criticized and belittled would stay put in disgrace for a long time. How? Let's see what a poet says about a tribe:

Had I been in a match with such a Hashemite whose maternal uncle were the sons of Abdul Madan, I would have taken this match lightly. But just see, what type of lowly people I have been asked to fight.

A poet says about Bani Anf:

This tribe is the 'nose' of the world, and rest of the tribes are 'tail'. Just how could there be a relationship between a nose and a tail.

Besides praise and criticism, some poets used to present exaggerated poems in honor of the rich chieftains. When Mughirah bin Sh'abah goes in the court of Persian Army Chief, Rustam, what he sees is that people bow down to show their respect for him. Even people would go into prostration and doorsteps are kissed and great titles like Your Honor, Your Exalted Excellence, etc. are given even to ordinary aristocracy. Seeing this, Mughirah wonders and says:

I have not seen any nation more stupid than yours. We the Arabians do not consider one another as gods. And some of you are worshipping others. These acts are a cause of shame for you.

In short, to stop Arab poets from creating troubles and to free the Muslim Nation from flattery and sycophancy, it was ordered that "All the praises are but for Allah" and that's it. Just see how this one Ayat might have stopped disarray while how the minds of Arab poets might have be freed of man-worship and praises and obsequiousness and diverted to write poems in the praises of Allah. Moreover, how lessons of high morality might have been given to the entire Arab nation and whatever one got, whether directly (e.g., light, air and other related natural bounties) or indirectly (e.g., knowledge, service, rewards and presents, etc.), was all because of Allah's Benevolence.

(2)

وَإِذْ قَالَ رَبُّكَ لِلْمَلَٰٓئِكَةِ ۝

Here a question arises as to what angels are? 2:30

Ans: man got logic because of environment and because of the combination of earth and fire. If that is the case, then why the rest of universe that too is decidedly composed of the same elements, is deprived of logic. Greek philosophers had acknowledged the presence of uqul-e-A'shrah in the universe. The other name of these very brains is angels.

We observe various living things and of different types: for example earthworm, fish, and quadruped. Then there are different types of quadruped for example, mouse, cat, rabbit, deer, wolf, bear, cheetah, tiger, etc. After all these, comes the man. Is man the last destination of life? Could we not think of another creature that might be invisible? A stone does not have sex, anger and brains. Animal does have sex and anger but no logic. Man has all the three attributes. And then can we not think of another creature that has brains but no sex, no anger?

In human world, man works as supervisor in various walks of life. Someone is a judge, another one is a military commander while someone else is a governor. But then could it not be that there are small-scale supervisors looking after clouds and wind and heat that in Vedic are called 'deity' [devta] and in the Qur'anic jargon 'angel'?

(3) Muhkamaat[50] *and Mutashabihaat*[51]

There are two types of Ayaat in the Qur'an: Commands and Similarities. Let's see what these mean:

Commands

Its root is 'hukm' and various derivatives of 'hukm' are:

a) Hukm Hukama, Qazi wa Fazal, i.e., he made a decision or gave details

b) Ahkam, Atqan, i.e., proved through arguments or gave strength

c) Tahkum, Tasarruf wa faq Mashiyattah, i.e., brought changes as he wished

d) Al-Hukmatah: Justice, knowledge, philosophy

---

[50] The word *muhkamaat* is derived from the root *uhkima* which means to decide between two things. It means judgments, decisions and in technical language refers to all clearly decided verses of the Qur'an, mostly those concerning legal rulings, but also to other clear definitions such as between truth and falsehood etc.

[51] Derived from the root '*ishtabaha*' meaning 'to be doubtful'. Qur'anic verses that are not clear and hard to understand.

Rescuer [Al-Munjid]

In light of the literary research, 'Muhkamaat' means those Ayaat that are proven through arguments are detailed, where Allah might have given the details of His wish, that have philosophy and justice and that must be acted upon.

Examples

Allah has repeatedly said that nations that break the rules of law are criminals and as such, cannot live longer. To support this argument, Qur'an mentions at several occasions Pharaoh, Nimrod, A'ad-o-Samud[52] and some other destroyed nations. Therefore, Allah cannot make a nation with bad moral character His deputy.

Western scholars have after centuries of search and research declared that before the formation of earth and skies, there was just smoke. This means that different elements were in the form of smoke flying all around. And then Allah willed that those particles should take the shapes of sun, and moon and earth and Saturn, etc. Therefore all these bodies were given the forms of stars and started revolving in their respective orbits. Qur'an attests the theory of western scholars through this Ayat:

And then Allah decided to create skies. Then the entire universe was smoke. Allah commanded earth and skies to come along and start work, whether they liked it or not. Both of them answered that they were available like most obedient servants.

---

[52] Allah states in the Quran that He had created people of phenomenal size the like of which He has not created since. These were the people of A'ad where Prophet Hud was sent. They were very tall, big, and very powerful. Later these people turned against Allah and the Prophet and transgressed beyond all boundaries set by Allah. As a result they were destroyed.

This and many more Ayaat have proved the authenticity of modern knowledge.

Mutashabihaat

There is a Hadeeth about mutashabihaat [the doubtful ones] that says that no one, save Allah, knows its details. But this Hadeeth does not seem to be correct because modern discoveries have proved lot many such verses to be beyond doubt. For example when Pharaoh drowned, Allah said:

Today, We will conserve your body so that you become a lesson for the coming generations.

For good thirteen hundred years, our scholars wondered as to what is meant by "conserving the body". During the first quarter of 20th Century, when the body of Pharaoh was discovered, the above Ayat that was in the category of "doubtful" has now shifted to "authentic".

Not just in Qur'an even in the universe, there are millions of 'truths' that are 'hidden' from us. Just one hundred years back, who knew what was ether. What is the true nature of color? How many elements do we have? How many stars are there in the universe and what is the status of their orbits? All these were secrets of Nature. In other words, these were 'the doubtful ones' that have been explored and proven to be 'the authentic ones'.

Western scholars said that there were billions of 'highways' in the universe that are used by billions of stars and moons to tread upon. Allah said:

I swear by these heights that have a network of highways.

Western scientists said that this earth has seen such an age when it had no mountain chains. These were rather submerged in water upto 10,000 ft [3,000 m] deep and there was water all around. Allah says:

A time has passed when the Throne of Allah was spread just on water.

Plant specialists say that some plants are male and some female. If any of the two is eradicated, their development and growth would stop and with that, the plants. Allah has declared:

Earth creates complete pairs of male and female.

Sir James Jeans says that after studying the astrology for good forty years, I have concluded that to understand an author, it is a pre-requisite to first read his books. By the same analogy, to understand Allah, one must first read the Heavenly Book, the Qur'an. The more we study the Book of Allah, the more the curtains are removed from His greatness and wisdom, and appear to be coming closer to the horizon. And when He comes closer, eyes and heart drops in prostration. Himalayas look like a mound from a distance but from nearby, it shudder the spines even of a tiger. Likewise, ignorance is the distance which, when comes between man and Allah, looks small. As against this, knowledge is the ladder that takes us closer to Allah. Approaching Allah, we get dumbfounded by the mere glory and sublimity. Now let's just see what Allah thinks:

See those mountains having red and white and black layers of stones ... Remember! Only the knowledgeable can be afraid of Allah.

The crux of these explanations is that hundreds of Qur'anic Ayaat that were (so-called) doubtful are now scientifically proved. 'Doubtful' are in fact those hidden facts that could be made bare only through knowledge. Let's keep it in mind that 'knowledge' does not mean 'the so-called knowledge' of mullah that it should remain limited to puddings and roasted chickens. It is rather that unlimited knowledge of nature whose institutions can only be found in the West.

Inspite of the fact that discoveries have solved the

mystery of 'doubt' of some Ayaat but the Qur'an has hundreds of Ayaat that are still a mystery; and Allah knows how long they would remain so. Allah says:

Allah created you from the wombs of your mothers. <u>This was a creation after another creation, in three darknesses</u>.

Read all the literature about cosmography of fetus. You won't be able to find the explanation of the 'underlined' sentence. Recently a friend returned from the States who had great interest in biology. He said that in the USA, a biologist had discovered the fact that cells that make genes, split into three parts: one part is till the back, second, from back to neck, and the third makes the human head. And nature has created layers among the three groups. Quite possible, 'three darknesses' might mean these three layers. Similarly, 'seven skies' is a mystery. Western researchers have till now been able to discover only three 'transparent walls' one of which stops electrical impulses, second, sound and the third stops ultra-violet rays boiling like a volcanic mountain, just a few hundred miles above. If Allah would create a breach in these 'transparent walls', life on earth would come to an end within no time.

When these mysteries would be solved, no one knows. Each day there is a discovery. And a day would definitely come when all the 'doubtful' Ayat would be transformed to 'clearly decided verses'. But rest assured, it will not be the Muslims doing it. It will rather be again the non-Muslims, the Europeans. As for the Muslims, they will remain under the misconception that they are the "chosen ones" and would go straight to the Paradise. Remember what Ross Keppel said about Muslims; though jokingly?

Ayaat that look 'doubtful' are because of our lack of knowledge. The is like an author who has the feelings (of ignorance) about maths and of course, the ups and downs of music for a mullah. But the same are decided knowledges for a mathematician and a musician. Similarly, some of the facts are fictions and doubts for us. That will however one day be seen by those who have the vision and insight and not the ones who do ablution, pray and expect Allah to send all of his bounties to his wellbeing. Allah says:

In fact the Qur'anic Ayaat are those realties the explanation for which is with Allah.

Explanation of the 'Mother of Books'

Whether the system of Cosmology of Galen was correct or wrong, we don't know however this much we can say that it was the mother of all the systems that followed. Today, a lot of changes have occurred in Darwin's Theory of Evolution. But we have no escape to acknowledge that his theory was the father of all the theories that followed his theory. Had Darwin not presented this queer thought, the other researchers might not have considered that even now. Hipparchus[53], Theory of Months and Year; of Democritus[54], Atomic Theory; and of Heraclitus[55] Theory of Revolution of Earth were all the initiators of debate on such important theories.

---

[53] Hipparchus of Nicaea (c. 190– 120 BC), was a Greek astronomer, geographer, and mathematician of the Hellenistic period. He is considered the founder of trigonometry but is most famous for his incidental discovery of precession of the equinoxes. He is considered the greatest ancient astronomical observer and, by some, the greatest overall astronomer of antiquity. He was the first whose quantitative and accurate models for the motion of the Sun and Moon survive. He developed trigonometry and constructed trigonometric tables, and solved several problems of spherical trigonometry. With his solar and lunar theories and his trigonometry, he may have been

See next page

Now let's go out from the world of knowledge to the world of morals and ask the people that do nations get destroyed if they lie and are dishonest? Everyone that you ask would say where is the relationship between these vices and the national existence? Who could make them understand that right from Hazrat Adam till this day, thousands of nations have been destroyed just because of these two vices. These are the basic elements that invite other evils. Or the thought that worldly pleasures can be achieved through Eiman, is again a quaint thought. All these theories and thoughts have been described by Allah in details in the Qur'an. And these theories are basic, necessary for national existence and according to Qur'an, are 'Mother of Books'.

Qur'an turns our attention to the following modern theories in details or in brief:

---

the first to develop a reliable method to predict solar eclipses. His other reputed achievements include the discovery and measurement of Earth's precession, compilation of the first comprehensive star catalog of the western world, and possibly the invention of the astrolabe, also of the armillary sphere, which he used during the creation of much of the star catalogue. It would be three centuries before Claudius Ptolemaeus' synthesis of astronomy would supersede the work of Hipparchus.

[54] Democritus (c. 460 – c. 370 BC) was an ancient Greek philosopher. A pupil of Leucippus, he was an influential pre-Socratic philosopher who formulated an atomic theory for the universe. His exact contributions are difficult to disentangle from those of his mentor Leucippus, as they are often mentioned together in texts. Their speculation on atoms, bears a passing and partial resemblance to the nineteenth-century understanding of atomic structure that has led some to regard Democritus as more of a scientist than other Greek philosophers. He was well known to Aristotle. Many consider Democritus to be the "father of modern science".   See next page

a) Theory of Evolution

b) Theory of Particles

c) Theory of Earth's Orbiting

d) Theory of Sun's Orbiting

e) Theory of Female Plants

f) Theory of Existence of Aslah

g) Theory of Ether

h) Theory of Life after Death

i) Theory of Death in Life (i.e., sleep) and

j) Theory of Happiness and Sadness

And many many, more theories.

If today, Herzel has proved that sun orbits, he has not done something special. Why? Because it is already mentioned in the Qur'an! Same is true of so many other researchers. Problems and theories mentioned in the Divine treatises and the Qur'an are those basic things that were used to raise the level of human knowledge to its present heights.

---

[55] Heraclitus of Ephesus (c. 540-480) stands primarily for the radical thesis that 'Everything is in flux', like the constant flow of a river. Although it is likely that he took this thesis to be true, universal flux is too simple a phrase to identify his philosophy. His great truth is that 'All things are one', but this unity, far from excluding difference, opposition and change, actually depends on them, since the universe is in a continuous state of dynamic equilibrium. Day and night, up and down, living and dying, heating and cooling – such pairings of apparent opposites all conform to the everlastingly rational formula that unity consists of opposites; remove day, and night goes too, just as a river will lose its identity if it ceases to flow.

Interpretation

Qur'an has certain Ayaat regarding Metaphysics that can be justified however if a person who interprets it with bad intentions, a lot of chaos can be raised. Wrong interpretation of *'Kahtimun-Nabiyeen'* has resulted in nine prophets till now. The non-Qur'anic explanation of the Ayat "*Li ullil kitaba ....*" resulted in the birth of Mu'atazils; "*Yaghfiruz-zunubaba jamee'an*" caused Majah; "*Wa lahul asma-ul-husna*" created Ma'alumiyah; "*Wa ma tashawan illa an-yasha-Allah*" resulted in *Jabariyah*; and the wrong interpretation of "*Wa man-yasha falyoumin*" resulted in *Qadriyah*. How much damage have these sects inflicted to our basic principles, should be asked by the historians.

The Purpose

Following is the main purpose of what has been said above:

a) that with the evolution of knowledge, 'doubtfuls' are being converted to 'factuals';

b) that facts explained by the Qur'an are those foundations [Mother Book] that resulted in the sky-scrapping buildings of knowledge; and

c) that there is a possibility of wrong interpretation of the 'doubtfuls' and a lot of pugnacity can be created because of that

After these explanations, let's see what the following Ayat has for us:

Allah has given you a book that has some Ayaat as "Muhkam" and those are the "Mother of Books". Then there are certain "Mutashabihaat" as well that are misused by the bad-intentioned people to create chaos. Correct explanation of these mutashabihaat are either known to

Allah or those who posses great knowledge. Such people believe in facts and they say that fountain head of truth is Allah. And it is a fact that whether there are mutashbihaat or muhkamaat, it is the wise man that can benefit from them.

(4) Diversity of Day and Night

Indeed, in the creation of the heavens and earth, and the alternation of the night and the day, and the [great] ships which sail through the sea which benefits people, and what Allah has sent down from the heavens of rain, giving life thereby to the earth after its lifelessness and dispersing therein every [kind of] moving creature, and [His] directing of the winds and the clouds controlled between the heaven and the earth are signs for a people who use reason. Baqarah, 164.

The difference of day and night is a great blessing. Because of the nearness or farness of sun, we have simultaneously winter and summer, and spring and autumn. If you get embarrassed by the intense heat of Africa, go to Europe. And if the snows of Russia trouble you, go to India or Australia.

Had there been just one type of season in the entire world, the man, who likes diversity, would have been fed up with monotony. If sun was to be static at one place, people in some countries would have died of heat and of others, of cold.

.... And Allah determines [the extent of] the night and the day........Muzammil, 20.

Apple ripens in winter and melon in summer. If there were cold in the world for ever, man would have been deprived of all the fruits of summer. It is just because of the movement of sun, that heat and cold are almost equally distributed over the world. That is why everywhere one can get fruits of all types.

The sun and the moon [move] by precise calculation.

Rahman, 5.

Sun does not set rather becomes invisible from one part of the world. The morning of schools with some intervals, start in Delhi, then Peshawar, then Iran, Arabia, Africa, and then after crossing Atlantic, to America. When in Madras it is 5:22 p.m., at that time in Mexico, it will be 5:20 a.m., midday in London, evening in Shanghai, and in Egypt, afternoon. In Australia, people would be sleeping and the people in Berlin would be preparing lunch.

This change of seasons and differences in day and night are great blessings of Allah. It is very much in the right of Allah to make the hottest day of June 21, two years long, or make the night of December 21, six years long. But do you know its implications? The long day of June 21 would cause fires all around while the cold night of December 21 would freeze the blood of all the human beings and animals alike. And in both the cases, life would be wiped. Allah says:

> Say, "Have you considered: if Allah should make for you the night continuous until the Day of Resurrection, what deity other than Allah could bring you light? Then will you not hear?" Say, "Have you considered: if Allah should make for you the day continuous until the Day of Resurrection, what deity other than Allah could bring you a night in which you may rest? Then will you not see?" And out of His mercy He made for you the night and the day that you may rest therein and [by day] seek from His bounty and [that] perhaps you will be grateful. Al-Qasas, 71-73

(5) Circumlocution of Winds

The ever-changing direction of winds is also a blessing of Allah; so that clouds could be moved to any part of the world. Wind in fact is a sort of 'pillion' for clouds. If due to some reason, winds stop blowing, then electricity moves it. Sometimes wind speed reaches upto 120 miles [ca. 194 km] an hr. Storms of such a velocity can even pick frogs and fruits and throw them elsewhere and the people would start thinking that these are coming from the skies.

Clouds are generally at a height of about 16,000 ft [ca. 4,850 m]. Had the clouds been lower, everything down here would have been soaked in moisture. And had clouds been too high up, hails would have formed and while coming down, would have torn through ceilings, doors and windows destroying everything including our livestock. Moreover, if because of greater distance, we were not able to see the clouds, then rain, snow and hails would have been taking us by surprise, farmers' harvest would have been destroyed and the world at large would have borne a great loss.

Had there been rain with equal intensity everywhere, there would have been jungles all around. The number of snakes and other poisonous animals would have increased tremendously, frogs in the night would not have allowed us to sleep. Because of excessive greenery, man might have started hating landscapes and the tillable land would have been converted into wilderness. It would have been impossible to move easily, and thus journeys of days would have taken months and this land would have been a hell. In fact, the 'habit' of wandering of clouds is Allah's blessing in disguise.

> And [His] directing of the winds and the clouds controlled between the heaven and the earth are signs for a people who use reason. Baqarah, 164.

(6) Life and Death

There are different types of animals. Some crawl, others run, still others fly, till one reaches the status of man. Then in man, there are thousands of different stages: from primitive to the most advanced. In other words, in evolution of life, thousands of stages have passed. If that's true, then would it be difficult for Allah to develop another stage, i.e. the creation of Hereinafter? Not at all!

And you have already known the first creation, so will you not remember? Al-Waqi'ah

The way youth is better than childhood and old age is better than young age, likewise, death is the upper stage of life where life would reach its extreme stage.

Think, that how we made different stages of life that are superior to each other. Similarly, Hereinafter is also a higher and better stage. Bani Israel, 21.

What is Hereinafter? What would be the status of life over there? And what shape would life take? No one knows. We have decreed death among you, and We are not to be outdone. In that We will change your likenesses and produce you in that [form] which you do not know. Al-Waqi'ah, 56:62.

What will be after death, no one knows. I personally believe that a man who remains busy for his entire life, in developing a particular facet of life, completes only after his death. For example, a man remained busy in philanthropy. After death, his efforts would become a reality. But, if a person remains busy in destructive activities, then after death would his mission be completed? Only Allah knows.

Is Life a Dream?

Sometimes I feel that this life is not the life but a dream of life. Our real life was in action before we were born and in fact, will be again in action, but after death. The way a traveler feels asleep and starts seeing a decent dream. Similarly, we have also been taken over by sleep while on our way to Hereinafter. And during the sleep, we woke up, got education, got pension, became old and died and just by coincidence, our eyes opened and found out:

Dream it was, whatever we saw and heard, and was a fiction.

Each night while sleeping, we see that we are eating, playing, appearing in exams, feel happy to pass, cry over agonies and if a snake follows us, we make noise. But in the morning when our eyes open, we come to know that the entire dream of last night was just a fiction. If in case we do not wake up for forty years, we would consider our life during sleep to be our real life. Here naturally, a question arises: is life a reality or a dream?

The Prophet says:

People are sleeping and will wake up when they die.

Each night the drama of sleep makes a declaration that there is no dearth of bodies. Our bodies remain on the bed while our souls sitting wander around. That 'dream body' passes through happy and sad states, the same way as the physical bodies. If that is so, then is it not possible that our souls enter a similar 'dream body' after death and our near and dear ones are with us as we are each night in dream? What is dream? A light experiment of death and Hereinafter! That is why Allah says:

Allah takes the souls at the time of their death, and those that do not die [He takes] during their sleep. Zumr, 42.

Allama Iqbal has given some unusual arguments about the permanence of life, and says:

a) When after each evening, morning comes, then is there no morning of the evening of death?

b) When seed falls on earth, it becomes a tree. Will man become nothing after going into the earth?

c) These blue ignescents are glowing since millions of years. Man is like sun in the company of universe, then is our sun inferior to the stars?

d) Before flying, a bird wraps its wings. Death is like wrapping up of wings. Does this mean that there would be no further flight?

e) Death of a bunch is a message of cheeriness for the

flower. If so, then is death of man not the message of flourishness?

f) You are enjoying on a river bank. A ship arrives from the east and disappears in the blue waters towards west. Same is the case of man: death hides it from eyes but cannot erase.

g) Look, there is a spring coming down from a mountain. At the point of impact, there is a world of drops. The same drops flow and mix in a stream. The same way like waterfall, life came down from extreme heights. Life is water drops, millions of types of people appeared that after sometime, mixed in the larger stream of life. Name of this meeting is death but in fact, this is the real life.

h) A car maker makes full efforts that his car should be strong and stable. Allah is the maker of man. Will He not like to see His creation to be strong and stable?

Rain and Death

When it rains, earth's internal potentials wake up and make the landscape a bed of colors and fragrance. Death is like rain over the 'earth of human bodies' that makes the life more beautiful, more attractive and more colorful.

When a nation become lazy, become greedy and indulges in profligacy, death rains on them like mercy and such nations become alive once again. Sick Turkey was given a lease of life by the sword of Allied forces. Old Russia was re-invigorated by the German firework while the death and destructions of WW-II have made the world more beautiful.

And it is Allah who sends the winds, and they stir the clouds, and We drive them to a dead land and give life thereby to the earth after its lifelessness. Thus is the resurrection. Fatir, 9.

Fear of Death

Almost all the people are afraid of death. Some are so because they are cowards and they fear darkness, whether of night or of grave. Alas! Had they known that death is not darkness; it is rather an illuminant world where mild rays of moon play in springs, and sensualities dance. Some are afraid of death lest they are sent to Hell. This fear can be cured by becoming chaste. And still, there are some who want to live to see the end of WW-II or see the decision about the fate of India[56]. This thought can be controlled through different ways. First, it is quite possible that even after death, we can remain in touch with the happenings of this world. In this regard, certain Ahadeeth are available. Second, then why should I be worried about the story where a cow came and a donkey went. Third, a lot of political revolutions came before our birth and we were not there. India was ruled by Chandra Gupta Mauriya[57], Bikram

---

[56] The author lived and wrote this book while 2nd World War was still raging and the British were still ruling the un-divided India.

[57] Chandragupta Maurya (340 BC – 298 BC) was the founder of the Mauryan Empire and the first emperor to unify India into one state. He ruled from 322 BC until his voluntary retirement and abdication in favor of his son Bindusara in 298 BC. Prior to his consolidation of power, most of South Asia was ruled by small states, while the Nanda Dynasty dominated the Gangetic Plains. Chandragupta succeeded in conquering and subjugating almost all the Indian subcontinent by the end of his reign. His empire extended from Bengal and Assam in the east, to Afghanistan and Balochistan, eastern and south-east Iran in the west, to Kashmir in the north, and to the Deccan Plateau in the south. It was the largest empire yet seen in Indian history.

Jeet, Asoka[58], and the Mogul Emperor Akbar, but we were not there. The same land has the privilege where Ram Chandra Jee and Krishna Jee were born and we were not around. Sometime in the past, Mehmood of Ghazni[59] trotted from here like a hurricane, but alas, we were not there. If all these changes and revolutions came in our absence and we have no regrets, then why to worry when tomorrow Jawahir Lal Nehru or Mohammad Ali Jinnah would be the president of India and we won't be around.

Some people are afraid of death because they cannot tolerate the separation of their near and dear ones. They must know that death cannot bring separation. Each night while sleeping, we meet our children and brothers and sisters. Then is it not possible that their sleeping bodies would be with us when we die? If we can meet here in dreams, why not that context be continued then?

Still there are more people who say that their children are small and without any source. Their only source of

---

[58] Ashoka Maurya (304–232 BC) was an Indian emperor of the Maurya Dynasty who ruled almost the entire Indian subcontinent from ca. 269 to 232 BC. He reigned over most of present-day India after a number of military conquests. His empire stretched from the parts of the ancient territories of Khorasan, Sistan and Balochistan, Afghanistan and possibly eastern Iran to Bangladesh, Assam in the east, and as far south as northern Kerala and Andhra Pradesh. The empire had Taxila, Ujjain and Pataliputra as its capital.

[59] Mahmud of Ghazni (971 – 1030), was the most prominent ruler of the Ghaznavid Empire. In the name of Islam, he conquered the eastern Iranian lands and the northwestern Indian subcontinent from 997 to his death in 1030. Mahmud turned the former provincial city of Ghazna into the wealthy capital of an extensive empire which covered most of today's Afghanistan, eastern Iran, Pakistan and northwestern India.

living is their fathers' earnings. They are afraid because if they die, their children would be doomed. Such people must be sure that each and every act of Allah is for their betterment. If Allah sees that the children would have no one to support them, and even then He calls their father then He must have thought of something better for them; something that is beyond our inferior faculty of thinking.

Moreover, we see new countries in dreams and meet new people. With some of them, we even develop a relationship of love. When we wake up in the morning, there is not even a trace of that relationship. It is just possible that this life is a dream and when we wake up after death, we may not have even a faintest though of this world crossing our minds.

One forgets ones relatives in dream. It is quite possible that we forget our relatives and when we wake up after death, we may meet them again.

Anyhow we are not familiar with the contours of life-after-death. The Qur'an while referring to the life of a martyr, has tried to keep the stance of that world hidden from us.

"They are dead." Rather, they are alive, but you perceive [it] not. Baqarah, 154.

Death is Anyhow a Blessing

This is so because:

a) This keeps the nations alive

b) Those in troubles, get rid of them

c) Death is a new world and anything new is more attractive

d) Death will unfurl the mysteries of life

e) Death is sort of transport that will take us to Allah

Then they His servants are returned to Allah, their true Lord. Unquestionably, His is the judgment, and He is the swiftest of accountants. An'am, 62.

(7) Allah is a Mathematician

In the past pages it has been said that the setting of universe was done from elements. The protection of this 'setting' is a miracle. Making water from hydrogen and oxygen and its protection is an extremely time-consuming responsibility, being diligently handled by a Supreme Power. Today if this Power removes its control, the entire universe would go wayward. Elements would dissolve and run towards their center and all that would be left, would be just smoke. Life is the second name of contexture of elements and death is the dissolution of elements. This contexture and dissolution occur in accordance with the Will of Allah.

To create different things from these elements in precise proportions is not possible without Supreme Knowledge. How various things have been created from mixing a number of elements and in exact proportions, can only be understood by a Chemist.

This is a fact that all the plants and animals are composed of oxygen, hydrogen, carbon, nitrogen, and some salts. Though elements are just these few but the number of compounds prepared can be judged from the fact that today, we know of about 1,400,000 plants and 300,000 animals. Composing such a lot of things from such a small number of elements, is a living example of the extreme Miracle of Creation, and there is a proof for that:

And He is the subjugator over His servants, and He sends over you guardian-angels until, when death comes to one of you, Our messengers take him, and they do not fail [in their duties]. Then they His servants are returned to Allah, their true Lord.

Unquestionably, His is the judgment, and He is the swiftest of accountants. An'am, 61,62.

(8)

[All] praise is [due] to Allah, who created the heavens and the earth and made the darkness and the light. Then those who disbelieve equate [others] with their Lord. It is He who created you from clay and then decreed a term and a specified time [known] to Him; then [still] you are in dispute. An'am, 1-2

Man was made of dark clay but Allah established lights in it at several places; phosphorus in bones, devitrification in eyes, and the light of senses in brain.

Man has wrath, sex, moral darkness but also the light of wisdom.

Coal is all darkness and fatal. But it is because of it that nations live. Petrol is it the sweat of coal that is used by nations to get power. Light in cities is because of coal. Trains are running because of coal. Now just think how intense is the craftsmanship with which light and darkness within coal have been combined.

Diversity in universe is of various types, like solids, for example iron, stones, liquids, and then, lighter than liquids like smoke; lighter than smoke like gas; lighter than gas like light; lighter than light like ether; and lighter than ether i.e. spirit. Spirit is subtle and body is dense and their blend has given rise to the beauty of Universe.

Knowledge is such a power that can create light out of darkness. Today, scientists in western countries are getting light with the help of steel, coal, etc. Muslims have given up on it since centuries. And thus have been rendered the sleep of death; even if they are (nominally) living.

After passing through different stages of helplessness, childhood, youth, old age and finally, man reaches the stage of wisdom. Same way the mankind after passing through hundreds of stages of barbarism and ferocity, finally attained the status of knowledge and wisdom. Just imagine that how many stages a man had to pass through to travel to light from darkness. Had there been no wisdom, there would not have been any need for light. Had man not passed through the period of darkness, we would not have been able to appreciate the value of knowledge and its application.

As said earlier, life is the contraption of various elements while death is the diffusion of those elements. That is why Allah says:

It is He who created you from clay ... An'am.

When Hazrat Eisa [Jesus] made a bird from clay, everybody was wonderstruck. Each day, Allah creates millions of animals and birds but alas, no one feels to wonder.

(9)

Inclining [only] to Allah , not associating [anything] with Him. And he who associates with Allah - it is as though he had fallen from the sky and was snatched by the birds or the wind carried him down into a remote place. Hajj, 31.

In the above Ayat, 'Teer' can be considered as aeroplane and 'reeh' as gas. Today, each aging nation can be killed with the help of these two means.

Those who make laziness, greed, and selfishness their ways of life, they are thrown from throne to floor by those who act, are brave, and hardworking such that all the facets of their life pulverized. India's history is replete with such events.

(10)

Allah is the Light of the heavens and the earth. The example of His light is like a niche within which is a lamp, the lamp is within glass, the glass as if it were a pearly [white] star lit from [the oil of] a blessed olive tree, neither of the east nor of the west, whose oil would almost glow even if untouched by fire. Light upon light. Allah guides to His light whom He wills. And Allah presents examples for the people, and Allah is Knowing of all things. An-Nur, 35.

Allah is Noor (Light) that is restless to appear. And this entire universe is also all Noor. Therefore Allah is noor over noor.

This earth was created from sun and sun was taken out from galaxy. Off-springs of noor are also noor. Therefore we must acknowledge that from a particle of desert upto the stars in skies, everything is made up of noor. Some things are apparently black but have a world of noor into it. Strike stone with a stone, and produce fire. Petrol and oil are brimming with noor. Electricity is dancing in the monsoon clouds. Gardens and farmlands are full of flowers that look like ambers. Light and glows at the waterfall of Jogindar Nagar is such that the entire Punjab looks like one enormous light bulb. Silkworm makes beautiful silk for those who love to wear soft and smooth clothes. Stone turns into sculpture and iron into sword and makes us wonder.

Each scene of universe is a complete lighthouse. Somewhere noor is naked, for example in glow-worm and sun but elsewhere, is undercover, for example in iron, coal, oil, wood, and water. Water is composed of two gases, both of which are inflammable. The entire universe is composed of electrons and these particles are somewhere in the form of stars, elsewhere flowers and fruits. In short, each and every vein of universe is full of waves of noor, restless to appear, bare and naked.

Allah is the Light of the heavens and the earth. The example of His light is like a niche within which is a lamp, the lamp is within glass, the glass as if it were a pearly [white] star lit from [the oil of] a blessed olive tree, neither of the east nor of the west, whose oil would almost glow even if untouched by fire. Light upon light. Allah guides to His light whom He wills. And Allah presents examples for the people, and Allah is

Knowing of all things. Nur, 35.

(11)

Do you not see that Allah drives clouds? Then He brings them together, then He makes them into a mass, and you see the rain emerge from within it. And He sends down from the sky, mountains [of clouds] within which is hail, and He strikes with it whom He wills and averts it from whom He wills. The flash of its lightening almost takes away the eyesight. Nur, 43.

My respectable friend Pir Ghulam Waris, Professor of Chemistry, Govt. College Hoshiarpur has explained the above Ayaat (printed in Tarjuma-e-Qur'an) as follows:

a) *Yuzji subhana*: 'Zaja' means slowly moving, moving with a spear, getting saturated, i.e. Allah slowly moves the clouds after when they get saturated with water. Since spear shines, it may mean electricity.

b) *Yoallifo bainahu*: Alaf is mutual struggle. If in a drop of water positive electricity is produced then the nearest particle will get negative and the next, positive electricity. These drops with opposite charges attract one another and the more they come closer, according to the rule of 'inverse square' their mutual absorption would keep on increasing. It is also called synthesis. '*Baina*' explains that this attraction is inherent in all the drops of cloud.

c) *Ruka mann*: Stacking; conjoin to reduce the volume; making dense. This word tells all these conditions that are created in water molecules after being electrocuted. Each drop of rain is composed of numerous water particles. Geometricians know that when a bigger sphere is prepared from smaller ones, its outer surface reduces in area compared to the smaller spheres. And this way, the intensity of electric current increases manifold.

d) *Wadaqa*: Coming out slowly, becoming papulose. Obviously rain drops come in trickles. Their 'bellies' being full of water, are papulose while electricity warm them up or electrocute them.

e) *Min Khilahe hi*: 'Khalal' means amidst, sourness. Scientists know that if electric current is passed through a conductor, it will appear on its surface. Water is non-conductor but because of the acidity that mixes with raindrops while passing through air, make it conductor. And because of electricity, the outer surface of a raindrop gets electrocuted. The acidic material that comes with raindrops, serves as manure for earth while electricity infuses life in the dead body of earth. If by '*khilahe hi*' was not meant the acidic material, then probably the word *baihah* or jofa would have been used.

f) *Wa yanzolo minas same min jibale fiha*. And He sends down from the sky, mountains [of clouds].

Mufassirin[60] explain it like this:

And Allah sends rain from skies i.e. from mountains.

This explanation has been under so many objections:

[60] Those scholarly people who can explain various Qur'anic verses in reference to the context.

First, from skies i.e. from mountains has 'that is' which does not seem to be needed. Why would Allah not tell straightway whether from mountains or skies? Second, when in the entire Qur'an, rain is sent from skies then in this very Ayat, where was the need to mention mountains. Third, *Yanzal*: there is no mention of what Allah descended from the skies. Fourth, mufassirin consider the word 'rain' has been expunged. Now the question is why would Allah need to expunge something?

And then Hazrat Ibne A'bbas has done some further wonder by recognizing the existence of mountains in the sky and said that clouds are always developed in sky-based mountains and then rain down. That is why this Ayat means that "Allah rains from the mountains of skies".

In fact this Ayat was a riddle till this day but scientific discoveries have clarified it. *'Jabbaal'* is the plural of *'jabl'* and *jabbaal* means mixing water in clay. Experts in rains have discovered that formation of drops is not possible without dust particles. Each raindrop prepares around dust particles. If that is so, then the Ayat would mean:

And Allah sends such drops from skies that have dust particles mixed with it.

g) Lightening of electricity is so intense that it makes the eye plate senseless. It is because the entire blood of eyes accumulates around the plate. If we do not shut the eyes immediately, eyes would burst because of blood pressure. That is why we loose the sight for some time and world gets dark. And when blood spreads to where it belonged, eyesight returns.

The flash of its lightening almost takes away the eyesight. Nur, 43

With these explanations, Ayat would be translated as:

Don't you ponder that Allah moves clouds and bring them close by. Because of electricity, drops get closer and then acid-mixed drops come down from skies. And Allah brings down such drops that are accumulated around dust particles. Some places have rains as Allah wills and at others, no rain. It is quite possible that electricity might blind the man.

We need 100°C to boil water. To convert 100 gm water into gases, we need 236° temperature. Now it is the bounty of Allah that each day millions of tons of water is converted into gases without our efforts. It has been calculated that the amount of vapors needed just to irrigate 16 square miles area would need 500,000 tons of coal and over all India, 10-minute rain would need a trillion tons of coal costing 450 trillion rupees. This amount is 30,000 times more that the yearly income of the Government of India.

All these discoveries about rain have been made during the last fifty years. And the Prophet knew about 1400 years ago. Now be honest and tell what other proof would be needed to prove that Qur'an is a Divine Book?

(12)

But those who disbelieved - their deeds are like a mirage in a lowland which a thirsty one thinks is water until, when he comes to it, he finds it is nothing but finds Allah before Him, and He will pay him in full his due; and Allah is swift in account. Or [they are] like darkness within an unfathomable sea which is covered by waves, upon which are waves, over which are clouds - darkness, some of them upon others. When one puts out his hand [therein], he can hardly see it. And he to whom Allah has not granted light - for him there is no light. Noor, 39,40.

On warm sand, lower air gets lighter and the upper one heavy. The procedure is that if a ray of light passes through two medium, it will deflect. That is why that if a portion of a stick is immersed in water, it will appear to be wiggled. The same rule applies to mirage: eyesight after passing through dense and light air gets wiggled and a tree's roots seem to be above and its top below that gives the impression of the presence of water.

Like the prisoners of mirage, renegades' sight also gets wiggled. They try their best to get what in fact is bad for them. But for this, they pay a heavy price.

Divine Code is the only light that prevents eyes from seeing things as if they were wiggled. In today's times, when the darkness of greed and personal gains are all around and the sun of advice is wrapped in the midriff of sins, the disease of seeing the things distorted has become extremely widespread. Wherever you see people with all such filthy thoughts whether religious or political, social or financial, they will invariably consider their opinions to be the ultimate truth.

If civilized people wish to come out of cruelty and darkness and move towards such a future where soft rays of the Sun of Divinity provide solace and where the heavenly clarinet's intoxicating tunes are causing serenity and ecstasy and joyance.

وَمَنْ لَّمْ يَجْعَلِ اللّٰهُ لَهُ نُوْرًا فَمَالَهُ مِنْ نُوْرٍ ۞

Who ever Allah not guide will remain not guided.

Acts of renegades are like the mirage of wilderness. This

is what a thirsty man considers to be water and when he reaches there, nothing except Allah who immediately make him face the consequences of his actions. This is because Allah does not delay justice. Their bad deeds are like the darkness of ocean where waves upon waves rise. Black clouds are hovering and there is darkness upon darkness so much so that one cannot see his own hand. It is true that a person, who cannot move towards his destination, looses the path.

(13)

Though at night our sun sets but other suns that are thousands of times larger and brighter, remain in the universe. In the presence of those millions of suns, the spreading of darkness over the land surface is one of the greatest workmanships of Allah. Had there been no darkness, there would have been fire all around and simultaneously, because of restlessness, our brains would have burst. In other words, night is a great blessing of Allah.

The way an engine pulls the train, same way darkness follows the sun, i.e. sun is also the leader of darkness. Each prophet came to the world like a sun and along with him, are the glories (of Allah). The moment he leaves this world, then on the world of spirits, darkness spreads, the way sun sets on earth.

Have you not considered your Lord - how He extends the shadow, and if He willed, He could have made it stationary? Then We made the sun for it an indication. Furqan, 45.

(14)

Water around the world has so many shapes. If here it is frozen, there it is liquid, and elsewhere it is gas. Somewhere it is fruit juice, elsewhere it is oil, milk, blood and petrol. When we drink water, it reaches every where through blood vessels. From there, it collects impurities and throws some of it through lungs and rest, through kidneys. Similarly, mountain springs laden with minerals, reach us and after collecting the refuse of our towns, drop in the ocean. In other words, 'use of water' is a miracle of cosmology and creation. Petrol, blood, milk, clouds, rivers, and springs are all the miracles of water usage. The flood of electricity is the result of waterfalls. These moving engines are because of steam. In other words, the world of water is the world of immense power and horror, the study of which is extremely necessary. How great relationship does water have with our national and individual life, how big a miracle is its synthesis, and useful it is by converting it into steam and making electricity and thus how much incremental comforts and facilities has water afforded to us? To think over all these things, is the duty of Muslims. And those who do not do it, they according to Qur'anic jargon, are not Muslims. Allah says:

> And it is He who sends the winds as good tidings before His mercy, and We send down from the sky pure water. That We may bring to life thereby a dead land and give it as drink to those We created numerous livestock and men. And We have certainly distributed it among them that they might be reminded, but most of the people refuse, show ingratitude. Furqan, 48-50.

And the elemental spirit! Even a drop of water cannot be destroyed. It rose from the river and became cloud. From there it rained on the desert and again went into the air. It rained into a garden and becoming juice, went into the fruit. From there, came into our stomach where it either became part of our body or went out through our kidneys. And if dropped in the ocean, it went back to its home. That drop of water remains present in one or the other shape. If water being a compound can remain alive, then the spirit, that is fundamental, must not perish in the first place. The way rays of sun find the drop of water in the desert and take it to the heights of skies, similarly, all the drops of life that are lying in the various parts of human body, would reach the unlimited universe.

(15)

[The time of] their account has approached for the people, while they are in heedlessness and turning away. No mention comes to them anew from their Lord except that they listen to it while they are at play with their hearts distracted. And those who do wrong conceal their private conversation, [saying], "Is this [Prophet] except a human being like you? So would you approach magic while you are aware [of it]?" The Prophet said, "My Lord knows whatever is said throughout the heaven and earth, and He is the Hearing, the Knowing." But they say, "[The revelation is but] a mixture of false dreams; rather, he has invented it; rather, he is a poet. So let him bring us a sign just as the previous [messengers] were sent [with miracles]." Not a [single] city which We destroyed believed before them, so will they believe? Anbia, 1-6.

A bird looks after its chicks in a nest. It brings food for it and makes it sleep under its cozy wings. And when the chicks grow, they leave the nest. Same is the state of earth. We grow on it, sun gives us light and energy, clouds rain, trees and plants give us fruits and food. After sometime, we leave this cradle and go to the other world.

(16)

الرَّحْمٰنُ ۝ عَلَّمَ الْقُرْآنَ ۝ خَلَقَ الْإِنْسَانَ ۝ عَلَّمَهُ الْبَيَانَ ۝

The Most Merciful Taught the Qur'an, Created man, [And] taught him eloquence. 55:1-4

Look at the unlimited benevolence of Allah that He gave us a complete code (the Qur'an). Creation of man is one of the greatest things that Allah could do. He gave him the power to speak (so that he could explain the Godly Treatise).

Let's listen to some poems from the Book of Nature:

ٱلشَّمْسُ وَٱلْقَمَرُ بِحُسْبَانٍ ○

The sun and the moon [move] by precise calculation. 55:5

These changes of weather and this diversity of trees and fruits is the result of the orbiting of sun and moon. To think over it and then explain it, is the duty of mankind.

وَٱلنَّجْمُ وَٱلشَّجَرُ يَسْجُدَانِ ○

And the stars and trees prostrate. 55:6

Is it possible that grapes have the taste of apple or banana changes into the shape of mango? Not possible because all the things in universe are following a set code of action. And it is because of this obedience that we see balance, regularity and system all around.

وَٱلسَّمَآءَ رَفَعَهَا وَوَضَعَ ٱلْمِيزَانَ ○

And the heaven He raised and imposed the balance. 55:7

Nations lose their worth by not ensuring justice.

وَأَقِيمُوا ٱلْوَزْنَ بِٱلْقِسْطِ وَلَا تُخْسِرُوا ٱلْمِيزَانَ ○

And establish weight in justice and do not make deficient the balance. 55:9

Today, not a single nation can be seen on the surface of earth willing to do justice to mankind. Everywhere there is loot and plunder. Greedy nations are throwing fire over each other. Towns upon towns are being destroyed and old civilizations are being wiped out. Nations are being destroyed in months and weeks and human blood has become cheaper than water. Why so? Because nations have given up on justice.

Nations remain alive through justice, the way earth because of rain. Apparently, this earth is dry and lifeless but when the clouds of spring rain on it then all around are flowers and greenery. Same way, when the clouds of justice rain on a habitation then till horizon, it is all garden. After mentioning 'Al-Mizaan', green pastures point towards such a fact.

وَالْأَرْضَ وَضَعَهَا لِلْأَنَامِ ۝ فِيهَا فَاكِهَةٌ ۝ وَالنَّخْلُ ذَاتُ الْأَكْمَامِ ۝

And the earth He laid [out] for the creatures. Therein is fruit and palm trees having sheaths [of dates] 55:10-11

What is man by himself? A drop of water? Or sun-baked clay? When He created a balance in his emotions, his individual life became lustrous. When He tried to create balance in the world, his national life brightened.

خَلَقَ الْإِنْسَانَ مِنْ صَلْصَالٍ كَالْفَخَّارِ ۝

He created man from clay like [that of] pottery. 55:14

Today, western wisdom has declared that right from the outset, sun kept shining on sea shore. It is because of that phenomena that life started from the coast.

Mountains mean baked clay, water and fire. In other words, by using the word *fakhkhar*[61] Allah testified to the western theory.

The way fire is hiding in earth, stone, coal, and tree, similarly, there is fire of anger and sex in man. Only those people are considered great who do not let this fire erupt; rather try to create balance in it. And those who cannot control that fire, become all fire. They may, more appropriately, be called devils.

وَخَلَقَ الْجَانَّ مِنْ مَارِجٍ مِنْ نَارٍ ۝

And He created the jinn from a smokeless flame of fire. 55:15

After years of research, western scientists have claimed that pearls are developed in sweet water and coral in salt water. The Qur'an testifies to this in these words:

From both of them [sweet and salt waters] emerge pearl and coral. Rahman, 22.

If this Ayat is not explained this way, then '*minhuma*', its

---

[61] An earthen shard, or crock, a fire hardened, or cooked earth. That cooked earth or earthen crock that produces sound when it is clanked or tapped. Man was also made from this kind of clay or mud as said in the Ayat above.

pronoun (both of them) becomes useless. And then it cannot be explained anymore.

Millions of years earlier, oceans had large animals. All of them disappeared as they were defenseless; the way innumerable nations disappeared after losing the capabilities to live. Allah is present right from the outset; and will remain so for ever. Why, because He is the Strongest One and because He has the fury and grandeur.

Everyone upon the earth will perish, And there will remain the Face of your Lord, Owner of Majesty and Honor. Rahman, 26,27.

The greatest treasure of life is Allah who is begged by everyone and everything of us for life. What is life? Acting on the Qur'anic injunctions! Intelligence of the universe is like studio that is expanding by day with the addition of innumerable attractions. And these excesses are a testimony to the versatility and pinnacle of imagination of the Creator.

Whoever is within the heavens and earth asks Him; every day He is bringing about a matter. Rahman, 29.

Justice is Life of Nations, Injustice is Death

Wherever in the world, there is justice, there the life is blooming: is there anyone who could circumvent the rules of life and avoid punishment? Or run away from earth? This earth is a castle that has deep oceans all around and above, is air. Somewhat above are poisonous rays, electrified atmosphere that a little freedom from earth's gravity, and a star attracts so forcefully that fire would erupt from all our body parts, even hair.

O company of jinn and mankind, if you are able to pass beyond the regions of the heavens and the earth, then do pass. You will not pass except by authority [from Allah]. Rahman, 33.

If we consider the meaning of 'sultan' as 'power', and

purpose as 'knowledge', then its explanation would be:

Such a power due to which you could enjoy the exosphere!

(17)

In today's world, coal is the most significant source of energy. With the usage of its energy, western powers are making tremendous strides. And we the pitiable Muslims have been reduced to shame of both the worlds. Allah knows why Muslims couldn't see (and understand) this Ayat:

And have you seen the fire that you ignite? Is it you who produced its tree, or are We the producer? We have made it a reminder and provision for the travelers. Alwaqi'ah, 71-73.

Coal has the rays of sun latent in it while in man's heart, eternal sun's rays are implicit. Black coal can make a man live and if a man becomes human being, he can generate stupendous amount of goodness to his fellow beings.

(18)

Stars are causing tremendous light because they are following a set procedure. Today if they intend to disobey the Order, they will just perish by colliding with one another. The way moons and stars grandeur is subject to a specified code, likewise man can never shine if he does not follow the constitution, mentioned in all the divine books.

Then I swear by the setting of the stars. And indeed, it is an oath - if you could know - [most] great. Indeed, it is a noble Qur'an. Al-Waqiyah, 75-77.

(19)

Qur'an is the call of life and the Prophet, life itself. Today we see with our own eyes that nations are alive just because of coal and steel. In other words, all the industrialized countries are acting upon certain principles of the Qur'an. As for the (so called) followers of Islam, they

have no idea what is going on in the world: they are long
dead. And those that are (the living) dead, cannot be the
followers of the Prophet. And those that are dead or are
dying, can never be called the followers of Prophet.

O! you, who have believed, respond to Allah and to the
Messenger when he calls you to that which gives you life. And
know that Allah intervenes between a man and his heart and
that to Him you will be gathered. Anfal, 24.

To spread the message of Allah in the world, it is
necessary that alongwith mercy, there must be valor and
overpowering instincts, something not possible without
arms and ammunition. Just who could be willing to listen to
a weak and incapacitated nation?

.... And We sent down iron, wherein is great military might
and benefits for the people, and so that Allah may make
evident those who support Him and His messengers unseen.
Indeed, Allah is Powerful and Exalted in Might. Hadid, 25.

Allah knew that the period of arms and ammunition
would come but after the completion of the sequence of
prophethood. That is why the word '*bil-ghaib*' has been
used.

(20)

Earth has quakes because the hidden treasures of earth
and the mountains from deep oceans could appear. These
quakes are not some incidental phenomena. These rather
appear with the full consent of Allah and there is a specific
strategy behind all this.

Qur'an is a complete code of human life that has been
given to us so that quakes could appear even in our hearts
and the springs of knowledge could provide relief to
everyone.

Like man, other entities of the universe have also been
placed under a system of existence that is followed with
great alertness. But man, the one who breaks his own

system anywhere and everywhere, is getting a thorough beating. Had the system of life for man (the Qur'an) been given even to a mountain, it would with all its readiness, have followed all of its sections and clauses and would have moved, burst, spring, and a world of bounties would have been thrown out.

If We had sent down this Qur'an upon a mountain, you would have seen it humbled and coming apart from fear of Allah......Hashar, 21.

(21)

Nun. By the pen and what they inscribe, You are not, [O Muhammad], by the favor of your Lord, a madman.....Qalam, 1,2.

In this Ayat "*beniamatah Rabbika*" demands explanation. If we consider "*ba*" of "*beniamatah*" as compurgatory, then its meaning would be "swear on your Rabb that you are not *majnoon*". And if take the meaning of "*Niamatah*" as "bounty" then it would mean "pen and what the pen wrote (the Qur'an) is testimony to the fact that by the Grace of Allah, you are not mad".

After acting on the various clauses of the Qur'an, the Muslims have proved that each and every Qur'anic direction is the ever-lasting message of life. Then how could there be any justification calling its "Greatest Expositor" as mad. Such a lot has been written about the wonderful life of our Prophet and his revolutionary messages that no one else has been considered worth of writing even a fraction of what has been written about him. Then is the voice of all the humanity not the declaration of this fact that:

مَآ أَنتَ بِنِعْمَةِ رَبِّكَ بِمَجْنُونٍ 68:2

If "*yastorun*" is taken as 'future', then this Ayat becomes good news that followers of Islam would generate so much knowledge and expertise that they will be acknowledged as scholars of the world. At that time the world would say the leader of such big historians, philosophers, geographers, cosmologists, and mathematicians cannot be a mad man.

Besides the believers of Islam, even the bigoted western scholars like, for example, Noldke, Nicholson, William Moore, and Draper had to acknowledge the greatness of our Prophet. Notwithstanding the fact that they severely criticized our Prophet but along with that, they have written beautiful essays about his knowledge, statesmanship, wisdom, politics and other qualities. This seem to be the explanation of *"Ma anta biniamatihi Rabbika bimajnoon"*.

(22)

What a message of intoxication and hiatus by the dim moonlit night that when it dawned, the entire universe unfurled its infinite beauty. And when the sun rose, the atmosphere was filled with yet another type of (inner) light spreading its wings all around.

This life is like the moonlight, old age is the dawn of next day, and death, the setting of sun. After that, the atmosphere would be full of light.

No! By the moon. And [by] the night when it departs. And [by] the morning when it brightens, Indeed, the Fire is of the greatest [afflictions]. Mudassar, 32-35.

(23)

Prophets conveyed the message of justice and beneficence and devoted their lives to control mischief. Because of them, the entire world kept on dividing into two camps: pro and con. Former got the right over both the paradises - worldly and of Hereinafter – and the latter, got only death and destruction.

After looking at this state through the historical perspective, the fact becomes evident that there is no escape for those indulging in wickedness.

By those [winds] sent forth in gusts. And the winds that blow violently. And [by] the winds that spread [clouds]. And those [angels] who bring criterion. And those [angels] who deliver a message. As justification or warning. Indeed, what you are promised is to occur. Mursalat, 1 to 7.

(24)

There is a special similarity between a poet and a magician. A magician would show the unreal as fact and the poet would present the ideal things interesting for eyes and hearts. Poet spends all of his energies over the use of appropriate words and remains far away from the world of reality. He by nature likes exaggeration, deprived of courage and persistence, mad for color and beauty, and a toy in the hands of emotions. He does not have an opinion but rather keeps on changing his stance every now and then. Since poetry is an easy hobby that does not need use of brains, knowledge and research, and a poet writes poems for getting admiration, that is why they are easy going and lewd. Same is the case with his admirers.

Those who follow poets, are wayward. Don't you see that they don't keep themselves confined to any principles? They keep on wandering in all the valleys and their sayings never materialize. Alsha'arah, 224 to 226.

After a cursory look at the history of Islam, the fact becomes bare that poet has always been the precursor of downfall and lethality. Before the Prophet, Arabia had thousands of poets and concurrrently, the entire nation indulged in orgy and moral degradation. When that nation opened its eyes, they founded an enviable Sultanate and with that, poets just vanished in thin air. After a few hundred years, this courier of death and degradation resurfaced. History is testimony to the great narrators and poets during the reign of Abbasids. Hammad remembered one hundred thousand poems. Abu Timam had fourteen thousand and Asma'a had learnt sixteen thousand couplets by heart. Once, Abu Samim narrated the poetry of a number of poets to Haroon-ur-Rashid, whose alliteration took one and a half days to complete. These poets had definitely influenced the caliphs while the last few caliphs became lazy and easy-going and were thus swept by the Tartar invaders.

Muslims of Spain reached their downfall only when hundreds of poets were born, so much so that even official correspondence was done in poetry.

In Iran, Ghaznavese, Timurites, and Saljuqese came like a flood but sat like froth. Immediate reason of their downfall was poetry. Through poems, the kings were given the impression of being indispensable and of owning the skies and the earth. As a result, they became prey to their own illusions and chicanery. There were about 400 poets in the court of Mahmud Ghaznavi. And who doesn't know about the court poets of Malik Shah and Sanjar. To the other end of the spectrum, Safvi Dynasty ruled for about three hundred years but did not encourage even a single poet to charm the rulers. Reason is obvious: poets sprout only to ensure the downfall of a dynasty. In India, ascendancy of Urdu poetry started during the reign of Mohammad Shah Rangeela. And that was the time when the downfall of Mughals surfaced. During the days of Shah Alam Sani, Nawab Asif-ud-Daola and to top it all, during the reign of Bahadur Shah Zafar – the last Mogul Emperor - poetry became so widespread that in the storm of distich, the twinkling lights of the Empire came to its logical end.

Today (in 1942), the downfall of India has reached its last limits. Poetry is in full swing. Every now and then, poets gather and enjoy. A couple of admirers sit together and a poet looks to towards the gathering to get laurels for one distich that he repeats several times. The listeners may or may not understand what the poet says but keep on saying "once again" and don't tire of praising, time and again. In return, the poet pretends humility by saying that it is all because of your love and encouragement, otherwise "where do I stand" last part of the sentence being very true. After the Mushaira[62], the poet keeps on asking "How was it"? I had no time but on the insistence of Secretary so and so, I developed a few distiches but did you enjoy? The (so-called) admirers of the poet would laugh loudly and say, "By God! Why are you being so full of humility? Your poetry was incredible and today if Mir[63] and Daagh[64] and Amir Minayee[65] were alive, they would have kissed you hands in reverence.

Why don't England, Germany and Russia have that much frequency of poets as in India? Are the hearts of those people devoid of human feelings? Does a mother over there not love her children? Is nature not beautiful over there? Yes, all of it is there, but the difference is that their best brains are busy in unfurling the mysteries of nature and solving political, economic, moral and knowledge-based

---

[62] A sort of poetic symposium

[63] Mir Taqi Mir, whose real name was Muhammad Taqi and whose pen name was Mir was a leading Urdu poet of the 18th Century A.D. He was one of the pioneers who gave shape to the Urdu language itself. He was one of the principal poets of the Delhi School of the Urdu *ghazal* and remains arguably the foremost name in Urdu poetry often remembered as *Xudā-e suxan* (god of poetry).

[64] Nawab Mirza Khan (1831–1905), commonly known as Daagh Dehlvi was an outstanding poet famous for his Urdu *ghazals* and belonged to the Delhi school of Urdu poetry. He wrote poems and *ghazals* under the pen name *Daagh Dehlvi*.

[65] Ameer Minai, an Urdu poet of eminence was born in 1826 at Lucknow and died in 1900 at Hyderabad. A popular poet both with the people and the aristocracy, he was held in high esteem by his contemporary poets like Ghalib and Daagh Dehalvi.

problems of their nations. And here, we are holding "poetic symposiums' and trying to tie down the wings of bulbul with the veins of tree leaves, besides locating the thin, rather the non-existent, waist of the beloved.

Prophets and other reformers were in consonance with solid realities of the world. All of their doings are clear like "two-and-two-four". To the other end of the spectrum, poets deal with fantasies. This indulgence in fantasies, speculations, and virtuosity do not permit them to get the strength of determination, or high ideals, or other equally noble traits. Now let's be honest to ourselves and think on how could a nation bring revolution or have a reformer while indulging in poetry and remain a do-gooder or ameliorator?

And We did not give Mohammad, the knowledge of poetry, nor is it befitting for him..... Yasin, 69.

There are exceptions in the world of poetry. Both in east and west, certain poets have come who went far above the age-old repetition of "bulbul and flower" and used this genius for higher ideals. For example, Iran's Sa'adi[66] and Rumi[67]; Goethe[68] of Germany; and in India, Balmik[69], Baba

---

[66] Sa'adi was one of the major Persian poets of the medieval period. He is not only famous in Persian-speaking countries, but has also been quoted in western sources. He is recognized for the quality of his writings and for the depth of his social and moral thoughts. Sa'adi is widely recognized as one of the greatest masters of the classical literary tradition.

[67] Rumi (1207 – 1273) was a 13th-century Persian poet, jurist, theologian, and Sufi mystic. Iranians, Turks, Afghans, Tajiks, and other Central Asian Muslims as well as the Muslims of South Asia have greatly appreciated his spiritual legacy in the past seven centuries. Rumi's importance is considered to transcend national and ethnic borders. His poems have been widely translated into many of the world's languages and transposed into various formats. In 2007, he was described as the "most popular poet in America.   See next page

Guru Nanak[70], Tagore[71], and Iqbal[72] are those reformers who delivered their messages in poetry. They were the

[68] Goethe (1749 – 1832) was a German writer and politician. His body of work includes epic and lyric poetry written in a variety of meters and styles; prose and verse dramas; memoirs; an autobiography; literary and aesthetic criticism; treatises on botany, anatomy, and color; and four novels. In addition, numerous literary and scientific fragments, and more than 10,000 letters written by him are extant, as are nearly 3,000 drawings.

[69] Valmiki is celebrated as the harbinger-poet in Sanskrit literature. He is the author of the epic *Ramayana*, based on the attribution in the text of the epic itself. He is revered as the A*di Kavi,* which translates to *First Poet,* for he invented *sloka* that set the base and defined the form to Sanskrit poetry.

[70] Guru Nanak (1469 – 1539) is the founder of the religion of Sikhism and is the first of the ten Sikh Gurus, the eleventh guru being the *living Guru*, Guru Granth Sahib. His birth is celebrated world-wide on Kartik Puranmashi, the full-moon day which falls on different dates each year in the month of Katak, October-November.
Guru Nanak travelled to places far and wide teaching people the message of one God who dwells in every one of God's creations and constitutes the eternal Truth. He setup a unique spiritual, social, and political platform based on equality, fraternity love, goodness, and virtue.

[71] Tagore (1861 – 1941), was a Bengali polymath who reshaped his region's literature and music. Author of *Gitanjali* and its "profoundly sensitive, fresh and beautiful verse", he became the first non-European to win the Nobel Prize in Literature in 1913. In translation his poetry was viewed as spiritual and mercurial; however, his "elegant prose and magical poetry" remain largely unknown outside Bengal. Tagore introduced new prose and verse forms and the use of colloquial language into Bengali literature, thereby freeing it from traditional models based on classical Sanskrit. He was highly influential in introducing the best of Indian culture to the West and vice versa, and is generally regarded as the outstanding creative artist of modern South Asia.

See next page

people with special mental faculties and their imagination touched the divinity. In their poetry, one could find a blend and proportion of spirituality and worldly good. They can in no way, be compared with seasonal poets whose only objective would be to make capital out of their poetry.

(25)

The greatest miracle of Allah is the creation of universe itself. If the nerve-shattering grandeur of this universe is not sufficient to convince certain wayward persons, then the splitting of Nile, conversion of stick into snake, or the appearance of angles in human looks will not be any use either.

Each prophet at the time of calling toward Allah, invited his people to think over the creation of universe. For example:

---

[72]   Sir Muhammad Iqbal (1877 – 1938), was a philosopher, poet and politician in British India who is widely regarded as having inspired the Pakistan Movement. He is considered one of the most important figures in Urdu literature, with literary work in both the Urdu and Persian languages. Iqbal is admired as a prominent classical poet by Pakistani, Iranian, Indian and other international scholars of literature. Though Iqbal is best known as an eminent poet, he is also a highly acclaimed "Muslim philosophical thinker of modern times". His first poetry book, Asrar-e-Khudi, appeared in the Persian language in 1915, and other books of poetry include Rumuz-i-Bekhudi, Payam-i-Mashriq and Zabur-i-Ajam. Amongst these his best known Urdu works are Bang-i-Dara, Bal-i-Jibril, Zarb-i Kalim and a part of Armughan-e-Hijaz. In Iran and Afghanistan, he is famous as Iqbāl-e-Lāhorī (Iqbal of Lahore), and he is most appreciated for his Persian work. Along with his Urdu and Persian poetry, his various Urdu and English lectures and letters have been very influential in cultural, social, religious and political disputes over the years.

Said Pharaoh, "And what is the Lord of the worlds?" [Moses] said, "The Allah of the heavens and earth and that between them, if you should be convinced." Shu'ara, 23,24.

Hazrat Ibrahim calls his nation towards Allah that has the following qualities:

Who created me, and He guides me. And it is He who feeds me and gives me drink. And when I am ill, it is He who cures me. Shu'ara, 78-80.

Hazrat Noah says:

And I do not ask you for it any payment. My payment is only from the Allah of the worlds. Shu'ara, 145.

Hazrat Hud (Prophet) diverted the attention of his nation A'ad towards the universe in these words:

Provided you with grazing livestock and children. And gardens and springs. Shu'ara, 133,134.

Hazrat Shoaib (Prophet) invited the people of Aikah to think over Allah this way:

And fear He who created you and the former creation. Shu'ara, 184.

These are some of the samples otherwise open any divine book and you will come across a number of miracles and warnings of Allah.

(26)

At the defeat (of Allied forces) at Dunkirk (May 29, 1940), the Daily Telegraph wrote in its June 18, 1940 editorial:

The more we feel sorry, the lesser would it be that during the last 20 years, we made our youth learn two things: Tennis and Golf. We did not prepare them for Struggle for which today, we are paying the price.

In his radio broadcast of 9:30 p.m. on June 22, 1940, the President of France Marshal Petain said:

Compared to WW-I, this time we had greater number of armies, greater quantities of arms and ammunitions and other requisites. Our allied nations were also many. Still, a question arises: what are the reasons of our defeat? After thinking over this problem, I have reached the conclusion that we were not defeated by Hitler, we were rather defeated by our own youth whose only pastime was eating and enjoying.

Today the world has realized that what Islam said, was in our good. Fasting was made mandatory to make the people sturdy and tolerant. Zakat was ordered, lest we start worshiping wealth like greedy people. The offering of Namaz was made mandatory to have moral and spiritual cleansing, to observe discipline, obedience to leader and regularity and to ensure punctuality in our affairs. Europeans though wrongly considered palatial houses, cars and cinemas as the ultimate objective of civilization and progress. Today they have come to know that what they considered civilization, was in fact nothing but death and destruction (now Muslim countries who got rich since Dr. Burq's days followed the same path and became poor role models for the new genarations).

.....And indeed, Hell will encompass the disbelievers. Taubah, 49.

Consumers of the poison of new civilization! And those who yell about the new civilization! Remember that there is no salvation except following the system of divinity. If you cannot act according to the laws of nature, then just for one time accept the divine message and see that all of your problems would be solved. And that is through justice: justice with self; in service, with assistance, with rules and justice with colonies. Then justice with neighboring countries and justice with people of other countries. Justice is that elixir that will make your national life and your politics, government and the entire world would pray for your long life.

And establish weight in justice and do not make deficient the balance. Rahman, 9.

(27)
A Good News

During the life of Prophet Mohammad when Zoroastrians defeated the Romans near Basra (Iraq), they taunted Muslims that though Christians were their near ones but the Iranians defeated them. On this, the following Ayat was revealed:

The Byzantines have been defeated. In the nearest land. But they, after their defeat, will overcome. Within three to nine years. To Allah belongs the command before and after. And that day the believers will rejoice. Rum, 2-4.

In this Ayat, two good news were told: that in just few years, Romans would defeat the Iranians; and two, there the government of Allah would be established that will make the Muslims happy.

Hazrat Abu Bakar asked the Prophet the meaning and purpose of *"baz sanin"* as given in the verses mentioned above. The Prophet said that it may happen in three to nine years. Just seven years after this Ayat, Romans defeated the Iranians and exactly after nine years, the Muslims captured Damascus. This way, both the good news proved to be true.

These are just a few historical facts that cannot be falsified. I wonder over the wisdom of those who in the presence of such facts, try to falsify the Qur'an.

The Point: the war was fought between Romans and Iranians. In the first war, Iranians won. Very strange that Allah mentioned the defeated Romans but did not mention the Iranians. This was probably a signal towards the fact that Roman Empire would stay and the Iranians would just be wiped out the way their mention was omitted from the Qur'an.

Translation: Romans were defeated near the Arabs, but after a few years, they became victorious. On this land (in the days of Hazrat David), was the government of Allah and again that government would be established. That day, Muslims would be very happy.

(28)

Woman is beautiful in youth. The same beauty becomes the basis of love between husband and wife. In old age, both beauty and love go on *long leave* and instead, affection takes its place. In the following Ayat, expression of love for close of the kin[73], points to this fact:

And of His signs is that He created for you from yourselves mates that you may find tranquility in them; and He placed between you affection and mercy. Indeed in that are signs for a people who give thought. Rum, 21.

(29)

The way honey-making is in the nature of bee, likewise, making love and be affectionate is in man's nature.

Question: If goodness is in nature of man, then why does he feel happy while, e.g., stealing or indulging in fornication?

Answer: such people do so because of certain circumstantial compulsions otherwise they too hate indulgence in undesirable acts. As an example, if dacoity is committed in the house of a thief, or if someone keeps bad intentions for the daughter of a fornicator, he will immediately flare up in rage. This proves that even such people consider a sin or a crime, a sin and a crime. Otherwise if they would consider these as good acts, they would not be angry with such people but would rather have been patting such people.

---

[73] Say: No reward do I ask of you for this except the love of those near of kin. 42/23

[Adhere to] the fitrah of Allah upon which He has created [all] people. No change should there be in the creation of Allah. Rum, 30.

Making use of its natural instincts, honey bee is making honey. Nature of plants is making plants while tree is busy in its own right and trying its wee bit to make beautiful world of fruits and greenery. Man's nature is better and varied. If a bee can perform such a wonder (honey-making!), what is it that man cannot do by using its full potential and talent. But the problem is that he is running away from his own system.

Indeed mankind, is ungrateful to his Allah. Adiat, 6.

(30)

There is such a lot of cooperation in various facets of nature that they look like members of the same family. To prepare food for man, land, air, sun, mountain, and ocean all combine their energies and work in unison. When after fall, a spring flows with all its beauty and romance, then for the recreation of plants, all the components of universe start performing their functions. Sun heats up the desert, winds take the vapors up and move towards the Himalayas, where clouds are formed that rain on 'dead' earth and with that, its treasure of plants wakes up. Bacteria of earth start its own function and this way, recreation of plants occurs.

Neither the creation of first was a problem for Allah nor of the second. In the realm of human creation, we daily see the first creation while in case of plants, each year, recreation occurs. The machinery of universe has the tremendous potential of creation and sun, wind, and ocean are all parts of the machine that come into action for the benefit of even a very tiny particle, called man.

A man who wants to assemble a bed, first plans and then using his feet, goes to the market and brings necessary material. His eyes see and his hands weave. Same way, universe is like body, various parts of which work together and make the things happen.

Your creation and your resurrection will not be but as that of a single soul......Luqman, 28.

(31)

Saddul A'ram

Ma-arib was a famous city of Yemen that has a long range of mountains to its southwest. A stream used to flow originating from southwest towards Onah Valley in northwest. A rule of Ma-arib named Abd Shamas constructed a dam on its water that became known as Saddul 'Aram. Its length was 2,400 ft [727 m] in east-west direction and was 42 ft [13 m] high and 450 ft [136 m] wide. Two canals were taken out of the dam that used to irrigate two orchards, one to the left and other to the right of the city. When the people of Saba indulged in profligacy, and forgot about the maintenance and upkeep of the dam, it burst and the entire city was submerged; and disposed to the dustbin of history.

The story of Saddul 'Aram was neither documented in history nor in the minds of men. Qur'an has removed the screen from that incident and today, the archaeological remains of the city are testimony to what the Qur'an had already said about it.

There was for [the tribe of] Saba' in their dwelling place a sign: two [fields of] gardens on the right and on the left. [They were told], "Eat from the provisions of Allah and be grateful to Him. A good land [have you], and a forgiving Allah." But they turned away [refusing], so We sent upon them the flood of the dam, and We replaced their two [fields of] gardens with gardens of bitter fruit, tamarisks and something of sparse lote trees. [By] that We repaid them because they disbelieved. And do We [thus] repay except the ungrateful? Saba, 15-17.

A'arazwa may also mean people who shied from repairing the dam.

(32)
Route of Noah's Flood

A German researcher has proved that in ancient times, America and Africa were jointed and in-between part used to be called Atlantis. Because of a quake, the in-between part sank and the two continents separated. To support this theory, he gave three arguments:

a) The eastern coastal plants of America and the western coastal plants of Africa are exactly the same. This may be because both were the same chunk of land.

b) Like the pyramids of Egypt, similar archaeological sites have been discovered in Mexico that leads to the belief that earlier, these two continents were one piece of land that had similar civilization and architecture.

c) And finally, pottery and statues excavated from both the continents have great similarities.

Researcher believed that Noah's Flood occurred in Atlantis and was the result of a massive earthquake. Some other researchers contend that it occurred in Limoria; a piece of land that connected South Africa with Arabia but has now sunk. Yet another historian opines that this flood occurred in the north of Iraq because of flooding of Euphrates and because of that, a very large and advanced city called Ore was destroyed in 3500 B.C.

The last theory seems plausible because besides Qur'an, an incident "History of Ancient Malmal" also testifies it where it was written that:

In the kingdom of Kaldiah, a deity called Ba'al felt very angry with the people. He gave news of the flood to King of

Kaldiah, Kisouthrous and ordered him to make a boat and keep pair of all the things in it. And then it rained till all the adjacent area sank in water and the boat stopped at the mountain of Armenia.

The Qur'an says:

The boat of Noah stopped at the mountain of Jodi[74]. The History of Old Malmal is exactly like the one stated in the Qur'an. There is just a difference that in Qur'an the man who possessed the boat was named Noah while the one mentioned there was Kisouthrous. Since names change in different languages, for example, we call Hazrat Masih as Eisa and Christians call him Jesus Christ; Daud is David and Yahya is Johanna. Same way, it is quite possible that Kisouthrous of ancient times became Noah in Arabic.

Both the statements make it clear that the flood occurred in Iraq, in its northern parts.

(33)
Islamic Farm

On numerous occasions, the Qur'an has mentioned the nation brought up by the Prophet. At one instance, the Qur'an says:

Muhammad is the Messenger of Allah; and those with him are forceful against the disbelievers, and merciful among themselves. You see them bowing and prostrating [in prayer], seeking bounty from Allah and [His] pleasure. Their mark is on their faces from the trace of prostration. That is their description in the Torah. And their description in the Gospel is as a plant which produces its offshoots and strengthens them so they grow firm and stand upon their stalks, delighting the sowers - so that Allah may enrage by them the disbelievers. Allah has promised those who believe and do righteous deeds among them forgiveness and a great reward. Fatah, 29.

---

[74] A mountain at the border between Syria and Armenia

Chapter-XII

Rationale Behind Certain Surahs

Wal Fajr

When a suspected criminal has no evidence to defend himself, he swears by Allah to prove his innocence. In other words, he gives the evidence of Allah. Therefore 'swear' would mean evidence, argument, and proof is the Surah Al-Fajr.

Explanation of words:

Fajr: morning.

Layal 'Ashr: 'ten nights' mean 'nights of Hajj'. We give great importance to Hajj. This is because Muslims from all over the world wear similar dress and each year, gather at one point to display their strength, unity and organization.

Ashaf'a: even numbers

Alwatr: those numbers that cannot be divided by 2, i.e. la'ad. The way one and one make eleven, likewise in the beginning of Islamic era, Muslims, after uniting, had become a huge force. Today, they are scattered and disunited and are getting thorough beatings. While referring to numbers, it was also intended that Muslims would be the inventers of Algebra; though Algebra was invented by a Muslim mathematician Al-Khwarizmi[75].

---

[75] Algebra was invented by the Muslim mathematician Al-Khwarizmi in the book he wrote in 820. Algebra is the Arabic word "al-jabr" for "equation" in 1820. He is rightly known as "the father of Algebra". In fact, many ancient civilizations developed some sort of algebraic methods of solving problems, as far back as the Babylonians

Look at the irony of fate that today, most of the Muslims fail in Maths.

Iram Zat-ul-A'mad: All the Arabs are the children of Iram while 'Aad-o-Samood were their ancestors who had migrated from Iraq to Arabia. With the exception of one branch 'Amaeqa' all the rest have disappeared who ruled Iraq and Egypt from 3460 to 281 B.C. and were called R'atah. Iraq was ruled by different nations during different periods. For example, Marbeen, Kaldani, Ashura, Dolta-al-Babaliyah.

Ah-Ula: The last one was purely Arabian Government that had eleven rulers. One of them was called Hamurabi[76] who developed a code of governance for his rule having 283 clauses.

A'ad-o-Samud entered Arabia in 334 B.C. and founded their government in Yemen that was known as the Government of Moi'enibin. That government was larger than the government of Saba Har. An English travellor obtained 237 epitaphs from these. This shows that this government was spread from Persian Gulf to the coast of

---

[76] Hammurabi (died c. 1750 B.C.) was the sixth king of Babylon (1792-1750 B.C.). He extended Babylon's control over Mesopotamia by winning a series of wars against neighboring kingdoms. Although his empire controlled all of Mesopotamia at the time of his death, his successors were unable to maintain his empire. It has been said that Hammurabi was Amraphel, the King of Shinar in the Book of Genesis 14:1.

Hammurabi is known for the set of laws called Hammurabi's Code, one of the first written codes of law in recorded history. These laws were inscribed on stone tablets standing over eight feet tall (2.4 meters), of unknown provenance, found in Persia in 1901. Owing to his reputation in modern times as an ancient law-giver, Hammurabi's portrait is hanging in many government buildings throughout the world.

White Sea. This government was finally destroyed by the Qahtanese.

Some historians opine that Egyptian Pyramids were constructed by A'ad rulers and probably this Ayat "arm zatul A'amad" means Egyptian Pyramids.

Translation of Ayat:

By the dawn And [by] ten nights And [by] the even [number] and the odd And [by] the night when it passes, Is there [not] in [all] that an oath [sufficient] for one of perception? Have you not considered how your Lord dealt with 'Aad - [With] Iram - who had lofty pillars, ... Al-Fajr.

It means that the morning of prophethood has dawned and Muslims are uniting at one center and are getting from one to two and two to four (i.e. increasing in numbers geometrically). They are laying the foundations of art and science. The dark clouds of infidelity and ignorance are clearing. Can a nation under such circumstances exist that has no organizational structure, are not united, have no leader like the Prophet Mohammad and do not indulge in knowledge and wisdom? Men of wisdom were sure that all such nations would be destroyed like A'ad-e-Erum. And finally it did happen that way.

The way infinite numbers have been developed just from one number and no change has occurred in the original number, likewise from One Allah, millions of things sprung and even then, He is there without any change, like the original number.

'One' has nothing at the back nor is there any example in infinite numbers like 'one'. Same is the condition of Allah that He is Indivisible and Unparalleled.

The Number 'One' is the source of all the rest of numbers. Erase it and all the rest of numbers would automatically be erased. Same is the status of Universe and Allah.

Everyone upon the earth will perish, And there will remain

the Face of your Lord, Owner of Majesty and Honor. Ar-Rahman, 26,27.

Az-Zariyat

When sun shines over water, it transforms into vapors and goes up. From there, it rains and the earth becomes a garden and streams and rivers are flooded.

The Prophet is a sun that shines on human world and make able, hardworking, good natured people and takes nations to the climax of manners, behavioral, and civilizational heights. From there, they rain like the rain of providence and create gardens and flowers while lazy and worthless people are drowned like straws in the flood of progress and prosperity.

Right from the outset till this day, the code of conduct has remained the same. Though some of the sporadic instructions as laid down in the Divine Books differed somewhat but principles were the same. There are millions of suns orbiting in the universe in great precision. Their movements differ from one another but all of them are subject to just one code. Likewise, all the prophets had differences regarding intermittent instructions but invited everyone to just one great Categorical Imperative and present one Constitution though in different scripts and languages. If there could be no place for objection to the movement of stars, then why making a fuss about the sacred education where differences are only cosmetic in nature?

By those [winds] scattering [dust] dispersing And those [clouds] carrying a load [of water] And those [ships] sailing with ease And those [angels] apportioning [each] matter, Indeed, what you are promised is true. And indeed, the recompense is to occur. By the heaven containing pathways, Indeed, you are in differing speech. Az-Zariyat.

At-Tur

Hazrat Musa went to Koh-e-Tur[77] to get the code for human emancipation. Towards this end, thousands of prophets attained prophethood like Hazrat Adam. Construction of Ka'bah was also the same – that people from various social strata gather at one point and think over the peace and prosperity of the Ummah. This system of stars and suns is for our learning. And then those boiling oceans have been deliberately kept within the earth so that these may ooze treasures out from time to time for the benefit of mankind.

Now let's be honest and think: Will Allah not ask us about his benevolence and bounties that He so graciously gave us? Will the non-believers of the 'codes of prophets' and those unfamiliar with the respect and usage of Ka'abah, and after eating fruits ripened by the sun and sleeping carelessly, go unpunished for their (wicked) exploits? Never!

By the mount. And [by] a Book inscribed. In parchment spread open. And [by] the frequented House. And [by] the heaven raised high. And [by] the sea filled [with fire], indeed, the punishment of your Allah will occur. Of it there is no preventer. Tur, 1-8.

---

[77] According to the Book of Exodus, Mount Sinai is the mountain at which the Ten Commandments were given to Moses by God. Early Old Testament text describes Mount Sinai in terms which some scholars believe may describe the mountain as a volcano, although the word is omitted. This theory is not shared by all scholars. According to the Hebrew Bible, after leaving Egypt and crossing the Red Sea, the Israelites arrived at the foot of the holy mountain and gathered there in anticipation of the words of God.

Wan-Najm

The way each star is a guide for the world, similarly, the prophet was leader and teacher of mankind. The way a star is a source of light the same way the Prophet was the chairman of the light of guidance. The way a star moves on its orbit, likewise the Prophet traversed the Right Path. The way there is a Supreme Supervisor closely watching the movement of each star, likewise the Prophet too was under the supervision of Allah. And the way a star sets but does not perish, likewise the Prophet too is alive through his teachings and his followers. The way the Prophet laid the foundations of a grand government, some of its structures are still intact. Even today, democracy acknowledged as an international entity and the world is reverting to that system.

By the star when it descends, your companion [Muhammad] has not strayed, nor has he erred, Nor does he speak from [his own] inclination. It is not but a revelation revealed, ... An-Najm, 1-4.

The literary meaning of 'huwa' is both 'setting' and 'rising'. *Huwa hoya aza gharba wa huya iza a'la wa sa'ad.*

Translation of this Ayat:

Swear by the star that appears from the horizon and moves straight on its (pre-determined) path, likewise your friend (The Prophet) does not deviate even a little. He does not say anything canard but rather conveys Our Message.

A devoted and obedient student gets frequently impressed by the character of his teacher such that his acts completely cover the student's life and tries to follow what the teacher does.

We in our fore, have a student like the Prophet, and the Creator of Universe as his Teacher and Guide. This system of teacher-student relationship started through communication and later, became so intimate that there was hardly any distance between the two.

Taught to him by one intense in strength - one of soundness. And he rose to [his] true form, while he was in the higher [part of the] horizon. Then he approached and descended and was at a distance of two bow lengths or nearer. And he revealed to His Servant what he revealed. An-Najm, 5-10.

Interpreters of the Qur'an consider *Shadid-ul-Qawa*[78] as Gabriel and the 'object' in *Fawaha ila a'bdohu* as Allah. This however seems like a fantasy. To me if we consider *Shadid-ul-Qawa* as Allah, it will add luster to the explanation. This way we might also get rid of finding the object of *Fawaha*.

Surah Al-Badar

a) Mecca was considered the House of Allah even during the times of ignorance. There, killings and quarrels were strictly prohibited. But unfortunately, the Meccans used to torture the Prophet over there. If in the most sacred city, a most revered man is not safe from the excesses of non-believers, what would be the status of human beings in other cities, is not hard to imagine.

b) Think over the birth of human being. After staying in the darkness of womb for nine good months, he is born with great agony. He then consumes a lot of energies to be brought up. Not a single moment of his life is free of problems. Family upkeep, difficulties of education, and worldly problems follow the man till his death. In that case, why should a man not strive to take some additional pains and try to ascend the mountain of eternal life?

[78] To put it extremely lightly, this would mean someone with extremely strong nerves

c) Man consumes all of his life in quest of tranquility. Even then, he hardly manages it. This means that man's emancipation is elsewhere; in some other hands.

Does he think that never will anyone overcome him? Al-Balad

d) Man has always been complaining that he earned millions but could not get satisfaction. Alas! Had he known that satisfaction does not come with material wealth. It is rather a bounty that can be had by properly using ones life and limbs. What is the proper use of limbs? Its answer is available from within. As Allah says: *We have shown both the paths – bliss and misery - to man.* It is now upto him which path he chooses for himself.

e) All the great reformers of the world had been bearing great physical agonies and imprisonments. Even then they remained satisfied and happy. Why? Because after making proper use of their limbs and mind, they used to get the bounty of satisfaction.

I swear by this city, Makkah - And you [O Mohammad] are free of restriction in this city - And [by] the father and that which was born [of him], We have certainly created man into hardship. Does he think that never will anyone overcome him? He says, "I have spent wealth in abundance." Does he think that no one has seen him? Have We not given him two eyes? And a tongue and two lips? And have shown him the two ways? But he has not broken through the difficult pass. And what can make you know what is [breaking through] the difficult pass? It is the freeing of a slave, or feeding on a day of severe hunger, an orphan of near relationship, or a needy person in misery. And then being among those who believed and advised one another to patience and advised one another to compassion. Those are the companions of the right. But they who disbelieved in Our signs - those are the companions of the left. Over them will be fire closed in. Al-Balad.

Al-Shams (The Sun)

Man's emancipation hinges on chastening of heart and mind. This can be achieved by good manners and the study of nature. The light of sun and moon and the study of earth and skies leaves such a lasting impression on heart and soul that man's inner-self becomes restless to reaching the last of the rewards that Allah has promised to the chosen ones.

The way the beauty of our world is indebted to sun, likewise man's spiritual finery is contingent upon chastening at the alter ego. The way clouds stop sunlight, likewise the darkness of sins shield the inner lights of a man and this way, heart becomes abode of darkness.

The greatest role in good acts and attitudes is the study of nature. This to one side, opens the latent strengths of a man and on the other, the greatest secret of nature – Allah – becomes bare to the inquisitive eye.

I was a hidden treasure. I wanted to be known bare faced. For that purpose, I created man.

There are multitudes of beautiful scenes hidden in nature, each of which depicts the workmanship and supreme artistic abilities that could only be performed by the Divinity. Therefore the followers of Hazrat Ibrahim need to follow his vision while studying the nature and not the superficiality of polytheists that sometime bow before moon and at others, before sun.

Say, "Allah has told the truth. So follow the religion of Abraham, inclining toward truth; and he was not of the polytheists." Imran, 95.

In Surah Ash-Shams, Allah says:

By the sun and its brightness. And [by] the moon when it follows it. And [by] the day when it displays it. And [by] the night when it covers it. And [by] the sky and He who constructed it. And [by] the earth and He who spread it. And [by] the soul and He who proportioned it. And inspired it [with discernment of] its wickedness and its righteousness, He has succeeded who purifies it. And he has failed who instills it [with corruption]. Shams, 1-10.

Al-Lail (The Night)

Our world is not more than a particle compared to the universe. When night warps the scenes of world, it bares naked the infinite worlds of skies. As against this, if day uncovers the worldly versatilities, it at the same time, gradually vanishes the innumerable worlds from our sight.

Death is the evening of life. The moment it comes, all the worldly scenes would disappear and all those mysteries that were hidden during the prime of life, would become bare.

The aversion of day and night and of masculine and feminine is, in fact, part of a beautiful and perfected system. The way this disagreement (of day and night) is the beauty of nature, likewise the diversity of human races are cause to the beauty of human society. Actions of nations, civilization, and ways of human thinking differ widely. It is because of this diversity that the spirit of completion is alive. A nation's ascendancy creates envy in the hearts of others. If today, this spirit dies, then man's world would become the world of animals. And consequently, nations and individuals would stop striving to compete. And with this, the spirit of inquisition would die down.

Success is synonymous to struggle. Those who sacrifice life and wealth in constructive endeavors, do succeed. And those that shirk from such sacrifices, they are just grinded in the mill of time.

By the night when it covers, and [by] the day when it appears, and [by] He who created the male and female, indeed, your efforts are diverse. As for he who gives and fears Allah, and believes in the best [reward], We will ease him toward ease. But as for he who withholds and considers himself free of need, and denies the best [reward], We will ease him toward difficulty. And what will his wealth avail him when he falls? Al-Lail

Al-Azha [The Brightness]

A Hadeeth says that for some time, revelation stopped over the Prophet. This caused disturbance in his temperament. On the other hand, the non-believers started flouting him by saying that his prophethood has come to an end. After sometime, the following Surah descended:

By the morning brightness and [by] the night when it covers with darkness, Allah has not taken leave of you, [O Muhammad], nor has He detested [you]. And the Hereafter is better for you than the first [life]. And Allah is going to give you, and you will be satisfied. Did He not find you an orphan and give [you] refuge? And He found you lost and guided [you], and He found you poor and made [you] self-sufficient. So as for the orphan, do not oppress [him]. And as for the petitioner, do not repel [him]. But as for the favor of Allah, report [it]. Azha

The way the system of day and night has been established are the mercies of Allah. Likewise, revelation is the day of prophethood and its stoppage is like the night of prophethood. And both are the blessings of Allah.

Allah who had been so beneficent to an orphan that He brought him up, protected him from enemies, crowned him with prophethood, and took him up from an ordinary subject to the status of a sovereign. If Allah could do that, will He deprive him (the Prophet) of his blessings?

At-Tin [The Fig]

Fig is quickly digestible, laxative, mouth cleaner (inflammation, wounds, etc.), emollient (softens chest mucus), rich in sugar especially for those who burn a lot of calories, and removes sand from (urine) bladder. Tur is a famous mountain where Moses had the opportunity to speak to Allah. Mountains have generally a lot of minerals but Tur was the place of revelation as well. Mecca is where the Prophet was born and has the Ka'abah. If Allah can make mountains and towns the sources of bless, then how could the creation of man be an inferior act.

Babylon has the abundance of figs and around Jerusalem, olives were planted. Tur is related to Moses and Mecca to Mohammad. By referring to these four things, Allah has diverted our attention to those four prophets who were born in the lands of non-believers. Inspite of this, they became beacons of light and shone the world over. Had the nature of man been inferior, then how these reformers could have shined in that dark and wayward environment soiled in sin?

By the fig and the olive, and [by] Mount Sinai, and [by] this secure city [Makkah], We have certainly created man in the best of stature; ...... At-Tin, 1-4.

Al A'laq[79] [The Clot]

Recite in the name of your Lord who created - Created man from a clinging substance. Recite, and your Lord is the most Generous - Who taught by the pen - Taught man that which he knew not. Al-A'lad, 1-5.

If in 'Alamal insaan ..... 'qalam' is considered as the object of 'ilm', there would be greater beauty to its

---

[79] Also known as Surat al-Iqra (Read!)

explanation. That is, 'pen' has made a man learn what he had no idea of. And quite obviously, all the civilization and progress is the result of pen. Had we not received the thinking of our ancestors, we would still have been in the initial stages of civilization.

This was the very first Ayat that was revealed onto the Prophet in Cave of Hira[80]. Just think how forcefully we are being given lesson about universe to start with the name of Rabb who created man from leach.

Man was a leach in the womb of his mother for some time. Gradually it transformed in to man and then after passing through a number of stages, attained the status of prophethood. Then was it not possible that the Arabians could come out of the darkness and barbarism and on the path of radiance and welfare?

We respect father because he is our patron and (apparently) the provider (of food). We bow in front of our teacher because he is our moral guide. And we respect our guide that he advises us and guides us. Allah has all these characteristics to their extreme. He is our creator and giver, guide and path leader and He is our teacher and patron. That is why He deserves far greater respect.

Allah swore by the pen, overlooking man's mind and tongue, though write-up is the reflection of mental feelings. The reason is that mental reflections do wipe away, but the write-ups remain. In other words, a pen is the guard of man's feelings and that is why it commands great importance. These Ayaat seem to be such prophesies that

---

[80] Hira or the Cave of Hira is a cave about 2 miles [3.2 km] from Mecca, on the mountain named Jabal al-Nour in the Hejaz region of present day Saudi Arabia. The cave itself is about 12 ft (3.7 m) in length and 5 ft 3 in (1.60 m) in width. It is notable for being the location where the Prophet Mohammad received his first revelations from God through the angel Jabril.

after passing various stages of politics and civilization, Arabs would soon be the acknowledged leaders of the world. And the world saw that the prediction proved to be true.

Al-Qadr

The dictionary gives the following meanings of Qadr:

Fate; Division; Establishment; Decision; and Estimate

The descend of Qur'an was without doubt, distribution of bounty, determination of (true) path, and the cosmology of nation. Irrevocable decision of sending bad nations where they belong to and what they deserve. This sacred document (the Qur'an) was purported to bring a powerful moral and political revolution and to make the lowly the higher and the higher, the lowly. Therefore, it will not be wrong to say that Qur'an descended on such a night that was a decisive night for the community of nations. That was the night of the downfall of Kaiser and Qasra and of evolution and perfection of the followers of Prophet. That night, hundreds of revolutions and stimulations were gazing the nations of tomorrow. Old and outmoded system was breaking down and the sun of new system was rising from the horizon of humanity with all of its pomp and grandeur.

At that time, dark night of blasphemy and wickedness had wrapped the world while in the last part of the night, Qur'anic lights had started raining down from divine heights. And so the night that had brought to the mankind divine bounties, was no doubt, better than one thousand nights .... *Khahirum min alfe shahr.*

Alf Shahr (one thousand months) means the period of ignorance. Though that period spanned over hundreds of years but the last eighty years were the worst from all the angles. Then the Prophet laid the foundations of a new and young nation. Everything becomes perfect after passing through various stages of its life. A wheat plant matures in six months and a mango tree, in eight years. The speed of ascend of nations is very slow needing immense patience. It took the UK nine hundred years to become a powerful kingdom. Same is the case with other nations.

World is cognizant of the fact that during the last period of Umayyad Caliphate, the borders of Islamic Sultanate had spread up to Multan in the east while to the west, up to English Channel. Knowledge of science and arts was spreading all around and great philosophers, astrologers, and historians were appearing. And when the Abbasid Caliphate took over, there was a flood of knowledge. Thousands of men of letters and arts were born and propped and millions of books were written. That was the age when Baghdad was known for the best books. And according to Dr. Darpiere[81], Zubaida's personal library had six hundred thousand books. Once a war broke between Caliph Mamun-ur-Rashid and King of Rome where the latter was defeated. Look at the love of Mamun for books that just for one book (Akhitee), he returned the entire sultanate to the defeated king. During that period of radiance, the people of Iran provided the most service to knowledge. A great number of scholars, physicians, and philosophers were Persians. And this way, the Prophet's saying also proved to be true when he said:

Seek knowledge even if you have to travel too for (China).

That was the morning that dawned over Baghdad.[82]

Without knowledge no ruling nation can become civilized. The tartars trampled the entire Muslim world in

---

[81] Of "Fight between Religion & Science" fame

[82] Kufah is a city in Iraq, about 170 km south of Baghdad, and 10 km northeast of Najaf. It is located on the banks of the Euphrates River

no time but they were san education. And that is why historians still call them ignorant and wild. Knowledge is the ornament of individuals as well as the nations. And this is that sun that lights up their nights.

We descend this Qur'an in a deciding night. Al-Qadr.

Al-A'adiyaat [The Horse]

The creator of horses is Allah. And Allah produces his feed. All that a man does is that he brings fodder from the farm. For this small kindness, the horse runs and runs till it starts panting. On rocky lands, its hooves create ignescents. With no fear of swords and daggers, it attacks the enemy lines tearing the dust and there it goes. To the other side, man who has been created by Allah, gave him brain to think, provided wonderful means for his brought up, and even gave the control of sun and moon in his hands. But alas, even then he remained defiant and did not repay even as much as a horse does for just a bundle of grasses.

By the racers, panting, and the producers of sparks [when] striking, and the chargers at dawn, Stirring up thereby [clouds of] dust, Arriving thereby in the center collectively, Indeed mankind, to his Lord, is ungrateful…. Al-A'adiyat, 1 to 6.

Al'Asr [The Age]

History is replete with man's excesses, failures, and destructions. Hundreds of nations rose worldwide, spread and prospered. However, the moment they deviated from the laws of nature, the nature turned them to smithereens.

By time! Indeed mankind is in loss. Except for those who have believed and done righteous deeds and advised each other to truth and advised each other to patience. Al-A'sr.

Al-Fil [The Elephant]

Abraha bin As-sabah constructed a Ka'bah in Sana'a[83] and called it Flees and forced the people to go around it. Finding an opportunity, an enterprising man spread human faeces in it. That made Abraha very angry and arranged a powerful army having 13 elephants, intended to attack Ka'bah[84] to bring it down. It is said that when the elephants reached near Mecca, they stopped. If they were directed towards San'a, they would move, otherwise they would sit.

Near Mecca, where two hundred camels of Abdul Mutalib, the grandfather of Hazrat Mohammad, were grazing, were caught by Abraha. When Abdul Mutalib came to release his camels, Abraha said, "You are the leader of Quraish and caretaker of Mecca. Do you know that I have come to bring down Ka'bah. You are worried about your camels but not Ka'bah?" Abdul Mutalib[85] said that he

---

[83] Sana'a is the capital of Yemen. It is one of the oldest continuously inhabited cities in the world. At an altitude of 2,300 meters (7,500 ft), it is also one of the highest capital cities in the world. The old city of Sana'a, a UNESCO World Heritage Site, has a distinctive due to its unique architectural characteristics, most notably expressed in its multi-storey buildings decorated with geometric patterns.

[84] The Ka'bah, "The Cube", also known as the Sacred House is a cuboid building in Mecca, Saudi Arabia. It is one of the most sacred sites in Islam. Al-Masjid al-Haram, the most sacred mosque in Islam, is built around the Ka'bah. Muslims are expected to face the Ka'bah during prayers, no matter where they are. From any given point in the world, the direction facing the Ka'bah is called the Qibla.

[85] Shaybah ibn Hashim (ca. 497 – 578), better known as 'Abdul Muttalib or 'Abd al-Muttalib, since he was raised by his uncle Muttalib, was the grandfather of Islamic prophet Mohammad.

was only the owner of camels and must be worried about his camels. As for Ka'bah, it also has an owner who is much more powerful than me and He himself will look after it.

Meanwhile, a special type of bird came having pebbles in their beaks. These pebbles when dropped, would pierce through the bodies of elephants, horses, and soldiers.

Now here are two bottom lines that need solution: (i) bringing of pebbles by birds; and (ii) killing of men and animals by pebbles. The first riddle sill needs solution and man's knowledge has not yet been able to unfurl this mystery. The second riddle has been solved through the law of gravity.

Law of Gravity

If we throw a stone from a plane at a height of 10,000 ft, its speed would keep on accelerating after every second. After calculations, it has been found that this speed was 32 ft in first second, in second, it was 64 ft, in third, 96 ft and in fourth, the speed was 128 ft.

Now if we throw a stone from a height that takes two minutes to reach earth, then in the last second, its speed would be 3,480 ft, i.e., about half the speed of bullet.

If the birds threw stones from a height that took two to two-and-a-half minute, their speed must have been four to five thousand ft per second; sufficient to kill men and animals.

Have you not considered, [O Muhammad], how your Lord dealt with the companions of the elephant? Did He not make their plan into misguidance? And He sent against them birds in flocks, striking them with stones of hard clay, And He made them like eaten straw. Al-Fil.

Gnomic

One night, I met Allama Iqbal and Sir Syed Ahmad Khan[86] in sleep. Allama asked me, "Please explain Al-Fil." When I explained, he expressed his satisfaction by nodding. Meanwhile, my eyes opened.

End of Discourse

Every beginning has an end. After fourteen editions of "Two Qur'ans", it has reached its ultimate end. Meanwhile, tens of letters were received from all over the country. Some appreciated my efforts while others brought my weaknesses to the fore. I am thankful to both of these respectable readers. The former, because they considered my efforts worth consideration; and thus encouraged me. The latter because they corrected me. Since it is not to my liking to indulge in arguments, I did not reply a letter or two. I am very sorry for my discourteous conduct.

A lot of hidden corners of the universe have remained to be explored. Some were ignored because of the fear of protraction while in case of others, my deficient knowledge came my way. I have however shown the readers the true path leading to the understanding of universe. It is quite possible that someone else might throw light on all the facets of universe that will satisfy all the seekers of knowledge.

I am not a student of science. It is therefore quite possible that I might have wrongly interpreted the natural problems; in an unscientific way.

---

[86]   Sir Syed Ahmad Khan (1817 – 1898), born Syed Ahmad Taqvi commonly known as Sir Syed, was an Indian Muslim philosopher and social activist of nineteenth century India.

My respected brother Maolana Ghulam Ahmad Parwez complained that the topic had become too long. It is quite possible that other readers of *"Al-Bayan"* might chew me out. But as is said, *"It feels good when I prolong the story."*

When Arabian poets used to write on certain topic, they would start with their beloveds. Sometimes, it would be a few distiches on the topic but three-fourths of the poem would relate to the beloved. When Ka'ab ibne Zubair presented 55 distiches in honor of the Prophet, it had 40 distiches in the loftiness of the beloved.

Turfah used to write 29 distiches praising his beloved and Labeed bin Rabiah, 31. Same was the case with Umra al Qais, Umar bin Kalsoom, and other Arabian poets.

If you could bear with Kashaf, Mu'alim, Baizavi, and Jalalin's logic, Allama Fakhrud Din Razi's logical criticism and of other mufassarin, then I hope that my disjointed and irrelative explanations on Allah's workmanship would also be borne.

A farmer enters a lush green farm along with his bull. There an economist and a botanist are already present. Now each one the three looks at the farm from his angle. All that the bull needs is freedom so that it could just graze and fill its stomach. The farmer is estimating how much of the borrowed money he would be able to return after selling the produce. Economist thinks of the effect of this year's good harvest on the country's economy. And the botanist is down in thoughts about the structure of various elements of plant, ground-based bacteria, and the wonderful machine of leaves.

Qur'an is like the farm. Some looked at it from the viewpoint of admiration, others narrated its beauty like a poet. The preacher selected interesting stories on it. Mullah became intoxicated by the mere thought of *hoor* and drinks.

Edict-givers considered it a code of jurisprudence. Pir occupying the seats of their ancestors found Ayaat in the perspective of respect for him. A monk presented arguments in favor of leaving the worldly joys while some made it a book having short-cut methods of mantra and exorcism. But what I found in the Qur'an was innumerable ways to solve political, economic, and moral problems of mankind. And I have found that there is absolute unanimity between the words and deeds of Allah. What is the explanation of Qur'an and what is Qur'an; the subject matter of universe.

Allah has sent down the best statement: a consistent Book wherein is reiteration. The skins shiver therefrom of those who fear their Lord; then their skins and their hearts relax at the remembrance of Allah…. Zumar, 24.

I have tried my wee bit to remove the screen from what has been deliberately kept secret and shrouded in mystery. To what extent have I been successful, I don't know. All that I know is that He is definitely present and these flowers and stars are his reflection.

The way the bringing out of this spirit of universe from the shrouds and making it bare for the people to see, is the absolute human endeavor. Similarly, there is also a colorful world living in man's mind. Its appearance is the completion of humanity.

Thanks

It will be great thanklessness if I do not thank "Al-Bayan" and Kitab Manzil, Kashmiri Bazar, Lahore for their gestures that resulted in the communication of my message to the length and breadth of the country. New avenues of thinking have been opened and the Muslims of India have been rest assured of the Qur'an being *"Tafsilan likule shai"*. Had these two organizations not helped me, my voice would have remained suppressed, the way some (flower) bud gets withered before becoming a flower and no one would have made us aware of its fragrance.

Extracts

Books that I have made use of, are given below. Some books have just their names but names of authors have gone out of my memory. And now when I try to find them, I can't:

1) Tafseer-e-Jawair-ul-Qur'an, Vol. 25; Allama Jauhar Tantavi

2) Tabqat-ul-Arz (published by Anjuman-e-Tarraqi Urdu, Hind)

3) Mala Qadeema (published by Anjuman-e-Tarraqi Urdu, Hind)

4) Insaan and Chaopaya [Man and quadrupt]; Dr. M.L. Sethi

5) Nabataat aur Nabatati Khoraak [Plants and their food]; Dr. M.L. Sethi

6) Alqamar [The Moon]; published by Anjuman-e-Tarraqi Urdu, Hind)

7) Tazkara [Mentioning]; Allama Inayat-ullah Khan Mashriqi

8) Tafseer-e-Bayan-ul-Qur'an [Explanation of Qur'an with reference to context]; Maolana Abu-ul-Kalam Azad

9) World of Plants

10) Peeping into the Universe

11) Wonders of the sea

12) War inventions

13) Miracle of life

14) How our bodies are made

15) Wonders of science

16) Marvels of life

17) Great Design

18) Science during the last 3000 years

19) Science from day to day

20) A.B.C. of Chemistry

21) Animal World

22) Starland

23) Marvels of Geology

24) Natures Wonder Workers

10:10 وَأُخِرُ دَعُوٰهُمُ اَنِ الۡحَمۡدُ لِلّٰهِ رَبِّ الۡعٰلَمِیۡنَ۠

Sixty Guidelines From the Qur'an

I suggest the following check list in every mosque and schools in Islamic countries to remind all of us the good manners QURAN demands of us. (Publisher)

1. Respect and honour all human beings irrespective of their religion, colour, race, sex, language, status, property, birth, profession/job and so on [17/70]

2. Talk straight, to the point, without any ambiguity or deception [33/70]

3. Choose best words to speak and say them in the best possible way [17/53, 2/83]

4. Do not shout. Speak politely keeping your voice low. [31/19]

5. Always speak the truth. Shun words that are deceitful and ostentatious [22/30]

6. Do not confound truth with falsehood [2/42]

7. Say with your mouth what is in your heart [3/167]

8. Speak in a civilised manner in a language that is recognised by the society and is commonly used [4/5]

9. When you voice an opinion, be just, even if it is against a relative [6/152]

10. Do not be a bragging boaster [31/18]

11. Do not talk, listen or do anything vain [23/3, 28/55]

12. Do not participate in any paltry. If you pass near a futile play, then pass by with dignity [25/72]

13. Do not verge upon any immodesty or lewdness whether surreptitious or overt [6/151].

14. If, unintentionally, any misconduct occurs by you, then correct yourself expeditiously [3/134].

15. Do not be contemptuous or arrogant with people [31/18]

16. Do not walk haughtily or with conceit [17/37, 31/18]

17. Be moderate in thy pace [31/19]

18. Walk with humility and sedateness [25/63]

19. Keep your gazes lowered devoid of any lecherous leers and salacious stares [24/30-31, 40/19].

20. If you do not have complete knowledge about anything, better keep your mouth shut. You might think that speaking about something without full knowledge is a trivial matter. But it might have grave consequences [24/15-16]

21. When you hear something malicious about someone, keep a favourable view about him/her until you attain full knowledge about the matter. Consider others innocent until they are proven guilty with solid and truthful evidence [24/12-13]

22. Ascertain the truth of any news, lest you smite someone in ignorance and afterwards repent of what you did [49/6]

23. Do not follow blindly any information of which you have no direct knowledge. (Using your faculties of perception and conception) you must verify it for yourself. In the Court of your Lord, you will be held accountable for your hearing, sight, and the faculty of reasoning [17/36].

24. Never think that you have reached the final stage of knowledge and nobody knows more than yourself. Remember! Above everyone endowed with knowledge is

another endowed with more knowledge [12/76]. Even the Prophet [p.b.u.h] was asked to keep praying, "O My sustainer! Advance me in knowledge." [20:114]

25. The believers are but a single Brotherhood. Live like members of one family, brothers and sisters unto one another [49/10].

26. Do not make mockery of others or ridicule others [49/11]

27. Do not defame others [49/11]

28. Do not insult others by nicknames [49/11]

29. Avoid suspicion and guesswork. Suspicion and guesswork might deplete your communal energy [49/12]

30. Spy not upon one another [49/12]

31. Do not backbite one another [49/12]

32. When you meet each other, offer good wishes and blessings for safety. One who conveys to you a message of safety and security and also when a courteous greeting is offered to you, meet it with a greeting still more courteous or (at least) of equal courtesy [4/86]

33. When you enter your own home or the home of somebody else, compliment the inmates [24/61]

34. Do not enter houses other than your own until you have sought permission; and then greet the inmates and wish them a life of blessing, purity and pleasure [24/27]

35. Treat kindly -Your parents-Relatives-The orphans-And those who have been left alone in the society [4/36]

36. Take care of -The needy,-The disabled-Those whose hard earned income is insufficient to meet their needs-And those whose businesses have stalled -And those who have lost their jobs. [4/36]

37. Treat kindly -Your related neighbours, and unrelated neighbours-Companions by your side in public gatherings, or public transportation. [4/36]

38. Be generous to the needy wayfarer, the homeless son of the street,and the one who reaches you in a destitute condition [4/36]

39. Be nice to people who work under your care. [4/36]

40. Do not follow up what you have given to others to afflict them with reminders of your generosity [2/262].

41. Do not expect a return for your good behaviour, not even thanks [76/9]

42. Cooperate with one another in good deeds and do not cooperate with others in evil and bad matters [5/2]

43. Do no try to impress people on account of self-proclaimed virtues [53/32]

44. You should enjoin right conduct on others but mend your own ways first. Actions speak louder than words. You must first practice good deeds yourself, then preach [2/44]

45. Correct yourself and your families first [before trying to correct others] [66/6]

46. Pardon gracefully if anyone among you who commits a bad deed out of ignorance, and then repents and amends [6/54, 3/134]

47. Divert and sublimate your anger and potentially virulent emotions to creative energy, and become a source of tranquillity and comfort to people [3/134]

48. Call people to the Way of your Lord with wisdom and beautiful exhortation. Reason with them most decently [16/125]

49. Leave to themselves those who do not give any importance to the Divine code and have adopted and consider it as mere play and amusement [6/70]

50. Sit not in the company of those who ridicule Divine Law unless they engage in some other conversation [4/140]

51. Do not be jealous of those who are blessed [4/54]

52. In your collective life, make rooms for others [58/11]

53. When invited to dine, Go at the appointed time. Do not arrive too early to wait for the preparation of meal or linger after eating to engage in bootless babble. Such things may cause inconvenience to the host [33/53]

54. Eat and drink [what is lawful] in moderation [7/31].

55. Do not squander your wealth senselessly [17/26]

56. Fulfil your promises and commitments [17/34]

57. Keep yourself clean, pure [9/108, 4/43, 5/6].

58. Dress-up in agreeable attire and adorn yourself with exquisite character from inside out [7/26]

59. Seek your provision only by fair endeavour [29/17, 2/188]

60. Do not devour the wealth and property of others unjustly, nor bribe the officials or the judges to deprive others of their possessions [2/188]

Note: The above points are some of the lessons learnt from Quran that apply to our general living. In the end, the verses of Quran from which the lesson is drawn is given. The points above may not be word by word translations of Quranic verses.

Source: http://quranicteachings.co.uk/manners-of-life.htm

Dr.Tarig Al Swaidan discovered some verses in the Holy Qur'an that

mention one thing is equal to another:

i.e. men are equal to women.

Although this makes sense grammatically,

the astonishing fact is that the number of

times the word man appears in the Holy Qur'an

is 24 and number of times the word

woman appears is also 24,

therefore not only is this phrase correct in

the grammatical sense but also true mathematically,

i.e. 24 = 24.

Upon further analysis of various verses,

he discovered that this is consistent throughout the whole

Holy Qur'an

where it says one thing is like another.

See below for astonishing result of

the words mentioned number of times in Arabic

Holy Qur'an

Dunia (one name for life) 115.

Aakhirat (one name for the life after this world) 115

Malaika (Angels) 88 . Shayteen (Satan) 88

Life 145 ...... Death 145

Benefit 50 . Corrupt 50

People 50 .. Messengers 50

Eblees (king of devils) 11 . Seek refuge from Eblees 11

Museebah (calamity) 75. Thanks ! 75

Spending (Sadaqah) 73. Satisfaction 73

People who are mislead. 17 Dead people 17

Muslimeen 41 . Struggle (to achieve goodness) 41

Gold 8 . Easy life 8

Magic 60. Fitnah (dissuasion, misleading) 60

Zakat (Taxes Muslims pay to the poor) 32 .

Barakah (Increasing or blessings of wealth) 32

Mind 49. Noor 49

Tongue 25. Sermon 25

Desire 8. Fear 8

Speaking publicly 18. Publicising 18

Hardship 114. Patience 114

Muhammad 4. Sharee'ah (Muhammad's teachings) 4

Man 24. Woman 24

And amazingly enough have a look how many times

the following words appear:

Salat 5 , Month 12 , Day 365 ,

Sea 32 , Land 13

Sea + land = 32 + 13= 45

Sea = 32/45*100q.= 71.11111111%

Land = 13/45*100 = 28.88888889%

Sea + land 100.00%

Modern science has only recently proven that the water covers

71.111% of the

earth, while the land covers 28.889%.

Is this a coincidence? Question is that

Who taught Prophet Muhammed (PBUH) all this?

Reply automatically comes in mind that ALMIGHTY ALLAH taught him.

This is the Holy Qur'an

First Qur'anic Command: Seek Knowledge

Publilshers last word

BURQ has clearly proved that Quran is a packaged deal. The Muslims must get back to basics. The first Quranic word IQRA "Read" and soon followed by KALAM "Pen" can only open doors to Allah (SWT)'s universe and the knowledge gathered will benefit Mankind.

In summary Burq is saying as this poet (SHAH) said, salat, fasting, Haj, is all good but it is different route (serving HIS creations with knowledge which is made available in Quran for MANKIND) we can please HIM.

Unfortunately, the Muslim countries have left the message down. For example the recent UNESCO's report on illiteracy shows Pakistan's youth between 15 – 24 there are 70% illiterate. The report says 15 million boys and 25 million girls do not attend school. The report ranked Pakistan 180 in the literacy rate from 221 countries.

I thank my dear wife Jean for supporting my various projects and made our home a very happy one.

21:87 لَّآ اِلٰهَ اِلَّآ اَنْتَ سُبْحٰنَكَ ۖ اِنِّیْ كُنْتُ مِنَ الظّٰلِمِیْنَ ۟

The first commandment to MOSES (pbuh):
I am ALLAH, there is no other god but ME so serve ME (worship ME) and establish prayers for MY remembrance (Chapter 20:14)

The first commandment to JESUS (pbuh):
And HE commands me to establish prayers and pay poor due as long as I live (Chapter Mary 19:31)

The first commandment to MUHAMMAD (pbuh):
Read in the name of thy Lord ... (Chapter 96:1)

This leaflet is dedicated to memory of
Late Dr. A. Razzak Khan.